D1598648

WOMEN
FROM BIRTH
TO DEATH

WOMEN FROM BIRTH TO DEATH

The Female Life Cycle in Britain 1830–1914

edited by

DR PAT JALLAND
Visiting Fellow in History
Australian National University

DR JOHN HOOPER
Senior Lecturer in History
Murdoch University

HUMANITIES PRESS INTERNATIONAL, INC.
ATLANTIC HIGHLANDS, N.J.

First published in 1986 in the United States of America by
Humanities Press International, Inc., Atlantic Highlands, NJ 07716

Library of Congress Cataloging-in-Publication Data
Jalland, Patricia.
    Women from birth to death.

    Bibliography: p.
    Includes index.
    1. Women—Great Britain—History—19th century.
2. Women—Health and hygiene—Great Britain—19th
century.   3. Life cycle, Human—History—19th century.
4. Stereotype (Psychology)—History—19th century.
I. Hooper, John.   II. Title.
HQ1593.J35   1986   305.4′0941   85–27070
ISBN 0–391–03382–4

PRINTED IN GREAT BRITAIN

Table of Contents

Contents

The sense of curiosity is, as a rule, aroused in us only by the unfamiliar and the unexpected. What custom and long usage has made familiar we do not trouble to inquire into but accept without comment or investigation; confusing the actual with the inevitable, and deciding, slothfully enough, that the thing that is is, likewise, the thing that was and is to be. In nothing is this inert and slothful attitude of mind more marked than in the common, unquestioning acceptance of the illogical and unsatisfactory position occupied by women.

Cicely Hamilton, *Marriage as a Trade*, 1912, p.1.

Preface

There is a special problem in recovering women's past, because of the very limited historical records that have survived. Our direct inheritance from the rich theory and practice of nineteenth-century women's lives has been very meagre. Women who published books and essays were exceptional, and their writing was usually confined to those literary forms which were seen as appropriate for their gender, such as the novel. Men published more than women about the female life cycle, and played a major role in shaping the social images and stereotypes of women. Many of these male texts were produced for professional groups like doctors, and are only retained in major libraries. Exploration of the worlds of Victorian and Edwardian women now depends, for most readers, on the republication of significant nineteenth-century texts. This process is still at an early stage.

Collections of documents have so far emphasised the public activities and roles of Victorian and Edwardian women. For example, Patricia Hollis' excellent volume on *Women in Public 1850–1900* (1979) excludes 'Domestic and marital life, women's health and women's childbearing' (p. viii) in favour of the social consciousness of women and their claims for greater equality—at work, in education, the public service, politics and the law. The women's movement and the preoccupations of early feminists have dominated this phase of publication of sources on Victorian women. More recently there has been an increasing emphasis on the personal history of women within the family, which was the dominant framework of experience for most Victorian and Edwardian women, especially among the middle and upper classes. This emphasis is well illustrated by Eleanor Riemer and John Fout's *European Women. A Documentary History*

1789–1945 (Harvester Press, 1983), and the fascinating volume *Victorian Women. A Documentary Account of Women's Lives in Nineteenth-Century England, France and the United States*, edited by E. O. Hellerstein, L. P. Hume and K. M. Offen (Harvester Press, 1981). Riemer and Fout's book provides short extracts on women and the family and the female body, as well as the more conventional sections on women and work and women's politics. Hellerstein, Hume and Offen's *Victorian Women* offers a challenging alternative to the more traditional approach to women's history, based on the stages in the development of woman's life. Their selection of women's experiences ranges very widely, though their sources are richer for France and the United States of America than for Britain.

There is a clear need for more detailed and specialised documentary studies of women's history within national historical contexts, as well as more comparative analyses of important themes. Our volume explores women's life cycle in Britain from about 1830 to the First World War, from adolescence and menstruation to marriage and maternity, and from the menopause to death in the family. Selected extracts illustrate important stereotypes and conventions about women's nature in this period. This life cycle framework suggests a more personal and structural syllabus for the study of women's history, to complement their public history. Our historical selections are based on middle- and upper-class culture, which have left the richest literary deposits. Assumptions cannot be made about the relationship between the views in these documents and social practices, which are a complex and individual problem (e.g. in relation to birth control). There were differences between families and within classes, just as there were differences between authors in this volume. Victorian and Edwardian stereotypes about the nature of women were inventions subject to the pressure of other people's ideas, and to improvements in scientific knowledge and the impact of economic and social forces. Still, the structure and major themes of this book are based on common patterns in a wide range of Victorian and Edwardian 'non-fictional' texts. Many of our themes appear to reflect simple biological stages in women's lives, but the reader will rapidly discover that menstruation or menopause have a cultural specificity which makes Victorian and Edwardian views peculiar to their times. 'Biology' was partly a cultural construction, illustrated most vividly by conditions like hysteria.

Male authors played an important role in establishing and perpetuating Victorian and Edwardian stereotypes about the features of the female life cycle. The history of women necessarily includes those male constructions of female identity developed, for example, in advice books, educational tracts, and medical texts. Male doctors in particular were increasingly important in the nineteenth and early twentieth centuries as 'scientific' authorities on the nature and acceptable behaviour of women. Some doctors attempted to reshape perceptions of women through a gynaecological approach to the female body and its destiny. Fortunately, many women demonstrated a healthy scepticism about the more extreme medical theories on the female life cycle. However, these theories formed a powerful, deterministic framework of beliefs about women's potential which influenced male and female expectations of life.

Until the late nineteenth century and beyond, female authors were seriously disadvantaged as prospective authorities on the female life cycle by their lack of scientific training. The exclusion of women from the medical profession, except in secondary roles as nurses or midwives, was largely effective in England and Wales until the 1880s and 1890s. The number of female doctors increased from 25 in 1881 to 101 in 1891 and 477 by 1911, according to the census returns. Even these exceptional women were conditioned by their religious beliefs, the medical education they received, and the prevailing socio-medical fashions of their times (like eugenics). Gynaecology remained a male specialisation, though the practices of the few women doctors consisted mainly of female patients and their children.

The extracts in this volume can be read in a variety of contexts and from very different perspectives. We hope our readers will include social historians, students of women's studies, sociologists, literary critics, medical historians, and psychologists among others. The fragmentation of knowledge has made it difficult to address the fundamental problems of 'human nature' without offending the specialists in one field or another. This book can be read within particular frameworks, but it can also serve as a meeting place for readers exploring the meaning of female (and male) identity.

Our introductions to the major themes could have attempted to encompass all the perspectives suggested above, but that would have required a series of volumes. Instead, the introductions provide a brief survey of questions raised by the individual extracts, and some historical context to help locate these documents in the mosaic of Victorian and Edwardian thought. They include specific references to most of the authors whose work is included in the following section. The date of extracts is given in round brackets, and extracts are normally in chronological order within each sub-section. Each entry is numbered consecutively, and this number is given in square brackets in the introductions.

We are indebted to many people and institutions for their help. We are especially grateful to Dee Cook for her patient and conscientious work as research assistant, following up items from our lengthy lists of sources and organising copies. Kay Walsh and Simon Ville provided essential research assistance at different stages of the book's evolution. Gail O'Hanlon contributed many references on puerperal fever. Professor Olive Banks and Dr Barry Smith generously read the typescript and made useful suggestions. Genelle Jones took on the principal burden of typing—with great efficiency and humour; aided by Thea Burnett and Marilyn Walker. Grants for graduate research assistance and research materials were contributed by the Academic Staff Development fund of the Western Australian Institute of Technology, and the Special Research Grant fund of Murdoch University. Pat Jalland is indebted to the Department of History in the Research School of Social Sciences at the Australian National University for the award of a Visiting Fellowship in History from 1983 to 1986.

PART 1

The Female Life Cycle 1830–1914

Introduction

The nature of women in Victorian and Edwardian Britain was conceived by contemporaries primarily in biological terms, expressed in the inevitable cycle of female life from menstruation to menopause. Women's perceptions of their self-identity were framed by prevailing beliefs about these biologically determined 'Successive Phases of Woman's Life'. These phases provided the structural basis for Dr Mary Scharlieb's book *The Seven Ages of Woman* (1915) [see Document 5] and many other medical and literary texts (see 1.1 below). Different authors emphasised somewhat different features and phases, but the most important stages seemed physically self-evident and constant for all women in all cultures. Birth and childhood were followed by the years of puberty, from the onset of menstruation. Marriage was the social institution in which sexual experience and pregnancy usually occurred. Pregnancy, childbirth, nursing and child-care occupied the major functional epoch of a woman's life. The final part of the cycle was the process of ageing, the menopause and death.

These developmental stages were experienced by most women, but their personal and social significance was not physiologically determined. The concept and meaning of these stages was socially constructed, and some distinctive theories about the female life cycle were developed by Victorian and Edwardian writers. These models of female identity were inventions of a particular cultural time and place, which masqueraded as eternal truths legitimated by the findings of the biological, medical and other sciences. The question of women's 'nature' was increasingly to be referred to specialists in the human 'sciences', from doctors to anthropologists. Their texts should be read in this historical framework, as inventions which represent characteristic features of their cultural place. They were also forms of ideological control, whose social functions included the restriction of the social and economic activity of their women. These models of the female life cycle were social stereotypes which defined what was acceptable and unacceptable in terms of gender.

The number of epochs in the female life cycle varied considerably from author to author, from two to ten in the selections in this volume (see 1.1). The smaller the number of epochs, the more evident was the preoccupation with the physical differences between men and women, and the consequent limitations on female roles. For example, Dr MacNaughton-Jones (1913) [4] isolated two *'epoch-making'* periods in women's lives—puberty and menopause. This was a social interpretation rather than an objective scientific fact, and Dr MacNaughton-Jones recognised that the influence of medicine on women's attitudes was 'largely sociological, and spreads to circles wider than we have any idea of...'. Dr Mary Scharlieb (1915) [5] acknowledged that the concept of epochs in the female life cycle raised the problem of personal and social judgments about which epochs were most and least important: 'It is impossible to say which period of a woman's life is the most important.' However, even Dr Scharlieb's account of the seven ages of woman was dominated by 'the great crown and joy of a woman's life, motherhood', for it was clear to her that 'the natural vocation for every woman is that of wife and mother.'

Walter Johnson's four epochs of female life (1850) [1] emphasised the lack of gender difference before puberty, in dramatic contrast with the sex-peculiarities of the epochs of menstruation, childbirth and menopause. These exclusively female stages were seen as the key to the entire female constitution and its proper social activities. Further, the major diseases were also gender specific, and in women were tied to the three major epochs. E. J. Tilt (1852) [2] followed the traditional model of ten septenniads or periods of seven years which were common to both sexes. However, in practice Tilt focused on a smaller number of 'critical epochs' for women, especially puberty, childbirth and menopause. Dr Barnes' (1873) [3] concept of three epochs in the woman's life was based on the 'special proclivity to nervous diseases marked by convulsion' in the stages of menstruation, reproduction and menopause. Like the frog in breeding season, women were characterised by higher degrees of 'nervous excitability', 'an exalted degree of emotional sensibility', because of their generative function. Thus, women were seen as dominated by their uterine difference from men.

The social significance of these various models of the female life cycle was that they established the biological destiny of women as the paramount fact about female identity and social functions. If the major stages of female life were puberty, maternity and menopause, then reproduction—as potential, activity and loss—was the most important element of women's lives. Women who were women were potential mothers, actual mothers, or retired mothers. The purpose of the female life cycle was simply biological—the reproduction of the human species. As Dr Michael Ryan noted (1841) [6], the woman's 'destiny [is] to be united to a husband, and to become a mother.' The predominant 'influence of the uterus' was very much in the minds of Samuel Mason (1845) [7], J. M. Allan (1869) [8] and Mr Dendy (1869) [9]. Allan best captured the biological reductionism of this view in his definition of woman as 'an admirably constructed apparatus for the most mysterious and sublime of nature's mysteries—the reproductive process'. Ironically, this reductionist model was also applied to the male sex by the eugenicists in the early twentieth century. The species-function of males was also to serve the race, and 'the right fulfilment of Nature's purpose is one with the right fulfilment of their own destiny' (Saleeby, 1912) [14]. Every 'individual was evolved by Nature for the care of the germ-plasm', and determined by 'the unchangeable and beneficent facts of biology' (see also Chesser, 1913 [15]).

These views of the biological destiny of women often included a biological devaluation of women's capacity outside the domestic world of reproduction. The female mind was perceived as a function of the womb, and the female constitution was seen as weak and feeble outside its uterine activities (e.g. Ryan, 1841 [6]). The remarkable control of the uterus 'over the mind and reasoning powers' was illustrated by 'the greater frequency of insanity' alleged to occur among women, especially during the years of menstruation (Mason, 1845 [7]). Allan (1869) [8] argued strongly that there was 'sex in mind' based on the physiological differences between men and women, with a natural male superiority in reasoning power. However, women were compensated by a 'superior instinct' or 'marvellous faculty of intuition' appropriate to the familial world of sympathetic emotion (Allan, and Dendy, 1869 [9]). These fundamental sexual differences were seen as necessarily entailing a social division of labour in which women occupied the domestic sphere while men did all the 'outside work' (Eliza Lynn Linton, 1891 [11]). Sexual difference was translated into economic and social difference—every aspect of human life could be reduced to 'a question of sex', as interpreted by 'science'.

The influence of the sexist view of female destiny was recognised by many women. Some accepted the argument that 'women's absence of mental creative power is accounted for by their having so much of physical creation to do' (Cavendish, 1888 [10]). Others attacked the devaluation of women represented in the idea of different, sexually based intellectual and emotional capacities. Harriet Mahood (1901) [12] argued that 'women, broadly speaking, are only using half their consciousness' because of the dominance of the idea of separate spheres in education. In her view this 'half' consciousness should be replaced by full human consciousness for both men and women, though she recognised that this might not suit the convenience of men. Cicely Hamilton (1912) [13] also emphasised the dominant role of male attitudes in the formation of female consciousness, where even the language of love or maternity was a 'more or less careful, more or less intelligent copy of the masculine conception of her emotions'. The logical extension of the biological reduction of women was the 'animated doll', the reproductive machine whose efficiency was inferior to the rabbit's.

The analysis of female health, or more often female ill-health, was central to the economic and social devaluation of women in Victorian and Edwardian Britain. The stages of the female life cycle and the woman's reproductive destiny were identified by many doctors as special and peculiar sources of ill-health, resulting in 'the many weaknesses and complaints women labour under' (Solomon, 1817? [16]). The character of their life of pain and dependence, 'a long chain of never-ending infirmities', was endorsed by Christianity and explained by physiology, according to Tilt (1851) [18]. The most extreme form of this sexist view of health was the claim that woman's 'natural' state was invalidism (Allan, 1869 [19])—a view more often expressed in American than in British medical texts. Menstruation was synonymous with being 'unwell', a 'periodical illness', and the menopause could be even more debilitating. However, most doctors agreed that woman's primary function of childbearing was a natural and healthy process and not 'a state of disease' (e.g. Bull, 1837 [92]; Conquest, 1848 [93]). More research is needed on this complex question of medical theories about women's health, including comparative analyses of British and American medical texts. It is important to remember that medical views were not monolithic, and their ambiguities and contradictions arose out of scientific ignorance and divided opinions.

Women writers strongly attacked the infirmity theory of female health, for example in the name of the 'kindly ordering of Nature' (Duffey, 1873 [20]) and the power of 'right living' (Chesser, 1912 [23]). Health was seen as a function of diet, exercise and sensible behaviour rather than a life sentence determined by gender. The absurdity of the infirmity theory was well illustrated in the great bicycle debate when the threatened perils of cycling for women were exposed as 'a bogey' (Fenton, 1896 [22]). The decisive argument was statistical: females had lower mortality rates and lived longer than males (Chesser, 1913 [24]). Even female sexuality could be seen as a stimulating source of good health by the radical author Richard Carlile (1838) [17], though at considerable cost for the spinster. Eugenics, as an alternative 'science' of health, desexed the health question in order to 'purify the life stream'. The 'unhealthy and undesirable' of both sexes would simply be denied the right of parenthood, and 'the ideal of perfect health' could thus be approached (Chesser, 1912 [23]). The 'science' of health could be used to justify the termination of 'unhealthy' minds and races, rather than the devaluation of women.

Medical books and articles on female health usually focused on the peculiar biological features of women, especially menstruation, maternity and menopause. The common health problems of men and women were a separate territory of mainstream medicine. Doctors themselves recognised that the medical approach to women could be dominated by a preoccupation with the womb and its effects (Bull, 1837 [25]), and that relatively few doctors specialised in female medical problems (Ryan, 1841 [26]; Ruddock, 1888 [32]). The interaction of male doctor and female patient was always potentially on the boundary line between professional investigation and social and sexual indecency. The extraordinary sensitivity about these male/female encounters is illustrated by the concern about 'the indiscriminate use of the speculum' and other forms of 'unnecessary interference' which were seen as lowering the standard of British morality (F.R.C.S., 1857 [27]). This belief in speculum 'mania' was far more revealing about the mental state of the anonymous author than about the medical profession as a whole, or British women. But there were many other examples of the tensions implicit in male treatment of females (for example, diagnosis and care during pregnancy—see Part 3; and diagnosis and treatment of sexual disorders—see Part 4).

The process of medical specialisation was part of the professionalisation and institutionalisation of medicine in nineteenth-century Britain. The 'subdivision of medical practice' (Barnes, 1873 [29]) included the professional recognition of obstetrics and gynaecology as those areas of medicine dealing with distinctive female problems. Obstetrics included the study of childbirth and its anterior and subsequent processes, rather than 'simply the art of delivering women in labour' (Barnes, 1873 [29]). Gynaecology was the study of the physiological functions and diseases of women. Tilt (1882) [30] and Barnes (1890) [33] argued that British gynaecology was 'largely surgical, and the true solution of its most important problems is revealed by direct appeal to surgery' (Barnes, 1890). The surgical approach to women's diseases, or 'vivisection of the noblest kind' as Dr Barnes called it, was effective in treating some conditions, but it was a dangerous general model for gynaecological practice. Surgical solutions could, after all, be sought inappropriately—for 'nervous disorders' like hysteria, or for socially unacceptable personal practices (see Part 4—the Baker Brown controversy). Medical definitions of acceptable behaviour for women were reinforced by the ultimate threat of surgical intervention to reshape the female body, if the female mind could not be self-disciplined. Alternatively, doctors controlled involuntary admissions to asylums for women who transgressed moral codes which were redefined as medical laws, for example in cases of female promiscuity and nymphomania (Housman, 1911 [36]).

There was an obsessive quality about the pelvic approach to

women's health that worried even some gynaecologists, who saw harmful consequences for both patient and doctor if the dangers deriving from the pelvic organs continued to be over-emphasised (Kelly, 1909 [35]). Thus medical theory could be seen as a significant cause of mental distress and psychosomatic illness among women, because of their belief in the 'idea that woman's ills are mainly "reflexes" from the pelvic organs.' As Lady Stanley (1870) [28] noted to her mother, some women thought of themselves as either pregnant 'or else something odious with that most troublesome part takes place'. No wonder women looked out for, and discussed among themselves, the sympathetic 'woman's doctor', whose major assets included being 'cheerful, helpful [and] sensible' (Lady Lyell, 1895–1902 [34]). Unfortunately, the prejudice against medical women was felt to be strongest 'among the practitioners who devote themselves chiefly to midwifery and to the special diseases of women' (Sophia Jex Blake, 1887 [31]). The reservation of the female body for the male gynaecologist was one of the final barriers to women gaining knowledge and certainty about their own physiology. As Dr Kelly (1909) [35] noted, 'women suffer from the secrecy which, for them has surrounded all the phenomena of reproduction'. The secrets of the female life cycle would only begin to be publicly and widely disclosed in the second half of the twentieth century.

1.1 The Epochs/Ages of Female Life

1. The Four Epochs of Female Life: pre-puberty, menstruation, marriage and childbirth, menopause (1850)

Before commencing the discussion of the peculiarities of disease, it will be well to consider the peculiarities of health—or the physiological and social distinctions impressed upon the female sex. In early childhood the speciality of the sexes is not yet developed.... But in a short time all this changes; each assumes his proper and permanent character, and occupies his allotted station.... As soon as the portal is passed, and puberty accomplished, a complete moral and physical revolution is effected—menstruation is instituted; and, by a species of harlequinade, the changes immediately commence. The maiden's form, previously angular, and displeasing to the critical eye, is rounded off, inharmonious projections and sharp points disappear; and that charming fulness of contour, and ripeness of development, which marks the transition from maidenhood to womanhood is established.... The mental constitution undergoes no less alteration. The laughing familiarity of girlhood is succeeded by bashful reserve; even the incorrigible hoyden loses much of her defiant spirit. At the same time the 'bloom of young desire' gradually ripens in the soul, the heart throbs with ill-understood wishes, and a sighing, yearning aspiration extends into the future. All is doubt—all is fantasy—poetry and reverie. In ordinary minds this impulsion of the soul is speedily directed towards an earthly lover—and visions of love in a cottage, maternity, and endless bliss crowd the prospective....

The menstrual epoch is one peculiarly exposed to the incursions of disease. Should any accident disturb the natural course of the monthly secretion—should it become excessive, or deficient, or fail altogether, or delay its appearance, twenty different maladies are ready to distract the patient. First

Chlorosis, with pallid aspect and bruised eye, creeps up, and tempting the maiden with a savoury morsel of slate-pencil, passes by. Then Hysteria, the mimic, appears, and assumes in twenty seconds twenty different shapes. First, with tragic cry, and writhing his flexile limbs, he apes the behaviour of Inflammation. Anon, starting to his feet with vehement gesticulation and fluent rant, he plays the part of Madness. Then with folded arms, and eyes nailed to the ground, he stands the personification of Melancholy. In a moment he again changes his character; another change, one more, and he is gone.

Puberty once established, in the natural order of things the female marries, and this third epoch is generally one of care and probation. After a short time the uterus enlarges, and the juices of the mother are drawn off for the nourishment of her offspring. If the woman be ailing and weakly, this state of pregnancy is attended with manifold dangers and distresses; and these dangers and distresses are increased tenfold at the time of delivery. Then, under unfavorable circumstances, arise fevers, hemorrhages, convulsions, and sometimes temporary alienation of mind. The perils of childbirth happily evaded, other occasions of disease come into play. Suppression of milk may take place, and milk fever, abscess of the breast, and other casualties, may ensue. Or if none of these appear, but the mother, from want of judgment, or from prudential considerations, neglect to wean her child after the lapse of a reasonable period, the prolonged drain upon the system generates a peculiar malady, which may be denominated the nurse's fever. If, however, the married female escape this penalty of indiscretion, and happen to prove more than ordinarily prolific, even this circumstance will favour the production of various harassing complaints. Local weakness, attended by profuse discharges, displacement of the womb, enlargement of the veins of the lower extremities, flaccidity of the abdomen, aches and pains in the loins and neighbouring regions, are frequently set up. These affections react on the general health, and indigestion, nervousness, uneasiness at the pit of the stomach, flatulent distension of the intestines, constipation, and all its afflictive concomitants appear.

The fourth epoch, that which commences at the turn of life, as it is called, or grand climacteric, and is signalised by suppression of the menses, is far less eventful than the preceding. During this epoch, however, cancer commits extensive ravages, attacking the breast, the womb, or the ovaries. But if the female remain exempt from its attack, this season is one of comparative repose, of quiet, which deepens gradually into the stillness of the grave.

In the above brief sketch of the diseases of woman, it is by no means meant that the maladies therein enumerated are *limited* to any period of life; thus hysteria may not attack its victim until after marriage or childbirth, and cancer may destroy the youthful patient, and even impress its fatal signature on the new-born infant....

Walter Johnson, *The Morbid Emotions of Women*, 1850, pp. 1–7.

2. The Critical Epochs of Life (1852)

Life is beset with critical epochs: first and second dentition, puberty, adolescence; and in women, marriage, child-bearing, and its consequences. These critical epochs are sometimes fatal to life, at others they exercise a prejudicial effect on the subsequent health, or again, on the contrary, they often strengthen the constitution, and terminate complaints hitherto deemed incurable. Another point is, that the importance of these critical epochs decreases as we meet them on descending the stream of life from infancy to old age; for the importance of an epoch is tested by its dangers, and these may be safely estimated by the amount of disease which it determines. For instance, the influence of the 'change of life', over the subsequent portion of woman's career, is less than that of puberty; and that of puberty is less than that of first dentition.... As we continue to live, every successive epoch is marked by a diminution of vital energy, until it becomes so impaired by increasing infirmities and old age, that there is not sufficient strength left to move the body, or to perform its most ordinary functions. Life, then, becomes gradually extinguished without a struggle.

In seeking to explain the rules by which health may be preserved at the various periods of life, we shall follow the example of many illustrious philosophers and medical men of both former and modern times, and divide the career of man into septenniads or periods of 7 years; for the 7th year, and the vicinity of each multiple of seven, is characterized by some great change in the human constitution. Thus the 7th year is that of second dentition, and the common belief fixes at that age the distinct perception of right and wrong.

At $1 \times 7 = 7$,   Infancy and Childhood
$2 \times 7 = 14$,   Puberty
$3 \times 7 = 21$,   Adolescence and full height
$4 \times 7 = 28$,   The full proportion of body
$5 \times 7 = 35$,   The greatest intensity of human power
$6 \times 7 = 42$,   The meridian of life
$7 \times 7 = 49$,   Physical decline. The physical strength has been ebbing since 42, and the decrease of reproductive power in women
$8 \times 7 = 56$,   Greatest mental vigour
$9 \times 7 = 63$,   The Grand Climacteric of the ancients
$10 \times 7 = 70$,   Mental energy fails, and signs of dissolution are everywhere to be detected.

E. J. Tilt, *Elements of Health and Principles of Female Hygiene*, 1852, pp. 26–7.

3. The Three Epochs of Woman's Life (1873)

There are three epochs, or rather stages in the life of woman, at which she exhibits special proclivity to nervous diseases marked by convulsion. In the first stage, that of infancy, the proclivity is common to both sexes, but still, I believe, more marked in the female....

The next stage of proclivity to convulsion begins with the advent of menstruation, and terminates with the cessation of that function. This stage, of course, includes, and is continuous with, that of sexual life or reproductive capacity. It is during this stage that the proclivity to convulsive action is the most strongly marked.

The third stage runs almost imperceptibly on from the second. It is difficult to draw a sharp line of demarcation between them. Theoretically, however—that is, physiologically—the two stages are distinct. The third stage begins with the decay of the reproductive capacity, and is prolonged for an indefinite period, ranging from one or two to five years, or more, but is seldom prolonged into the age of senility.

This third stage may be called the stage of aberrant nervous action. During the two earlier stages the nerve-force is employed, except when disordered by morbid influences, in the work of definite functions. These functions being at an end, and the organs by which they were performed undergoing the involution of decay, there follows a period of anarchy, during which nerve-force, no longer finding useful employment, goes astray in every direction, provoking the wildest and most extravagant manifestations. By-and-by, the stage of adaptation or readjustment arrives, the nerve-force generated finds appropriate occupation, and all settles down into comparative order and calm. . . .

If we now inquire into the conditions which raise the nervous system of women into this state of inordinate convulsive and emotional affectability, we are led to the irresistible conclusion that they depend upon influences springing out of the reproductive function. The great convulsive disorders of women are almost strictly limited to the period of activity of the reproductive organs.

Every function requires for its performance a supply of nerve-force directed *ad hoc*. The functions of ovulation, of gestation, of labour, and of lactation, which in turn dominate over the entire organism of woman, require a special and additional supply of nerve-force beyond that required for the ordinary functions of nutrition, locomotion, and thought.

The history of the animal kingdom abounds with illustrations of this proposition. I will draw but one from comparative physiology, and that shall be from the physiologist's devoted friend, the frog. In the spring, at the commencement of the breeding season, so great is the nervous excitability of this animal that a slight irritation of the skin, which at another time would produce no obvious effect, will induce almost tetanic convulsions.

It is easy to perceive analogous phenomena, sometimes quite as pronounced in the human female, at the advent of puberty, at the periods of ovulation, during gestation, and eminently during the act of labour.

It is a fact deserving to be remembered, that during all the three stages of life marked by convulsive proclivity there is an exalted degree of emotional sensibility. We might even generalise further, and affirm that emotional sensibility proceeds *pari passu* with the convulsive liability. Almost always co-existing, it might be said that the two conditions are convertible into each other. Certainly it may be said that each will often excite the other. Nothing is more common than for an emotion which, under ordinary circumstances, would be completely controlled by the subject, to evoke a fit of hysterical, epileptic, eclamptic, or vomitive convulsion, when the nervous centres are in a state which we may describe as *convulsive tension*. And on the other hand, if the convulsive fit be excited by reflex irritation, it is almost surely followed by an exalted degree of emotional sensibility.

It further deserves to be noted here that emotion takes a large part in every act or process of the generative function. In short, emotional affectability is the measure of convulsive liability.

Another proposition I would state is the correlative of the preceding one. It may not be quite so obvious in its truth, but I think I shall be able to show that it is equally constant. It is this: An energy which may be compared with, if not identical in nature with, convulsion, is an essential element in the leading acts of the generative function. I have known instances of an epileptic fit being repeatedly induced by the sexual act. I have heard of several other like cases. . . .

In the female, and especially so in the lower mammalia, the sexual aptitude is strictly periodic, like the ovulation upon which it depends. What idea can we form of periodicity, unless it be that it is dependent upon an accumulation of nerve-force in readiness to be used when the returning occasion arrives!

Then, as to the *influence of menstruation*, or rather of its *primum mobile*, ovulation. In all ages the frequent association of this function with epilepsy and hysteria has attracted attention. Hippocrates said, "Nubile virgins, particularly about the menstrual periods, are affected with epileptic paroxysms, apoplexia, and groundless fears or fancies". He thus records his observation that the emotional faculty was exalted as well as the convulsive. What was true then is true now.

It is a matter of frequent observation that the first attack of hysteria or epilepsy coincides with the first effort at menstruation, and that a fit is liable to recur at successive menstrual epochs. In girls and women who do not exhibit hysteria or epilepsy, vomiting is a frequent attendant upon ovulation.

Labour.—It is no stretch of hypothesis to describe labour as a series of convulsions. Convulsions, it is true, well directed to a specific end. So great is the nervous tension at this crisis that slight peripheral physical or mental irritation will easily provoke and maintain a renewal of the so-called "pain". The obstetric practitioner turns this irritability to account when he wishes to accelerate a labour actually begun, or to initiate the parturient process. When this irritability is in excess, or when some other cause impairing the cohesion of the ovum with the uterus is imported, spontaneous abortion or premature labour is the result; that is, if the nervous energy be well-directed towards the uterus; otherwise, it finds a vent in the production of convulsions.

Dr Robert Barnes, 'Lumleian Lectures on the Convulsive Diseases of Women', *The Lancet*, 12 April 1873, pp. 514–5.

4. The 'Epoch-making' Years of Puberty and Menopause (1913)

We are met to consider the physical and psychical phenomena which at two critical and eventful periods [i.e. puberty and menopause] of a woman's life influence her mentally and physically. We might call the years through which she is then passing the *epoch-making* ones of her life. The medical study of those years, in the light it throws on certain propensities and acts of the woman, has a most important relation to her attitudes to her entire social environment. Medicine, therefore, has here not merely a distinct function to discharge as regards the individual, but by the wise and tactful attitude assumed to relatives and friends in the ethical, moral and eugenical difficulties that often arise, its influence is largely sociological, and spreads to circles wider than we have any idea of. . . .

Dr H. MacNaughton-Jones, 'The Relation of Puberty and the Menopause to Neurasthenia', *The Lancet*, 29 March 1913, p. 879.

5. The Seven Ages of Woman (1915)

[The young girl, the young wife and mother, the nursing mother, the mother in "the noisy years", the woman in middle and old age.]

It is impossible to say which period of a woman's life is the most important. As each age comes under consideration one is tempted to say, *This* is the most important period. But the years between absolute childhood and the dawn of adolescence claim a very special attention, because on the management of the child during those years depends in a great measure her fitness for the momentous changes that immediately follow them....

Upon the successful management of the pre-pubertal period depends in a great measure the ability of the girl to endure without injury the extraordinary up-rush of developmental energy that will shortly occur.... She [the girl's mother] ought to tell her daughter what to expect, otherwise the girl may suffer a considerable nervous shock when the great event occurs. Much of a girl's happiness and health depends on her understanding the import of the changes that are occurring in her body. If she unfortunately believes that menstruation and its attendant phenomena are signs of illness, and if she is encouraged to treat them as if they were abnormalities, the foundation of nervous ill-health is likely to be laid. If, on the other hand, she is taught that these changes are beneficent, that they are necessary to her full development of womanhood, and that indeed they are the promise that after a few years she will be fit to receive the great crown and joy of a woman's life, motherhood, she will then view her condition not only with patience, but also with joy. The motherly instinct is deeply implanted in every young girl, and she will be willing, if necessary, to suffer restrictions on present enjoyment and activities in order that the change in her constitution may be satisfactorily accomplished, and that her health may be so well established as to enable her to play her part in life to the greatest advantage....

The natural vocation for every woman is that of wife and mother, and in the training of every girl provision should be made for the acquisition of definite and accurate knowledge of the essentials of domestic economy and mothercraft....

After a few months, if both husband and wife are in good health and if the powers of Nature have had fair play, there may be reason to hope for the blessing of a family, and with this hope there comes a new interest in life. It is very important that... both husband and wife should understand that it is really a privilege as well as a duty to fulfil the natural obligations of the married state.... The social value of young women consists chiefly in the perfection of their discharge of the duties of wife and mother. The mother in the nursery, and the mother throughout the 'noisy years' of the childhood and adolescence of her children, is a person of enormous importance both to her family and to the State....

Just as *evolution* or *development* is the keynote of life from birth to full maturity, and stability the keynote from maturity to the climacteric, so is *involution* the keynote of the years that succeed to this period. The acme of physical development is attained during the early part of adult life—probably between the ages of 20 and 25. Comparatively little difference occurs during the next twenty or twenty-five years, a slight decline in activity and powers of endurance may be noticed, but the woman who enjoys good health and comfortable circumstances ages comparatively little until the time of the menopause arrives.

This great change occurs somewhere about the fiftieth year; the actual time of its accomplishment varies much. As a general rule, the later the function of menstruation was established in youth the earlier is the menopause.... The average age of the menopause appears to have risen by at least five years during the last half century... older women are not graceful if they disregard the warnings of their gradually failing powers, and cling with pathetic but futile tenacity to the dress, the amusements, aye, and even to the duties, of former years. Old age may be beautiful, venerable, and much beloved, upon condition that the woman herself thoroughly accepts the new role assigned to her in life's drama. Gradually she must learn that diaphanous materials and bright colours do not suit her altered figure and her fading complexion. She must also learn that although artificial teeth are a great blessing, and although a suitable wig may be a charitable covering for a bald head, yet she is committing a sin against her personal appearance as well as against her self-respect if she dyes her hair.... It must also be remembered that 'old age' is a very relative term, and that capacity for work and for enjoyment depends not upon the woman's age, but on the elasticity and integrity of her tissues and organs. . . .

A consideration of the whole course of a woman's life has led us to believe that each period presents its own joys, its own difficulties, its own duties and its own rewards. We have learnt also that each period of life develops naturally from that which immediately precedes it, that its beauty, happiness, and efficiency depend inevitably on the preparation that has been made for it. We are therefore irresistibly led to the conclusion that comfort and happiness in old age can be secured only by preparation for it by a normal and beautiful life. As Thomas à Kempis says, 'Thou shalt always rejoice in the evening if thou hast spent the day virtuously.'

Mary Scharlieb, *The Seven Ages of Woman. A Consideration of the Successive Phases of Woman's Life*, 1915, pp. 1–2, 11–12, 51, 73, 264–5, 271–3, 276.

1.2 The Biological Destiny of Women

6. Functions Peculiar to the Female Sex (1841)

The character of woman's mind is chiefly determined by the part she bears in relation to generation. Her destiny to be united to a husband, and to become a mother, is perceived in the plays of her infancy, and afterwards becomes manifest in the commencing struggle in her bosom, between her modesty and her inclination for the other sex, as is seen in her lovely blushes, often united with a noble feminine pride and reserve, until she meets the man of her heart, when all these feelings are succeeded by a full and unlimited abandonment of herself to the object of her affection. Conjugal love has speedily, however, to submit itself to the stronger feeling of maternal affection, of the power of which we have many and the most extraordinary examples. . . .

It has long been a medical axiom, that women are more sensitive, weak, more influenced by moral and physical causes, and more liable to diseases than the other sex. The constitution is more feeble, and is peculiarly influenced by the mysterious process of reproduction, pregnancy, parturition, the puerperal state, and lactation, as well as by the other function peculiar to it. I have also to observe, that want of exercise in the open air, tight lacing, and constipation, are among the most common causes of female disorders and diseases. The natural sensibility is increased during menstruation. . . .

These facts being admitted, the treatment of diseases of women cannot be so active, as of those of the stronger sex; and we must never forget that indescribable, or perhaps mysterious influence on the female system, which predominates during the performance of any function peculiar to the sex, and is subservient to reproduction. It always guides a scientific practitioner, and causes him to be less active in his treatment of the ordinary diseases of women than of men....

Dr Michael Ryan, *A Manual of Midwifery*, 4th edn., 1841, pp. 61, 325–6.

7. The State of the Uterus (1845)

It is well known to all in any degree conversant with physiology, what an immense influence the uterus, more especially during the important changes which it naturally undergoes, has upon the female system.... It is indeed, as Sir Charles Mansfield Clarke observes, 'a fertile source of sympathy; and many symptoms referred to other parts arise from it.' Therefore it will be readily conceived, that any derangement of this organ, or defect in its regular functions, must, to a certain extent, influence the general health, in fact, the growth and healthy development, of the female; and in after-life, too, health or disease frequently bears an exact ratio to the state of the uterus.

So remarkable a control does it exercise over the mind and reasoning powers, that the greater frequency of insanity, among women in this country, has been referred to the mode and regularity with which menstruation is performed; for as soon as this function ceases, and the menstrual fluid is no longer secreted, the tendency to mental affections diminishes in a corresponding degree. The average number of persons attacked with insanity bears the proportion of five females to four of the other sex....

Among the more frequent symptoms of a disordered condition of the uterus may be enumerated headache: this is occasionally of a very severe character, and frequently referred to the back of the head: vertigo, or giddiness, prevails, vision is sometimes impaired, maculae, or spots of a blackish colour, float before the eyes, the mental powers gradually become impaired, the energies not infrequently languish, and a sort of nervousness resembling insanity follows.... Women, in consequence of the functions to be performed by the uterus, are liable to peculiar diseases ... depending upon peculiar organs endowed with special properties, and performing particular functions, [which] are certainly much more philosophically referred to derangements of the organ itself than to constitutional disorder....

Samuel Mason, *The Philosophy of Female Health*, 1845, pp. 1–3, 19, 104–5.

8. The Ultimate Destiny of Women (1869)

The assertions and claims put forward under the term 'Woman's Rights', are a challenge to anthropologists to consider the scientific question of woman's mental, moral, and physical qualities, her nature and normal condition relative to man. Nowhere, then, can the question be more appropriately and profitably discussed than in the Anthropological Society....

To prevent misunderstanding, let us define our terms. What is meant by the glib assertion, that woman is the equal of man? Is she equal in size? No. In physical strength? No. In intellect? Yes, replies the advocate; and if she received the same training as man, she would demonstrate her intellectual equality and her moral superiority to her masculine tyrant. I deny this assertion; and proceed to show why woman is incapable of receiving a training similar to that of man. My position is, that *there must be radical, natural, permanent distinctions in the mental and moral conformation, corresponding with those in the physical organisation of the sexes.* Examine male and female skeletons; study men and women physiologically, pathologically, in health and disease; observe philosophically their respective pursuits, functions, pleasures, tastes, aspirations; recall the part which each sex has played in history; listen to the conversation of men and women in society; compare the sculptured forms of the antique, and the portraits of the two sexes; study and contrast them artistically in the life-school; observe men and women as they mingle in the daily scenes of the world; and we shall find it difficult to accede to platform paradoxes—that there is no sex in mind, and that the intellectual diversity of the sexes is due to education alone!.... Although in some respects—such as grace, delicacy, beauty of form, complexion, etc—woman appears to recede more from, in other respects she approaches more closely than man does, to the animal type! Physically, for example, in the menstrual discharge,—if it be true that this is also a characteristic of female anthropoid apes, and of other mammalia. Mentally, the approach to the animal is more decided, and is seen in the superior instinct of woman compared with man. In reflective power, woman is utterly unable to compete with man; but she possesses a compensating gift in her marvellous faculty of intuition. . . .

In the animal and vegetable kingdoms we find this invariable law—rapidity of growth inversely proportionate to the degree of perfection at maturity. The higher the animal or plant in the scale of being, the more slowly does it reach its utmost capacity of development. Girls are physically and mentally more precocious than boys. The human female arrives sooner than the male at maturity, and furnishes one of the strongest arguments against the alleged equality of the sexes. The quicker appreciation of girls is the instinct, or intuitive faculty in operation; while the slower boy is an example of the latent reasoning power not yet developed. Compare them in after-life, when the boy has become a young man full of intelligence, and the girl has been educated into a young lady reading novels, working crochet, and going into hysterics at sight of a mouse or a spider. . . . Girls love best playthings connected with personal appearance—looking-glasses, necklaces, earrings, ribbons, lace, etc.; above all, dolls. The doll is the special amusement of girls. In thus playing at maternity by anticipation, nature affords a strong and unerring intimation of the ultimate destiny of woman.

For male and female there is no serious difference of opinion or object until the age of puberty. Then, how great the difference! The boy, springing into manhood, is at once and for ever developed, and, so far as sex is concerned, completed. Whereas the woman, for a period varying from twenty to thirty years, is an admirably constructed apparatus for the most mysterious and sublime of nature's mysteries—the reproductive process. The young man starts free; his sexual development once completed, all is accomplished: the young virgin is adapted for becoming a matrix, in which a process, involving her whole physique, may occur eighteen or twenty times within thirty years. Whether the menstrual discharge be peculiar to woman, or common to woman and other mammalia, it characterises women of all races in a normal state.

J. M. Allan, 'On the Differences in the Minds of Men and Women', *Journal of the Anthropological Society*, 7 (1869), pp. cxcvi–cxcviii.

9. The Influence of the Uterus (1869)

The constitution of woman was different from that of man. The sympathies of woman were more acute, and she expressed herself accordingly. She was better able than man to judge of character, and her sympathies were more fully called into action. Most of the distinctions in the characters of women might be traced to the influence of the uterus; to the condition of which were to be attributed hysteria, and other affections peculiar to woman. Women felt more acutely than men; but it should be considered that the occupations of man were so various that he could not concentrate his feelings; while women sat at home brooding, perhaps, over some sensational novel, and had their sympathies more strongly excited. Thus, they were unable to attain a stable state of mind, and went into extremes instead of concentrating their thoughts.

Mr Dendy, discussion of J. M. Allan's 'On the Differences in the Minds of Men and Women', *Journal of the Anthropological Society*, 7 (1869), pp. ccxvi–ccxvii.

10. Nature's Clearest Indications for Women (1888)

...Your idea that women's absence of mental creative power is accounted for by their having so much of physical creation to do, is splendid. Who can say how much of a mother's *mental* power must go to a baby's brain during those miraculous nine months, not to speak of all that she puts into the child during its first years?...

To a large extent I agree with you that you may trust to Nature, without interference, as to what work women can take up. But then I think those who insist on ignoring the very weakness which you so fully allow, are really running counter to Nature's clearest indications, and are perverse in wishing women to go at men's work till they drop, or at any rate till their poor babies and homes come to grief. It is not only weakness either that differentiates between men and women. They have their special *strength* for their own special duties, which men are quite devoid of . . . if women *will* undertake men's work their own must suffer. I don't only mean wives and mothers; single women have many motherly and home duties. . . .

Lucy Cavendish to Mary [Gladstone] Drew, 27 November 1888, Mary [Gladstone] Drew Papers, BL Add. MS. 46235, fos. 239–40.

11. Reproduction as the Ultimate End of Woman: the Normal Division of Labour (1891)

Be it pleasant or unpleasant, it is none the less an absolute truth—the *raison d'être* of a woman is maternity. For this and this alone nature has differentiated her from man, and built her up cell by cell and organ by organ. The continuance of the race in healthy reproduction, together with the fit nourishment and care of the young after birth, is the ultimate end of woman as such; and whatever tells against these functions, and reduces either her power or her perfectness, is an offence against nature and a wrong done to society. If she chooses to decline her natural office altogether, and to dedicate to other services a life which has no sympathy with the sex of humanity, that comes into her lawful list of preferences and discords. But neither then nor while she is one with the rest, a wife and mother like others, is she free to blaspheme her assigned functions; nor to teach the young to blaspheme them; nor yet to set afoot such undertakings as shall militate against the healthy performance of her first great natural duty and her first great social obligation. . . .

In the normal division of labour the man has the outside work to do, from governing the country to tilling the soil; the woman takes the inside, managing the family and regulating society. The more highly civilised a community is the more completely differentiated are these two functions. . . .

This clamour for political rights is woman's confession of sexual enmity. Gloss over it as we may, it comes to this in the end. No woman who loves her husband would wish to usurp his province. It is only those whose instincts are inverted, or whose anti-sexual vanity is insatiable, who would take the political reins from the strong hands which have always held them to give them to others—weaker, less capable, and wholly unaccustomed. To women who love, their 'desire is to their husbands'; and the feeling remains as an echo in the soul when even the master voice is silent....

This question of woman's political power is from beginning to end a question of sex, and all that depends on sex—its moral and intellectual limitations, its emotional excesses, its personal disabilities, its social conditions. It is a question of science, as purely as the best hygienic conditions or the accurate understanding of physiology. And science is dead against it. Science knows that to admit women—that is, mothers—into the heated arena of political life would be as destructive to the physical well-being of the future generation as it would be disastrous to the good conduct of affairs in the present. And social science echoes the same thing in all that regards wives and mistresses of honest families.

Eliza Lynn Linton, 'The Wild Women as Politicians', *The Nineteenth Century*, Vol. 30, July 1891, pp. 80–82, 86.

12. Woman's Standpoint—Sex Consciousness (1901)

Those who have the training of boys wisely aim at the highest possible development both in body and mind of the *human being*; the practice often falls short of the ideal, but that is the ideal. Now, what is the aim in the training of girls? To make them as perfect *women* as possible; not as perfect human beings as possible, but as perfect women. The idea of sex is never lost sight of, a method of education which would be positively dangerous in the case of boys, and which is only saved from the full consequences of its foolishness by the better moral nature and less strongly developed animal passions of girls. But still the girl grows up, having learnt to look at everything from the woman's standpoint, not from the larger standpoint of humanity. She never loses the consciousness of sex; it colours all her ideas; and probably in this fact lies the solution of the mystery that men are so often utterly baffled when they try to understand women. How can they possibly expect to do so? Men use their trained human intelligence and are not all the time looking at questions and events as male creatures. They forget that women, broadly speaking, are only using half their consciousness, the other half, the very one which would be common ground between them, being stunted or dormant. The emotional side of woman's nature is already strong, quite enough so for her own happiness; then why, in the name of all that is reasonable, foster it and cultivate it until it overpowers the intellectual and critical side? Better far to teach her that she ought to have more than one outlook upon life, that she ought not to stake all her chances of happiness on the satisfaction of one part of her nature, on the always risky speculation of marriage. It has often been said that marriage means much more to a woman than to a man; that marriage is a woman's whole life, while it is only an incident in the life of a man. This is of course the extreme view, but there is much truth in it: truth, that is, as a matter of observation of actual life, but wholly false as an ideal. Marriage ought to be much more than an incident in a man's life; but, on the other hand, it ought not to be the whole of a woman's life. Certainly this view has generally been urged upon women by men—it has suited their convenience—and women are always only too ready to believe what men tell them. . . .

Harriet E. Mahood, 'The Modesty of Englishwomen', *The Nineteenth Century*, Vol. 49, April 1901, pp. 598–9.

13. The Wife as Reproductive Doll (1912)

It is this consciousness, expressed or unexpressed, (frequently the former) of his own supreme importance in her destiny that colours every thought and action of man towards woman. Having assumed that she is incomplete without him, he draws the quite permissible conclusion that she exists only for the purpose of attaining to completeness through him—and that where she does not so attain to it, the unfortunate creature is, for all practical purposes, non-existent. To him womanhood is summed up in one of its attributes—wifehood, or its unlegalized equivalent. Language bears the stamp of the idea that woman is a wife, actually, or in embryo. To most men—perhaps to all—the girl is some man's wife that is to be; the married woman some man's wife that is; the widow some man's wife that was; the spinster some man's wife that should have been—a damaged article, unfit for use, unsuitable. Therefore a negligible quantity....

It is, I should say, quite impossible for any thinking man to entertain a real reverence and esteem for a section of humanity which he believes to exist solely in order to perform certain animal functions connected with, and necessary to, the reproduction of the race. After all, it is not upon the performance of a purely animal function that a human being should found his or her title to respect; if woman is reverenced only because she reproduces her kind, a still higher meed of reverence is due to the rabbit ... a person who is convinced that woman is a form of animated doll whereof the mechanism, when pressed on the right spot, squeaks out the two ejaculations of, 'I love you,' and 'Oh, my dear baby,' has a perfect right to describe her in those terms; but no woman has the right so to describe herself.

... As a matter of fact, her description of her emotions when she is in love or bears children is not, as a rule, a first-hand description; it is more or less careful, more or less intelligent copy of the masculine conception of her emotions under those particular circumstances. Thus the business-like aspect of love in woman, the social or commercial necessity for sexual intercourse is usually ignored by an imitative feminine art—because it is lacking in man, and is, therefore, not really grasped by him. When he becomes aware of it he dislikes it....

Cicely Hamilton, *Marriage as a Trade*, 1912, pp. 4–5, 112, 154–5.

14. Nature's Purpose for Women (1912)

Living Nature is not so fiendishly contrived as has sometimes appeared to the casual eye. On the contrary, the natural rule which we see illustrated in all species, animal or vegetable, high or low, throughout the living world, is that the individual is so constructed that his or her personal fulfilment of his or her natural destiny as an individual, is precisely that which best serves the race. Once we learn that individuals were all evolved by Nature for the sake of the race, we shall understand why they have been so evolved in their personal characteristics that in living their own lives and fulfilling themselves they best fulfil Nature's remoter purpose.... Since women differ from men, their sacrifice takes a somewhat different form, but in their case, as in men's, the right fulfilment of Nature's purpose is one with the right fulfilment of their own destiny....

It remains to state the most valuable end which this book might possibly achieve—an end which, by one means or another, must be achieved. It is that the best women, those favoured by Nature in physique and intelligence, in character and their emotional nature, the women who are increasingly to be found enlisted in the ranks of Feminism, and fighting the great fight for the Women's Cause, shall be convinced by the unchangeable and beneficent facts of biology, seen in the bodies and minds of women, and shall direct their efforts accordingly; so that they and those of their sisters who are of the same natural rank, instead of increasingly deserting the ranks of motherhood and leaving the blood of inferior women to constitute half of all future generations, shall on the contrary furnish an ever-increasing proportion of our wives and mothers, to the great gain of themselves, and of men, and of the future ... physiological and psychological facts ... demonstrate overwhelmingly the truth of the view that the individual was evolved by Nature for the care of the germ-plasm, or, in other words, was and is constructed primarily and ultimately for parenthood....

C.W. Saleeby, *Woman and Womanhood*, 1912, pp. 12, 14, 30–1.

15. The Essential Differences between Men and Women (1913)

Men and women are fundamentally alike, whilst essentially different. They are alike in the broad human sense; their essential diff erences are rooted in their sexual characteristics. What men find attractive in women, and women in men, are these different traits which may be expressed in the much abused yet expressive words, 'womanliness' and 'manliness'. It is the effeminate man—when it is not the prejudiced and jealous male—who dislikes woman and fears her emancipation. It is the abnormal woman whose conception of the movement after freedom is one of antagonism to the 'stronger sex'. What adds to the difficulty of modern life is that these abnormal types of men and women exist in sufficient numbers to affect popular opinion and to obscure the issue. A vast amount of energy is wasted in futile argument as to the relative superiority of men and women. We have insufficient data to make any decision possible. Even if woman is 'undeveloped man' or man 'rudimentary female,' no good purpose is served by insisting upon the fact. Both statements, after all, are true. Each sex contains undeveloped organs and functions which are more fully developed in the other. Each has mental and psychical qualities which the other possesses in less degree. Neither is superior to the other. Ability, power, character, like genius, are sexless. The lesson of biology is that, when sex exists, the two sexes are mutually dependent. Nietzsche expresses something of this idea when he says, 'The perfect woman is a higher and rarer type of humanity than the perfect man, but, at the same time, her influence can only be rightly exercised with the support and co-operation of man.' Sociologically, sex antagonism is destructive. Morally, it is opposed to altruism, to the spirit of sympathy and desire to promote the good of others which is the basis of social consciousness behind all the social progress of to-day....

The mothers of the race have special faculties and can give special service to the State in all that concerns the domestic welfare of the community and the betterment of home conditions, in legislation for the protection of children, and in the organisation of women's labour. In this period of transition there is danger that the special aptitudes of women are being misdirected, for a time necessarily so, because of the need of concentration. But the whole movement is meant to make for the uplifting of domesticity. Already there are signs that women are beginning to specialise in those particular occupations which, in spite of the cant associated with the phrase, remain our true vocation—in home making, child rearing, in the protection, preservation, and training of new life. . . .

Elizabeth Chesser, *Woman, Marriage and Motherhood*, 1913, pp. 245–6, 252.

1.3 Female Health

16. Female Disorders and the Plantation of Mankind (1817?)

Female disorders are certainly more complicated than those of men; who from their peculiar delicacy are subject to diseases, which men, as far as regards sensation, must be totally strangers to.

This consideration naturally inspires our sex with tenderness and compassion for the many weaknesses and complaints women labour under; at the same time it excites in us an ardent desire to aid and protect them on all occasions, as the objects of our felicity; and tenderly preserve them, as the plantation of mankind. . . .

Samuel Solomon, *A Guide to Health*, 66th edn., [1817?], p. 131.

17. Female Health and Intercourse (1838)

It is a fact that can hardly have escaped the notice of anyone, that women who have never had sexual commerce begin to droop when about twenty-five years of age, that they become pale and languid, that general weakness and irritability, a sort of restless, nervous fidgettyness takes possession of them, and an absorbing process goes on, their forms degenerate, their features sink, and the peculiar character of the old maid becomes apparent . . .

Healthy human beings so far differ from the generality of other animals, that their desires and modes of living lead them to desire intercourse at all seasons; and where debility is not produced by excess, health is confirmed by the stimulating and pleasing excitement. . . .

Richard Carlile, *Every Woman's Book or What is Love?*, 1838, pp. 35–6, 42.

18. Women in Pain (1851)

... man was created independent because destined to govern the family, society, and nature; while woman was made dependent, tied to hearth and home by a long chain of never-ending infirmities, as if to point out the destined sphere where her activity could find more happiness, although a paler glory. Instead, therefore, of despising herself on account of fetters, evidently necessary or they would never have been imposed, they should be worn with a proud humility, from the knowledge that in some mysterious way they seem to unite her more closely to her dearest earthly ties; from the remembrance also that if women have greater pains to endure, they are endowed with a greater capacity for joy, and that they derive infinitely more pleasure than men from the many forms of the one passion which alone harmonizes the terrible discordances of this world. In addition to these, Holy Writ suggests another, and truly the physiologist can adduce no better reason:—'In sorrow shalt thou bring forth children,' was said to woman with reference to uterine parturition, and this seems to me to hold good also in that periodical function which is intimately connected with the parturition of the germ by the ovary, and is therefore accompanied by pains of a similar nature, only much less intense. This is so true, that I do not consider the menstrual function to be healthily performed unless it be accompanied by at least some amount of spinal and ovarian pains. One of the most striking features of chlorosis is the total absence of such pains, and unless they reappear to some extent, a chlorotic patient can never be considered permanently cured....

E. J. Tilt, *On the preservation of the health of women*, 1851, pp. 70–1.

19. 'Damn Nature': Woman as an Invalid (1869)

Michelet defines woman as an invalid. Such she emphatically is, as compared with man. Woman is doubly entitled to man's protection; not only as smaller and weaker than himself, but as being, on account of her sex, more or less always unwell. Who does woman the greater service—he who ignores, or he who remembers this important physiological distinction between the sexes? This distinction is never mentioned on platforms, where men and women bray about the equality of the sexes; yet every medical man knows it underlies the whole question. This periodical illness of women is always ignored by theorists, whose object apparently is to produce an anti-scientific, superficial declamation to tickle the ears of groundlings; but it cannot be practically ignored with impunity. Outraged nature exacts a terrible retribution. Here, then, is to be sought the true cause of that predominance of the male intellect, ascribed by feminine frothy lecturers of both sexes to the tyrannical usurpation of man....

Even if woman possessed a brain equal to man's—if her intellectual powers were equal to his—the eternal distinction in the physical organisation of the sexes would make the average man in the long run, the mental superior of the average woman. In intellectual labour, man has surpassed, does now, and always will surpass woman, for the obvious reason that nature does not periodically interrupt his thought and application....

No woman ever passed through life without being ill. She suffers from 'the custom of women', or she does not. In either case she is normally or abnormally ill. Thus every woman is, according to temperament and other circumstances, always more or less an invalid. Therefore, no woman can pursue uninterrupted physical or mental labour. Nature disables the whole sex, single as well as married, from competing on equal terms with man....

It is superfluous to dwell on the importance of the maternal duties. The normal condition of woman being evidently marriage and maternity, it follows that women who fulfil this condition, and discharge thoroughly their conjugal and maternal duties, have neither time nor inclination to try to convert themselves into poor and imperfect copies of men. The functions of wife and mother are so essential, not only to the welfare but to the existence of the species,—so high and holy, that they cannot be abnegated or insufficiently discharged, without entailing the most disastrous consequences....

Woman's instinct and wishes do not lead her in the purely

intellectual direction. Her pleasures and duties are widely distinct from those of man. She is content, in most instances, to let others think for her, and trusts to that faculty, where she is really superior—her intuition—to discover the most proper person to do so. Nature has declared, in language which cannot deceive, that woman's chief mission is maternity. Woman craves to be a mother, knowing that she is an imperfect undeveloped being, until she has borne a child. There is a grand physiological truth expressed in the pathetic words of Rachel to Jacob: 'Give me children, or else I die'....

Any attempt to fix woman's condition in society, without taking into account the peculiarities of her physical conformation, must be worthless; and it is exactly woman's physical conformation which is utterly ignored by the advocates of sexual equality. To the transcendental school we may bequeath Fuseli's witty saying, 'Damn Nature, she puts me out.'

J. M. Allan, 'On the Differences in the Minds of Men and Women', *Journal of the Anthropological Society of London*, 7 (1869), pp. cxcix-cci.

20. Women's Health and Natural Law (1873)

CAN A NATURAL STATE BE CALLED A STATE OF INVALIDISM?—I have just been glancing at a modern American book, bearing the name of a well-known physician, and treating of the functions and diseases of women, and I have shut it in disgust on finding the same idea which Michelet has so sentimentally elaborated—namely, that woman's natural state is that of invalidism, and that all her peculiar natural functions are unavoidably attended with pain, inconvenience and disability. Speaking of a woman's monthly periods, this physician says: 'More or less pain, more or less prostration and general disturbance, at these epochs are universal and inevitable.' At the first glance I feel that, as a physician, he ought to know better. But on second thoughts I consider that, as a physician, he only knows of the cases of sickness and suffering, for those who do not suffer of course do not need his assistance. But there never was a greater mistake—a mistake which underlies all the others regarding woman's abilities and disabilities.

MENSTRUATION A PAINLESS FUNCTION.—A woman in complete health should menstruate with perfect freedom from pain, and with the least possible inconvenience. She will not even feel prostrated. The only difference at such periods is that she is more *liable* to weariness and prostration from over-exertion. This freedom from suffering is not rare. Menstruation is not a disease, nor should it reduce to a state of even slight temporary invalidism. When all the organs are in health and work in harmony, it will not do so. That it frequently does, I admit; but in these cases there is disarrangement. It is not the result of natural law....

IS PREGNANCY A STATE OF DISEASE OR OF HEALTH?—The first thing to be considered is whether pregnancy is a natural and healthy state or a state of disease. It seems an insult to nature and to the Creator to imagine that pregnancy was ever intended to be a sickness. It is the legitimate result of a law ordained by nature. If all the conditions are favorable, it ought to be attended with little or no inconvenience. I believe it is safe to declare that all its evil accompaniments are the result, not of direct laws of nature, but of violations of natural law. False states of society, false modes of dress, false habits of life, etc., all contribute to bring suffering at this time, much of which is undoubtedly the result of a wise and kindly ordering of Nature by which she averts more disastrous results....

Mrs E. B. Duffey, *What Women Should Know*, 1873, pp. 43–4, 165.

21. Sexual Functions and Female Mental Disorders (1890)

[Dr Hugh Fenton] said that no one who studied women or who was thrown amongst them and had to observe them could possibly overlook the fact that at certain sexual crises they were liable, with very slight determining causes, to have their mental balance overthrown, as, for instance, at puberty, marriage, maternity, and the menopause. When they bore these facts in mind it was impossible to disassociate mental disorders in the female from her sexual functions. This was certainly the case to a much more marked extent than in the male....

'Discussion on Sexual Function and Insanity', 22 October 1890, *The British Gynaecological Journal*, Vol. 6 (1890–1), p. 422.

22. The Effect of Cycling (1896)

Let it at once be said, an organically sound woman can cycle with as much impunity as a man. Thank Heaven, we know now that this is not one more of the sexual problems of the day. Sex has nothing to do with it, beyond the adaptation of machine to dress and dress to machine.

With cycles as now perfected there is nothing in the anatomy or the physiology of a woman to prevent their being fully and freely enjoyed within the limits of common sense....

The diseases of women take a front place in our social life; but if looked into, ninety per cent of them are functional ailments begotten of *ennui* and lack of opportunity of some means of working off their superfluous muscular, nervous, and organic energy. The effect of cycling within the physical capacity of a woman acts like a charm for gout, rheumatism, and indigestion. Sleeplessness, so-called 'nerves', and all those petty miseries for which the 'liver' is so often made the scapegoat, disappear in the most extraordinary way with the fresh air inhaled, and with the tissue destruction and reconstruction effected by exercise and exhilaration.

Anaemia is very prevalent among adolescent girls and with it languor, morbid fancies and appetites. There is no better antidote to this than free oxygenation of the blood, improvement in circulation helped still further by getting the patient out into the air and sunshine. It was expected that women specially might be exposed to injury from internal strains and from the effects of shaking and jarring when riding on the roads. In practice this has been found to be nothing but a bogey.... Already thousands of women qualifying for general invalidism have been rescued by cycling....

W. H. Fenton, 'A Medical View of Cycling for Ladies', *The Nineteenth Century*, Vol. 39, May 1896, pp. 797, 800.

23. Ill-health as Ignorance and Sin (1912)

This is a common-sense age. The idea that most of the ills of mind and body can be prevented is gaining ground. We are beginning to realize that health is the natural birthright of human beings and that we can be fit, healthy, happy and efficient if we exercise care and common sense. Ill-health is the fruit of ignorance and sin. Sin against the laws of nature, ignorance of the principles of health and hygiene.... If we are ill it is probably our own fault. Even if we are not personally to blame, illness is a disgrace to somebody, because it indicates physiological sins past or present. A great deal of ill-health is the result of infectious disease, perhaps contracted in childhood, and all infectious diseases are preventable and ought to be prevented.... When we are healthy and fit we do not succumb to the microbes of disease, even when we breathe or swallow them... women should keep the ideal of perfect health before them all the time....

Right living is the first essential. Most of the everyday ills of the flesh, from gout and dyspepsia to headaches and 'nerves' are the direct consequences of wrong living.... The perfectly healthy person is buoyant, self-confident, and expends her energy in useful work for others. The 'nervy' woman is self-centred, self-engrossed.... We can train our minds into good habits or bad, according to the kind of thoughts we indulge in....

The morality of the future will include the doctrine of *sane thinking*, the teaching that our thoughts, like our speech, can be controlled. Thought, like action, tends to become automatic, and every kindly, charitable and beautiful thought we harbour influences directly our character and our ultimate sense of happiness. The old teaching that we must be 'good' in order to escape punishment in the hereafter is giving place to a higher ideal that we must work, irrespective of any hope of reward, in harmony with the divine will. 'Goodness' is synonymous with health, health of mind and spirit. If we are perfectly healthy we are 'good'....

The development of Eugenics must necessarily affect human happiness and health.... Evil and disease can never be wholly eliminated from society. But by restricting the propagation of the unfit, and by encouraging a healthier public opinion on responsibility in marriage, we can, to a large extent, protect unborn generations from the social ills and diseases we suffer from today. The health and welfare of the race is largely in our own hands. We are beginning to understand the forces which make for happiness or unhappiness, health or disease, and we must apply our knowledge.

We must purify the life stream, improve the human stock by reducing the output of the unhealthy and undesirable, and increasing the number of fit, worthy, healthy and efficient men and women.... We must introduce a system that will make marriage 'permissive', that will deny the right of parenthood to the unfit... physical, mental or moral.... A higher birth-rate in the healthy and fit classes of the community is essential to the future prosperity of the nation....

Elizabeth S. Chesser, *Perfect Health for Women and Children*, 1912, pp. 3–4, 22–3, 36, 50–3.

24. The Greater Vitality of the Female? (1913)

We have in civilised countries hundreds of thousands more women than men. In England and Germany the women are a million in excess. Taking the figures for all Europe, there are approximately 1,024 women to every 1,000 men. And this in spite of the fact that more boys are born than girls. With the better protection of women at childbirth the number of males born alive might be considerably increased. In England, for example, 140 boys are stillborn for every 100 girls. This is partly due to the fact that boys have larger heads; but with proper care, with the provision of medical attendance for every necessitous mother at childbirth, many of these lives would be saved. In spite of this higher mortality of boys at birth, there is an excess of males born alive, the figures being 104 boys in England to every 100 girls; in France, 106; in Russia, 107; in Philadelphia, 110. We have a further loss of boy life after birth. More boy babies succumb in the first year than girls; it may be because the vitality of the female is greater, owing to her more important reproductive function and her greater biological value as a potential mother. It is certain that the better care of maternity would reduce the infant mortality rate, and the proportion of boys would therefore increase....

Elizabeth Chesser, *Woman, Marriage and Motherhood*, 1913, pp. 247–8.

1.4 The Gynaecological View of Women

25. The Controlling Female Organ (1837)

There is no organ in the body, with the exception of the stomach, that exercises a more extensive control over the female system than the womb....

Dr Thomas Bull, *Hints to Mothers for the Management of Health*, 1837, p. 55.

26. Doctors and Female Diseases (1841)

It has been, and, indeed, still is the case, that few consulting physicians or surgeons pay any attention to female diseases, unless the very small number who practice obstetric medicine....

Dr Michael Ryan, *A Manual of Midwifery*, 1841, p. 329.

27. Constant and General Use of the Speculum (1857)

I speak... of men, who, secured in the confidence of the public by the possession of their diplomas, and within the pale of the profession, are now rising into fame and fortune by the indiscriminate use of the speculum...[resulting in] the lowered and loosened state to which [the speculum] is rapidly bringing the morality of the country....

41

To believe in the necessity for this constant and general use of the speculum, is to admit a sad deterioration in nature itself. Either this, or that anterior generations were great sufferers without being aware of it ... the modern and multitudinous disorders attributed to the uterine system, are wicked inventions, put forth to sanction unnecessary interference. Why, if we are to believe these men, there is scarcely a patient who applies to them, that is not suffering from one or the other of these numerous affections. The womb, with them, is so invariably out of order or out of position, that disease and dislocation are more constant than its normal conditions.

Nor are these practices confined to the high priests in these temples of immorality, faith in their professions now pervades a large portion of female society... the mania has spread... and the consequence is, that some men in the general practice of our profession, are induced to shape their treatment less by the nature of the complaints, than the suggestions of their patients ... [who] remain long enough under treatment to familiarise [them] with indecency, and to enable the prenticed hand of the neophite to attain the *tour de maître* both in handling the instrument and the fee....

[These men] must not be allowed to jeopardise the modesty of the sex so long the pride and property of England....

F.R.C.S., *The Speculum: Its Moral Tendencies*, 1857, pp. 4–7, 11.

28. 'That Most Troublesome Part' (1870)

... I can't bear [Dr] Cumberbach having been wrong and so lost all this valuable time...she [dear Emily] has gone through so much that is horrid and painful and to feel that it has been for nothing is really too hard...I can't help thinking that your idea about the external application of leeches would do good....

...I am glad a cause is given for all her pain...though I fear the cure must take a long time...you see [Dr] Cumberbach was right about there being something wrong with that part [i.e. the reproductive organs]. After all, women, it seems to me must always be, either in a certain state [i.e. pregnant] or else something odious with that most troublesome part takes place. . . .

Lady Stanley to her mother, Lady Clarendon, 20, 24 December 1870, Hobbs-Derby/Gathorne-Hardy Papers, 30/25, 30/26 [Corpus Christi College, Cambridge].

29. Medical Specialisation—the Obstetric Approach to Women (1873)

How far that clear intelligence [Hippocrates, the Father of Medicine], or the still brighter genius of Harvey, who practised midwifery, would have approved the actual minute, and still proceeding, subdivision of medical practice, it is now useless to speculate. It is hopeless for any one man so to practise, and so to study, all the branches of medicine as to combine harmoniously, and profitably for science, the diverse materials that would accumulate upon him. He would be crushed under the overwhelming load.

There is nothing to be done, then, but to distribute the work amongst many workmen; and on all suitable opportunities to call them together to aid in building up the every-rising, but never-to-be-completed, Temple of Medicine.

Yet it must surely strike those who reflect, that subdivision of medical practice may be carried out to an injurious, even to an absurd, extent. The true medical mind will always refuse to look upon any one organ of the body as anything more than a dependent part of a whole. But the public seems to grow less and less reasonable upon this subject every day. I have recently been honoured by a visit from a lady of typical modern intelligence, who consulted me about a fibroid tumour of the uterus; and lest I should stray beyond my business, she was careful to tell me that Dr. Brown-Séquard had charge of her nervous system; that Dr. Williams attended to her lungs; that her abdominal organs were entrusted to Sir William Gull; that Mr Spencer Wells looked after her rectum; and that Dr. Walshe had her heart. If some adventurous doctor should determine to start a new speciality, and open an institution for the treatment of diseases of the umbilicus—the only region which, as my colleague, Mr. Simon, says is unappropriated—I think I can promise him more than one patient.

The fragmentary way in which medicine is studied, more especially in this town, undoubtedly interposes a serious barrier to the advancement of true knowledge. And it is not difficult to see that it acts injuriously upon the medical mind, disposing those who too exclusively study one branch to underrate the merit, and even the honesty, of those who study a different branch. This extreme splitting-up of medicine renders almost impossible the attainment of a full perception of pathology, or even of the import of any disease or symptom. It destroys the very idea of correlation, of the mutual reaction of different organs, and of the modes by which all the organs may be affected by one common condition.

It is a miserably narrow view to take of the practice of obstetrics to regard it as simply the art of delivering women in labour. The study of menstruation, of pregnancy, of labour, of childbed, and of the phenomena connected with these conditions, opens up to the earnest practitioner a rich mine of facts illustrative of many of the most interesting problems in medicine. Out of this mine he may extract materials in profusion which he would look for in vain elsewhere....

Not even surgeons witness more frequent or more instructive lessons as to the effects, immediate and remote, of rapid and profuse, or of repeated losses of blood.

Peritonitis in women must be continually misunderstood or misinterpreted, unless it be studied in connexion with puerpery, menstruation, and the diseases of the ovaries and uterus....

Dr Robert Barnes, 'Lumleian Lectures on the Convulsive Diseases of Women', *The Lancet*, 12 April 1873, p. 513.

30. Gynaecology: the Youngest Branch of Medicine (1882)

Gynaecology, or the accurate study of diseases of women, is the youngest branch of medical literature, for it began in 1816, with

Recamier and the better means of diagnosis that he introduced. The time that has elapsed since then, may be divided into two periods, the first extends from Recamier to Simpson, the second we are still in the midst of, and it dates from our illustrious countryman. The galaxy of Paris physicians who followed the lead of Recamier, had for object, to bring the sexual organs of women within the range of the general laws of pathology...inflammation was accepted as explaining most uterine diseases, and the therapeutical tendencies of this epoch were essentially medical without disparagement of surgery....

With Simpson began the more exclusive surgical tendencies that are still in the ascendant in England and America. He started the treatment of uterine displacements and flexions by pessaries, intra, and extra uterine....

Simpson devised the slitting of the womb for the cure of sterility, but when transplanted into America, his operation, in the hands of Dr Marion Sims, became one for the cure of most diseases of women. It is difficult for us simple-minded Englishmen, to withstand the American advocacy of surgical operations....

I gave it to be understood, that until Simpson made his mark, somewhat too large a part was given to inflammation for the explanation of uterine pathology. Since then, the tendency has been to undervalue the importance of this most important element of general pathology and of daily practice....

E. J. Tilt, *The Change of Life in Health and Disease*, 4th. edn., 1882, pp. vii–viii.

31. Medical Women (1887)

1. The first difficulty lies in some remaining jealousy and ill-will towards medical women, on the part of a section (constantly diminishing, as I believe) of the medical profession itself. Some twenty years ago the professional prejudice was so deep and so widely spread that it constituted a very formidable obstacle, but it has been steadily melting away before the logic of facts; and now is, with a few exceptions, rarely to be found among the leaders of

the profession, nor indeed among the great majority of the rank and file, so far as can be judged by the personal experience of medical women themselves. Unfortunately it seems strongest just where it has least justification—viz. among the practitioners who devote themselves chiefly to midwifery and to the special diseases of women. The Obstetrical Society is, so far as I know, still of the same mind as when, in 1874, they excluded Dr. Garrett Anderson, a distinguished M.D. from Paris, from their membership; and the Soho Square Hospital for Women has never revoked its curt refusal to allow me to enter its doors, when in 1878, I proposed to take advantage of the invitation issued in its Report to all practitioners who were specially interested in the cases for which the hospital is reserved. . . .

2. The second obstacle lies in the continued exclusion of women from the majority of our universities, and from the English Colleges of Physicians and Surgeons. . . .

Sophia Jex-Blake, 'Medical Women', *The Nineteenth Century*, Vol. 22, November 1887, pp. 704–5.

32. Healing and the Ailments Peculiar to Women (1888)

. . .In no department of the healing art, we apprehend, is quackery and mismanagement so prevalent as in that which appertains to the ailments peculiar to women. . . .

E. H. Ruddock, *The Common Diseases of Women including the Homeopathic and General Treatment of Ailments peculiar to Different Periods of Life*, 6th edn., 1888, p. iv.

33. Gynaecology as a Surgical Approach to Women (1890)

Before the recent advances of gynaecology, women, sane and insane, had to suffer from ills now known to be curable. . . .

Gynaecology is largely surgical, and the true solution of its most important problems is revealed by direct appeal to surgery. Not to extend this argument we may simply state that the surgery of the brain and spinal cord, and of the abdominal and pelvic cavities, is at once experimental and therapeutical. It is vivisection of the noblest kind. It teaches physiology, the rational basis of the healing art; it demonstrates pathology at the same time that it heals. The surgeon learns, the subject gains life and health....

Physiology points to the ovary as the ruling organ in woman, 'Propter ovaria mulier est quod est.' Accordingly we might expect that the disease of this organ would cause most disturbance of the nervous system. Evidence bearing upon this conjecture has been growing of late years; but it has long been foreshadowed. Thus Icard relates that Professor Coste had brought together in the Musée de France a fine collection of uteruses and ovaries taken from women of all ages who had committed suicide during menstruation. I wrote to Dr. Auvard asking him to examine this collection. He kindly did so. His report is that the specimens are all scattered and destroyed. Thus has a brilliant prescient idea aborted. But the example remains for imitation ... [ovarian or uterine] diseases we know are apt to entail nervous disorders, and we have seen that the nervous disorders, when complicating disease of the sexual organs, are frequently cured when the diseased organs are removed....

Dr Robert Barnes, 'On the Correlations of the Sexual Functions and Mental Disorders of Women', *The British Gynaecological Journal*, Vol. 6 (1890–1), pp. 391–2, 398–9, 402.

34. The Woman's Doctor (1895–1902)

Private

I have just received your kind letter—and from it I fear you are not better. Dr. Maclagan who applied the electricity would be naturally unwilling to think it had done so much harm, and I hope you may be going to consult another doctor.

Cadogan Place is so conveniently close that if I have a bad cold and I need a doctor I do send for him, but I do think he is not very

helpful and that there are others much more so. There is Dr.
Bowles in Upper Brook Street. He was a very famous woman's
doctor at Folkestone, so many people went to him from London,
that a few years ago he came to London. He is a most cheerful
helpful man—very sensible—I think he takes Sir Andrew Clark's
place somewhat. I have written *private* on this because one must
be so very careful in talking about doctors, but if you enquire
about Dr. Bowles I think you will find him well thought of.

Lady Lyell to Lady Campbell Bannerman, 27 November
[1895–1902?], Campbell Bannerman Papers, BL Add. MS. 41246,
fos. 261–2.

35. Gynaecology—the Pelvis as the Source of Ill Health (1909)

...it may be permitted here, in discussing the hygiene of the
growing girl, to emphasize the necessity of extreme care to avoid
the suggestion of pelvic disease to the young woman or to the
growing girl. Unfortunately, the possibility of giving or
withholding the suggestion is not often in the power of the
physician. The teaching of gynecology twenty-five years ago, with
the constant pelvic examinations, local treatment with douches,
tampons, etc., dilatations and curettage for 'the moral effect' has
fixed pretty firmly in the minds of women the idea that the most
frequent source of ill health of girls is to be found in the pelvis. A
prominent gynecologist of a generation ago told his patients that
if a woman knew the danger she was in from her pelvic organs she
would not step from her carriage to the pavement; the effect of
such teaching upon practitioners and patients has been harmful in
the extreme. It has hardly been possible in the present generation
for a neurotic or hysterical girl, or one suffering from
malnutrition, to reach the age of seventeen without having passed
through some more or less prolonged gynecological treatment by
the general practitioner, or, if she has avoided the physician,
without having used largely the various nostrums or local
applications of the patent medicine venders. It is difficult even for
a healthy girl to rid her mind of constant impending evil from the

uterus and ovaries, so prevalent is the idea that woman's ills are mainly 'reflexes' from the pelvic organs. If symptoms are suggestive of pelvic disturbance a young woman should be examined under an anaesthetic. Local treatment should be avoided unless absolutely necessary. On the other hand, pelvic examination when symptoms point to its necessity, must not be postponed by considerations of false delicacy. Here again women suffer from the secrecy which, for them, has surrounded all the phenomena of reproduction....

Dr Howard A. Kelly, *Medical Gynecology*, 1909, pp. 73–4.

36. Promiscuity and Insanity (1911)

I heard only the other day that whereas the man who (whether married or single) makes constant and promiscuous advances when circumstances favour him is a fairly well recognised phenomenon of modern society, the woman who does so—if she happens to be a married woman—is liable to be regarded as insane, and, by the connivance of her husband and the medical profession, to be shut up for life in a mad-house. I was told of two women, well known in society, who died in lunatic asylums, and whose only sign of insanity was this taste for promiscuity which some men look upon as quite normal in themselves.

That piece of injustice is merely another product of the extraordinary barrier which has been raised by silence against an honest and common understanding between the sexes of the weaknesses which they share, and of that mutual inheritance of disturbed and unhealthy conditions which some are ready to regard as normal in the one and insanely abnormal in the other....

Laurence Housman, *The Immoral Effects of Ignorance in Sex Relations*, 1911, pp. 23–4.

PART 2
Menstruation and Adolescence

Introduction

The history of menstruation was largely an oral record of superstitions until the twentieth century (see Aristotle [37]; *The Old Testament* [38]; Crawfurd, 1915 [39]). The 'mystery of the menses' [39] was fertile ground for the propagation of myths about the nature and significance of the menstrual flow. Separate spheres for the two sexes began at puberty, which was supposedly responsible for strength and vigour in boys, but weakness and vulnerability in girls. Women gained their dominant gender identity through the menstrual cycle which initiated the distinctive 'female economy' (Laycock, 1840 [41]; Johnson, 1850 [44]).

Until the Edwardian period, doctors were ignorant and confused about the nature and origins of menstruation. Dr Conquest (1848) [43] believed it depended on 'some established law of nature, of which we know nothing beyond its existence'. Medical ignorance was so great that bleeding from other parts of the female body was often assumed to be 'vicarious menstruation'. Ryan (1841) [42] believed it could proceed 'from ulcers on any part of the body', while Waller (1839) [40] agreed that blood could be discharged from different parts of the body 'in cases of obstructed menstruation'. Ryan reviewed changing theories about the origins of menstrual secretion, including the veins and the glands, but concluded that the 'uterine cavity' was usually the source. Female reproductive physiology was a matter for speculation throughout the nineteenth century, though there was a growing belief that ovulation and menstruation were somehow causally related. It was not until 1908 that Hitschmann and Adler proved this, and later researchers showed that ovulation usually took place about the middle of the intermenstrual interval and not during or immediately after the menstrual flow, as was previously assumed.

Inevitably ignorance bred fear and superstition. For centuries menstruating women had been treated as unclean and surrounded by powerful taboos. Johnson (1850) [44] described menstrual excess in terms of the vampire, sucking blood from the depleted woman. The nature of the vampire was rather uncertain—perhaps a disturbed 'economy' rather than a hyperactive uterus. But the metaphorical associations pointed directly to the repugnance and fear associated with the menstrual function: 'Hence it may be seen how much more perniciously morbid influences act upon woman than upon man'. Menstruation was a cause for revulsion, as God's curse on the sin of Eve. Not surprisingly it was a subject of embarrassment for women themselves, who used euphemisms such as being 'unwell' or 'out of order' (Waller, 1839 [40]). They rarely mentioned it in diaries or correspondence even with intimate female friends, except when discussing the possibility of pregnancy. Pejorative associations were so pervasive that medical authors found it necessary to stress the functional character of the menstrual process: 'Menstruation is a function similar to circulation, digestion, etc., and not a disease, as some have erroneously imagined' (Ryan, 1841 [42]). Dr Waller (1839) [40] still referred, critically, to the unfounded opinion of previous medical writers 'that the menstrual fluid possessed properties of a malignant nature' (see also Crawfurd, 1915 [39]).

The Victorian emphasis was placed on the extensive and painful symptoms of menstruation, and their association with female illness—at least for the upper and middle classes. The lists of 'many unpleasant symptoms' (Waller, 1839 [40]) were a feature of medical accounts of menstruation, including the 'Nervous and hysterical symptoms [which] frequently manifest themselves.' Ryan (1841) [42] was characteristically extravagant in his outline of 'the most common symptoms', since 'to attempt an enumeration of all those that may occur, would require volumes for their history.' His shorthand version included the possibility of 'disorder in all parts of the body, or cutaneous eruptions, convulsions, hysteria, and sometimes epilepsy may appear.' Walter Johnson's (1850) [44] 'secret history of uterine derangement' was based on the belief that 'no action of the [female] economy is so liable to disturbance as this [the menstrual secretion]'. Johnson's physician could 'read' the secret presence of disturbed menstruation in 'the blanched faces' and wrinkled brows of women in the metropolitan streets. Other causes of these symptoms, like poverty and poor diet, were outside the realm of 'The Morbid Emotions of Women'.

These attitudes were in large part a reflection and continuation of earlier myths about menstruation, as well as a recognition of the potential for expanding the role of the doctor in the female life cycle. Advice books were on strong ground when they commented that 'girls are kept in darkness relative to what is of so much importance' (Tilt, 1851 [45]). Adolescent girls received little if any instruction about menstruation. The convention of 'delicacy' restricted the range of socially acceptable subjects for women, including the omission of aspects of their own physiology: 'throwing a veil over the least noble of our necessities gives so great a charm to the relations of society' (Tilt, 1852[52]). Tilt gave mothers the key role in obtaining and transmitting knowledge about the proper management of their daughters' health (as did Weatherly, 1882 [53]). We will never know how many mothers failed to give this information, and how many girls suffered their first period in the horror, fear and shame of ignorance—as did Naomi Mitchison as late as 1909 (1975) [49].

The value and purpose of biological education was itself brought into question when the primary medical emphasis was placed on the 'intense pain' of 'so strange a necessity'. Tilt [45] and Ruddock (1888) [46] even advocated (in identical phrases) that the period of puberty should be retarded and the onset of menstruation delayed, so that proper training might bring girls 'to the full perfection of womanhood', prior to menstruation. The implications were that 'early' menstruation (before the age of fourteen) was potentially more dangerous, and a symptom of an unhealthy life (including, for example, excessive dancing and reading novels). The assumption that menstruation could be delayed by 'the frequent use of cold baths, free exercise in the open air' (Ruddock [46]), and by 'a wholesome subjection of every minute to rule and discipline' (Tilt [45]) provides a revealing insight into the Victorian desire for social control over nature.

The demystification of menstruation in the Edwardian period was only possible because of new scientific knowledge. Advice books were then more likely to take a positive approach, emphasising not 'making a monthly illness out of a natural function, and so setting up a false standard of health and disease in the mind of the inexperienced adolescent' (Scharlieb, 1915 [50]). Menstruation was redefined as part of good health, and for 'healthy girls under favourable circumstances neither the pain nor the discharge itself is sufficient to justify withdrawal from the usual duties and pleasures of life.' This change in approach had important consequences for perceptions of women's social capacities and physiological potential. In 1926 *The Lancet* declared that Victorian attitudes to menstruation had disappeared for ever, because of scientific advances and the need for women in the workforce during the First World War: 'Everybody now knows that women are not necessarily "unwell" once a month' (7 April 1926, p. 712).

At a practical level, one of the more useful Victorian contributions was the transition from rags and diapers to disposable 'sanitary towels', and the improvements in their design. Dr Galabin's (1880 [47], 1895 [48]) displays for the Obstetrical Society of London helped to advertise new models which encouraged greater mobility for women during menstruation, though the invention of the 'towel cremator' reflected earlier obsessions rather than making a major contribution for travelling women. Most women probably continued to soak their menstrual napkins overnight before boiling them in copper washtubs.

The belief that menstruation was incapacitating was used to support the idea of the inferiority of women, and to justify their inadequate education. It was part of the broader attempt to deny the capacity of young women to acquire an intellectual education largely reserved for males. Henry Maudsley argued in the *Fortnightly Review* in 1874 that women could not compete with men intellectually or professionally since they were 'more or less sick and unfit for hard work' for one week in every four during the best years of their lives ('Sex in Mind and Education', 1874, p. 480). Moreover, J. C. Webster (1892) [54] confidently claimed that 'science' itself 'points out the fatal perils awaiting female aspirants to intellectual fame'. Strong opposition was expressed by most writers to any 'system of forced mental training' (e.g. Laycock, 1840 [51]) for adolescent females, because vital energy would be diverted from the reproductive organs (see also

Spencer, 1904 [55]). Hysteria could result, until marriage cured the wayward girl. Mothers were even warned about 'the baleful effects of musical studies on the mind and passions' (Laycock [51]), and Weatherly [53] noted that girls should not be allowed music lessons during menstruation. The daily press was portrayed as a source of corruption rather than education, sending forth 'a wave of pollution' (Tilt, 1852 [52]) which threatened the virtue of the young, unmarried and properly uninformed woman.

The logical consequence of the separate evolutionary theory of the sexes was 'separate spheres' for male and female education as well as social roles. Education could be seen as 'a problem in applied biology' (Saleeby, 1912 [57]), where the proper objective was to teach middle- and upper-class girls to become good wives and mothers by instruction in 'womanly concerns' and ladylike accomplishments. From the 1870s, educational reforms for middle- and upper-class girls did not necessarily mean similar education for both sexes. Separate, gender-based curricula could be made to seem 'natural': 'Every woman should have a real knowledge of housewifery, hygiene and child management' (Chesser, 1912 [58]). Education for adolescent girls was usually defined in terms of woman's major social roles and prevailing models of biological capacity. Even Victorian feminists were divided about the appropriate curriculum for adolescent females.

The most striking examples of the biological devaluation of adolescent girls were afforded by the interpretation of two classic Victorian illnesses which were often correlated with menstruation. Chlorosis or 'Green Sickness' (see 2.3) was defined as an illness affecting adolescent girls, and was only later identified as anaemia, a blood disorder due to reduced red cells (e.g. Galabin, 1893 [64]). The symptoms overlapped to some degree with those at menstruation, but were initially seen as a consequence of delayed menstruation rather than the reverse (e.g. Solomon, 1817 [59]). The predominant causes were identified as peculiarly female in character, such as nervous depression, a sedentary life, or the grand passions (e.g. Johnson [62], Ryan [61]). Thus, 'moral' or psychological remedies were seen as an important part of the treatment. Chlorosis reached its apotheosis in Tilt's (1852) [63] vision of 'two-thirds of the women, of whatever class, who are seen walking the streets of large towns, [who] are more or less tinged with this complaint. Indeed, this state of semi-chlorosis is for woman the bane of a high state of civilisation'. The fact that women might require an improved diet or an increased iron intake during menstruation, pregnancy or lactation was all too frequently obscured by the preoccupation with moral and psychological problems thought to be largely peculiar to the female population.

The second disease which was usually seen as gender-specific and often associated with menstruation was hysteria (see 2.4), 'the most common form of nervous disease to which females are subject' (Laycock, 1840 [66]) and a malady 'of great magnitude' (Skey, 1867 [71]; also Tilt, 1852 [69], etc.). Hysteria was given a special importance by some doctors because it was largely 'peculiar to Females' (Laycock [66]; Carter, 1855 [70] etc.), and was thought by some authors to 'arise from a morbid condition of the uterus' (e.g. Ryan, 1841 [67]). Thus, in this view hysteria began with puberty and ended at the menopause (see also Barnes, 1873 [72]). The causes of hysteria were frequently extended beyond the uterus to a variety of female excesses including celibacy (Spencer, 1904) [76], too much sexual activity, masturbation, 'privation of sexual commerce after it had been long enjoyed', and indeed 'every thing that excites the general sensibility, and especially that of the genital organs' (Ryan [67]). Hysteria could cover the entire realm of the emotions, including depression, nervous fits and psychosomatic illness. Intervention was seen as necessary to establish personal and social control. Willpower must be opposed to feelings (Carter, 1855 [70]).

The great cures were 'moral treatment' to encourage restraint, and marriage to legitimate reasonable desire. Hysteria was represented as a contagious disease—'nervous affections are catching' (Tilt, 1852 [69])—so that isolation from other women, especially young companions, was part of the treatment. Recognition of the dangers associated with the sexist and wide-ranging approach to hysteria came slowly: 'The misery and unhappiness that have accrued to sensitive women through the misuse of these terms ['hysterical' and 'neurotic'] cannot be computed, and is all the more serious since the ignorant lay mind has become familiar with and places an entirely wrong interpretation on them' (MacNaughton-Jones, 1913 [77]). The misuse of the word 'neurotic' has become the modern successor to the misleading nineteenth-century use of 'hysterical'. The possibility that psychosomatic illness might be a real escape from unacceptable, excessively limited female roles and responsibilities was not widely considered until the twentieth century (e.g. Smith-Rosenberg, 1972: see bibliography).

The psychological devaluation of young Victorian and Edwardian women was completed with the invention of 'corset-mania' (see 2.5). This 'mania' was used to exemplify the fundamental opposition between female fashion and male intelligence: 'In truth, the habit of tight-lacing is a thing contrary to anatomy, to physiology, and even to common sense... this silly corset-mania' (Johnson, 1850 [78]). Women's predisposition to 'silly and wicked vanity' was castigated as an 'unnatural propensity' which could result in death, somehow associated with a grossly enlarged liver (Sheehy, 1871 [79]). It was even argued that the 'long train of evils, known as "female complaints"', resulted from this reliance on an external 'supplemental skeleton' (Duffey, 1873 [80]). Dr Kellogg (1885) [81] was deeply suspicious of the relationship between female fashion and vice, since he believed that corsets led to 'the unnatural excitement of the animal propensities', and women's clothing was responsible for 'generating unnatural local heat.' Appropriate medical advice was essential if hysteria and nymphomania were to be avoided. Dr Kelly (1909) [82] simply despaired of women being capable of wearing sensible clothes. Womanhood was a life-long condition; and the possibilities of reform were very limited in medical eyes.

2.1 Menstruation

37. Menstruation and the Moon: Classical Confusion

The onset of the catamenia in women takes place towards the end of the month; and on this account the wiseacres assert that the moon is feminine, because the discharge in women and the waning of the moon happen at one and the same time, and after the wane and the discharge both one and the other grow whole again.... With those in whom the ailment lasts but a little while, two days or three, recovery is easy; but where the duration is longer, the ailment is more troublesome. For women are ailing during these days; and sometimes the discharge is sudden and sometimes gradual, but in all cases alike there is bodily distress until the attack be over. In many cases at the commencement of the attack, when the discharge is about to appear, there occur spasms and rumbling noises within the womb until such time as the discharge manifests itself....

Aristotle, *History of Animals*, 582a, *The Works of Aristotle*, ed. J. A. Smith and W. D. Ross, Vol. 4, Book VII. 1, Oxford 1910.

38. Laws of Purification and Atonement (Leviticus, ch. 15)

And if a woman have an issue, and her issue in her flesh be blood, she shall be put apart seven days: and whosoever toucheth her shall be unclean until the even. And every thing that she lieth upon in her separation shall be unclean: every thing also that she sitteth upon shall be unclean. And whosoever toucheth her bed shall wash his clothes, and bathe himself in water, and be unclean until the even. And whosoever toucheth any thing that she sat upon shall wash his clothes, and bathe himself in water, and be unclean until the even. And if it be on her bed, or on any thing whereon she sitteth, when he toucheth it, he shall be unclean until the even. And if any man lie with her at all, and her flowers be upon him, he shall be unclean seven days; and all the bed whereon he lieth shall be unclean.

And if a woman have an issue of her blood many days out of the time of her separation, or if it run beyond the time of her separation; all the days of the issue of her uncleanness shall be as the days of her separation: she shall be unclean. Every bed whereon she lieth all the days of her issue shall be unto her as the bed of her separation: and whatsoever she sitteth upon shall be unclean, as the uncleanness of her separation. And whosoever toucheth those things shall be unclean, and shall wash his clothes, and bathe himself in water, and be unclean until the even. But if she be cleansed of her issue, then she shall number to herself seven days, and after that she shall be clean. And on the eighth day she shall take unto her two turtles, or two young pigeons, and bring them unto the priest, to the door of the tabernacle of the congregation. And the priest shall offer the one for a sin-offering, and the other for a burnt-offering; and the priest shall make an atonement for her before the LORD for the issue of her uncleanness.

Thus shall ye separate the children of Israel from their uncleanness; that they die not in their uncleanness, when they defile my tabernacle that is among them. This is the law of him that hath an issue, and of him whose seed goeth from him, and is defiled therewith; And of her that is sick of her flowers, and of him that hath an issue, of the man, and of the woman, and of him that lieth with her that is unclean.

Leviticus, 15. 19–33, *The Old Testament* (King James version).

39. Superstition and the History of Menstruation (1915)

Superstitions concerning the menses loom so large in the customs of primitive peoples and are so far from extinct among the lower orders of civilised nations as to be worthy of serious consideration. Many a farmer's wife in this country will still assure you that milk handled by a menstruous woman cannot be churned to butter or that hams will not take salt at her hands. That she has demonstrated the contrary in a series of experiments, month by month, year in and year out, has left unshaken the pillars of her faith: the foundations of faith stand firm in shifting soil.

The wise men of old stood baffled before the mystery of the menses. Pythagoras called menstrual blood the froth of the blood, and held that it contained the superfluity of the aliment. Aristotle explained menstruation as a process necessary to get rid of the excess of blood that had accumulated in the interior of the body of the woman, and his theory is ardently supported 1500 years later by his great commentator Averrhoes. Can it be honestly said that, apart from some suggestive evidence as to the interdependence of ovarian activity and catamenial function, medicine of today has any more satisfying explanation of the purpose of menstruation than theirs?

Where science has failed to establish a proof religion has seldom failed to establish a theory. The Levitical ritual was in no doubt that impurities collected in the woman's blood were discharged in the menstrual flux, so that she underwent a recurring series of purifications. To the men of the monasteries menstruation was a symbol of the essential sinfulness and inferiority of woman, polluted alike and polluting.... It must be remembered that till the middle of the seventeenth century, when the work of Harvey, de Graaf, and other pioneer embryologists led up to the discovery of the ovum in the human female, it was generally believed that the male semen and the female menses were the constituents out of which the child was formed, and by most the leading part was assigned to the menses....

Menstrual fluid has always been reckoned to possess a powerful influence over the affections of men, and has held pride of place as an ingredient of the love-charms administered by girls to would-be lovers.... The idea underlying these customs is that there resides in the menstrual blood some agent powerful for good or for harm; most of all is its power over the virility of the male, enfeebling him in the fierce struggle for the survival of the fittest.

The spirit of the woman resides in her blood and is transferable therewith to the male. It is a special aspect and a special application of the universal primitive blood-horror, founded on this same belief that the spirit of the person resides in his blood, and emerges with it for good or for harm. In addition, there is something unintelligible about menstruation, something uncanny, and the primitive mind explains it as due to some spiritual agency, which may harm the woman if she does not take certain precautions, and may pass from her and harm others if they neglect the prescribed precautions....

With the development of civilisation medical writers, from Hippocrates onward, actually recommended sexual intercourse during menstruation for sterility and other ailments; and in the Middle Ages it had become so common that preachers found it necessary to warn their congregations against it. The belief, of very ancient lineage, that coitus during menstruation led to the birth of monsters was formerly very widespread....

We see, then, that the circumstances of domestication and civilisation tend to an increase and a greater frequency both of oestrus and of menstruation; perhaps one other parallel condition may help us a stage further in the attempt to unravel the process of transformation. We know that in most mammals non-satisfaction of sexual desire by intercourse tends to a quicker return of heat than normal; and it may be that the greater frequency of menstruation in the human female may in part be referable to the fact that civilisation has brought it about that in the human female sexual desire is often compelled to go unsatisfied....

Dr Raymond Crawfurd, 'Notes on the Superstitions of Menstruation', *The Lancet*, 18 December 1915, pp. 1331, 1334–6.

40. Females Unwell and Out of Order (1839)

It may with truth be asserted, that of all the derangements of function to which the female system is exposed, there are none more common, or which excite more uneasiness, than the irregular performance of the uterine at its monthly periods... it is well known that the disorders producing it are generally of a very serious nature, and which, if not properly attended to, would prove highly detrimental, or even destructive to life itself. . . . In cases of obstructed menstruation, vicarious discharges of blood occasionally take place from different parts of the body; this has been specially noticed in those who are the subject of ulcerated legs, for at the time when the menses ought naturally to appear, these parts inflame, and a little blood is seen to distil from the surface of the sore; in fact, all diseased parts seem to grow worse, their vessels becoming more turgid at that period. The nervous system is also more irritable than at other times.

Menstruation is seldom completely established without the supervention of many unpleasant symptoms: there is pretty uniformly a feeling of languor and lassitude, head-ache, dull, heavy pains in the loins, hips, and region of the uterus, these frequently extending to the upper and inner parts of the thighs; the stomach is often sympathetically affected, the appetite bad, and the bowels confined. Nervous and hysterical symptoms frequently manifest themselves. After a longer or shorter continuance of some or all the symptoms just enumerated, a pale mucous discharge exudes from the vagina; this may in some instances be slightly coloured, but seldom assumes its sanguineous appearance until after several monthly periods. When the secretion is thoroughly established, and this will be known by its coming away in proper quantities, and of a red colour, these painful affections usually vanish, although in some females they recur with great violence, and with pertinacious regularity, throughout the whole term of menstruation, and these females rarely conceive. . . .

A doubt formerly existed regarding the part which furnished the secretion, whether the membrane of the womb or that of the vagina was employed in this office: this doubt has been, however, unequivocally set at rest, for in cases of recent inversio uteri it has been seen to ooze from the uterine membrane itself: the same fact has been also noticed in the dissection of females who have suddenly died whilst menstruating. Dr. Blundell had once an opportunity of seeing the discharge drop through the os uteri in a severe case of procidentia.

An opinion, altogether unfounded in fact, was entertained by many of our old medical writers, that the menstrual fluid possessed properties of a malignant nature. This notion probably owed its origin to the severe regulations enforced under the Jewish dispensation, respecting the conduct of women at this particular time. The discharge, however, seems to be as innocuous as any of the other secretions of the body.

In consequence of the monthly return of the evacuation, some physiologists have imagined that the influence of the moon was in some way or other concerned in its production. The late celebrated Dr. Mead entertained this opinion, for he states that the catamenia are equally with the tides the subject of lunar influence. This theory is too absurd to require any lengthened refutation; and I will merely observe, that an unanswerable objection is afforded by the well-known fact, that different females are menstruating every day throughout the year.... The menses, in popular language, has received various designations, such as *the courses*, *the terms*, *the flowers*, *the change*, and so on. More commonly, however, females during the flow call themselves *unwell* or *out of order*, or perhaps they will tell you they have not seen *them* for a longer period than usual, or *they* have been upon them for such and such a time. You should always be aware of their meaning when your patients thus express themselves, or they will have but a poor opinion of your knowledge of female disorders....

Dr Charles Waller, 'Lectures on the Function and Diseases of the Womb', *The Lancet*, 7 December 1839, pp. 393–6.

41. The Menstrual Function: A Necessary Interest (1840)

There is perhaps no one function which has excited greater attention than the menstrual: lawgivers, theologians, philosophers, of every age, and the whole mass of mankind have taken an immediate, because necessary, interest in the matter; and the consequence has been, that much stress has ever been laid upon its importance in the female economy. It would be useless to review at large the various opinions, respecting the causes of menstruation, which have been given to the world. By many it was thought, especially by the ancients, that something noxious was elaborated from the system during menstruation; and, as it occurred in most women every lunar month, the process was termed the menstrual purgation. Some called it 'the flowers,' because as these precede fructification in vegetables, so does menstruation indicate in women the capability of being fecundated. Another very general opinion, and held until recently, was, that the menstrual flow was blood, and indicated that there was a regular plethora, which this flow relieved; that such plethora was necessary in women, in order that the super-fluous blood might go to the nourishment of the foetus; and, as menstruation usually ceases during pregnancy, there was little doubt of the correctness of the theory....

Thomas Laycock, *A Treatise on the Nervous Diseases of Women*, 1840, pp. 40–1.

42. The Symptoms and Effects of Menstruation (1841)

Menstruation commences at puberty, is generally suppressed during pregnancy and lactation, or during suckling; but there are occasional exceptions, as some women perform this function during both the last-mentioned states.—(Deventer, Baudelocque, etc.) The aptitude for generation in woman commences with it, and this is lost at its termination. The secretion continues from puberty to old age, periods that may be called extremes, the spring and winter of female life, as they indicate the commence-ment and cessation of fecundity. Menstruation is a function similar to circulation, digestion, etc., and not a disease, as some have erroneously imagined....

The girl who is about to become puberous, and to menstruate, may be free from all disorder, or suffer from many unpleasant sensations, as cold shiverings, sense of weight and tension in the hypogastrium, pelvis, and with a feeling of bearing down, both in the vagina and rectum; pains in the loins, hips, inferior extremi-ties, as well as in the back, chest, and head, which cause lassitude and dislike to motion; there is sometimes headache, a sense of choking in the throat, noise in the ears, derangement of vision, of taste, or of smell: in fact, there is disorder of all parts of the body, or cutaneous eruptions, convulsions, hysteria, and sometimes epilepsy may appear. I know three sisters who are always attacked with epilepsy at the commencement of menstruation; and many who suffer most severely from the most intense hysteria, which in some approaches to catalepsy, and in others to idiocy. I have frequently seen cases of this kind both at the hospital and dispensaries which I attend. The appetite, in some cases, becomes bad or depraved, and the girl wishes for improper foods, as raw vegetables, chalk, oranges, etc. In some there is fever or haemorrhage from the nose, lungs, stomach or bowels. There may be vomiting, diarrhoea, colic, flatulency, and constipation. Boudelocque [sic] knew a woman who had vomiting and purging every month for three or four days, but she never menstruated. The secretions and excretions may be also deranged, as it is proved by ptyalism, incontinence of urine, diarrhoea or consti-pation, or more or less abundant perspiration. The countenance is somewhat altered, the eyes may become dull, and surrounded by a leaden colour or black circle. The respiration may be more or less impeded, there may be oppression of the chest, palpitation of the heart, spasmodic cough, and the voice may become hoarse or sometimes suppressed. I have known aphonia or loss of voice in such cases as those now under consideration. The sleep is more or less disturbed and unrefreshing. The imagination is rarely excited by lascivious ideas, at other times it is depressed: the individual becomes stupid, sad, nervous, and extremely hysterical. Women are more subject to nervous, hysterical, and spasmodic com-plaints during menstruation than at any other time. They are occasionally dejected and melancholy, and extremely fond of solitude and separation from society. Such are the most common symptoms which precede the first or any subsequent menstrua-tion; but to attempt an enumeration of all those that may occur, would require volumes for their history. All these symptoms may disappear on the eruption of the menstrual fluid, and all are easily explained by the origin and connection of the uterine nerves with the great sympathetic, in fact, with all others in the human body, for all are connected; and hence disorder or disease in any organ or part of the body, may derange the functions of the whole economy....

This secretion was said to proceed from the uterus by the

Greeks and Arabians, from the vagina (Columbo, Sue, Pineau, Bohn, Desormeaux), from the veins (Vesalius), from the arteries (Ruysch), arterial capillaries (Winslow and Meibomius), from the glands (Lister), from particular small receptacles (Simson), and from the venous sinuses (Astruc). The menstrual secretion incontestably proceeds from the uterine cavity in the great majority of cases, and this is the received opinion of modern physiologists....

It is likewise certain that the menstrual secretion may be vicarious, and issue from the surface of the vagina or vulva, or from ulcers on any part of the body. This is the case, perhaps, when a pregnant woman continues to menstruate regularly. This deviation is occasionally observed, and also when there is a vicarious discharge from the urethra, rectum, stomach, intestinal canal, air passages, or any part of the tegumentary surface of the body....

The presence of menstruation is vernacularly designated 'the courses, a change, the flowers, nature, indisposition, periodical or female health;' and among the middle and lower classes, the woman is said to be 'ill, unwell, out of order, to have a change, to be regular, or to be well in certain respects, or to be poorly.' The term poorly is also employed in all diseases by women in the humble rank of life....

It appears from the preceding sketch, that every process in the female economy is imperfect until the appearance of menstruation; it is the sign and establishment of health; without it beauty cannot exist, or will be speedily effaced; the order of vital actions will be altered; the mind become languid, and the body depressed. During its presence women are weaker, more delicate, and more susceptible of impressions; all their organs partake, more or less, in the condition of the uterus. The whole train of nervous sympathy is thrown into action; the vascular and nervous systems, the digestive and respiratory organs, are liable to derangement of function at this time. Hence, the universal rule of medical practitioners—a practice consonant with the prejudices of women themselves—is to omit all active medicines during the healthful function of menstruation. During the performance of this function all strong mental and corporeal exertions ought to be carefully avoided, as passions of the mind, travelling, riding in carriages or on horseback, long walks, dancing, and exposure to cold and moisture, every one of which causes may suppress the evacuation. Sexual intercourse is also most improper and dangerous....

The hygienic precautions relating to menstruation are scarcely ever duly attended to in this country. The young female, at the age of puberty, is not informed as to the change which is to occur to her; she is left ignorant on the subject; she is much astonished at the first eruption of the uterine secretion. The mental emotion thus excited, often interrupts the proper establishment of the evacuation for one or two years. She is not cautioned to avoid, during each periodical evacuation, exposure to cold, humidity, all strong emotions, violent exertions, walking, riding, dancing, etc., exciting aliments and drinks, etc., unless by the Hebrew persuasion....

It is well known that the first appearance of the catamenia will depend upon the state of constitution, mode of life, habits, etc., of the individual, and in the opinion of many, upon the manners of those with whom young women converse. It is also to be remembered that women, in general, are weak during the periodical evacuation, and are averse to sexual congress: the most abandoned of the sex will not allow it, unless impelled by the direst distress or profligacy. It has also been generally observed, that women of full habit, those who live luxuriously, those confined in warm apartments, and those who indulge in sexual commerce, menstruate most copiously. But we often observe individuals of full habits, who have the secretion sparingly, while pale and delicate women have it copiously. It is, in general, much increased by marriage, and may be rendered excessive, or painful, until it finally ceases....

Dr Michael Ryan, *A Manual of Midwifery*, 4th edn., 1841, pp. 63–6, 73–4.

43. The Periodical Indisposition of Females (1848)

That periodical indisposition of females, which, from its monthly recurrence, is termed *menstruation*, consists of a secretion resembling blood in its appearance, but not in its character, commencing in this country at about the age of fourteen, and recurring every twenty-eighth day, until the woman attains the age of from forty-four to fifty,—thus continuing for about thirty years.

This secretion constitutes a new and important epoch in the life of a female, and is one of the most decided and unequivocal evidences of womanhood....

The first appearance of the discharge is usually accompanied with lassitude, pain in the muscles of the back, groins, thighs, and breasts, headache, dark circles round the eyes, and distressing symptoms of indigestion. Slight exertion fatigues, and sometimes alarming derangement of the general health, occurs....

Various causes have been assigned for the periodical regularity of this discharge; but all that can be said on the subject, except what is merely conjectural, is, that it is a secretion (not blood) which is poured out in consequence of a determination of blood to the womb at stated times, depending on some established law of nature, but of which we know nothing, beyond its existence....

Dr John T. Conquest, *Letters to a Mother*, 1848, pp. 14–17.

44. The Menstrual Economy (1850)

The woman, in addition to the organs common to her and man, possesses a complete system devoted to the elaboration and sustenance of the New Being. In the presence, therefore, of morbid causes, the woman, possessing more organs than the man, will of course be so much the more liable to disease; just as two men are more exposed to disease than one man; but place the man and woman together under conditions of health, and they will enjoy equally its blessing....

It will now be necessary to say a few words concerning the grand physical characteristic of woman—I mean the menstrual secretion. Every one knows that the thirteenth or fourteenth year is a great epoch in a girl's life. About this time, sometimes earlier and sometimes later, but far more frequently later than earlier, her 'courses' (as they are termed by the nurses) are established, and she becomes marriageable. Upon the regular performance of this function her health and happiness seem henceforward to hinge; and it is not until the forty-fifth year of her life that it entirely leaves her. Now it so happens that no action of the economy is so liable to disturbance as this. Upon a slight cause, as fright or other emotion, it may be suppressed instantly, and refuse to return for months or years. On the other hand, it may be excessively increased in quantity, and more resemble the profuse bleeding from a recent wound than a natural evacuation; or it may be attended with intense pain, and the expulsion of a shreddy membrane.... How certainly can the physician, as he passes through the streets of the metropolis, read in the blanched faces and suffering aspects of hundreds a secret history of uterine derangement! He remarks the wrinkles stamped upon the brow of youth, the channels fretted in her cheeks; he observes the nervously hurried gait, the unsteady feeble progression, and recognises the vampire 'which at her heart, as from a cup, the life-blood seems to sip.'

These derangements, as I have before stated, supervene upon comparatively slight causes. Any cause of bodily debility, any mental or moral agitation is sufficient to induce these baleful results. Hence it may be seen how much more perniciously morbid influences act upon woman than upon man....

Walter Johnson, *The Morbid Emotions of Women*, 1850, pp. 11–12, 23–5.

45. The Strange and Painful Necessity (1851)

It may be said that it is only in the lower classes that girls are kept in darkness relative to what is of so much importance; but this is by no means the case. The same bad management equally prevails in the middle and the higher classes of society. Girls in affluent circumstances, and well educated, are, I know, often taken by surprise at the appearance of this function [i.e. menstruation]....

We constantly hear parents talk of 'bringing girls forward,' but all my observations, reading, and meditations on the subject, confirm me in the opinion which I have long entertained, that the art of educating girls in order to bring them to the full perfection of womanhood, is *to retard as much as possible the appearance of first menstruation.*

If there be any possibility of effecting this purpose, it must be by maintaining in its integrity an essentially English institution—*the nursery.* The nursery, in the usual acceptation of the term, means rational food, rational hours of rest and of rising, and rational exercise at judicious times. It means the absence of sofas to lounge on—the absence of novels fraught with harrowing interest; it means the absence of laborious gaiety, of theatres, and of operas—the absence of intimacies which are of a too absorbing nature, and a wholesome subjection of every minute to rule and discipline....

Young ladies delicately brought up, in the midst of every luxury, when first subjected to this chain, are often painfully affected by so strange a necessity. 'Am I to be subject all my life to this disgust?' is an expression which not unfrequently escapes a girl's lips; and if each revolving month brings back the same amount of intense pain, need we wonder if it should sometimes weigh heavily on the spirits, on the temper, and give rise to nervousness and hysteria, to increased repinings at their state, and to murmurings against Providence?...

E. J. Tilt, *On the preservation of the health of women*, 1851, pp. 20, 31, 70.

46. Retarding Puberty (1888)

Probably the most successful mode of rearing girls, so as to bring them to the full perfection of womanhood, is to retard the period of puberty as much as possible, at least until the 14th or 16th year. In carrying out this suggestion, it is of the highest importance to discontinue the use of hot baths, especially with the addition of mustard; also the indulgence in the use of hot, spiced, and stimulating food and drinks; living in over-heated and badly-ventilated rooms; excessive dancing, novel-reading, and late hours; for all these tend to occasion precocity, with frequent or copious or irregular menstruation. It is the duty, therefore, of the mother to enjoin on her daughter the frequent use of cold baths, free exercise in the open air, or in cool, well-ventilated rooms, to provide plain and digestible diet for her, and to insist on abstinence from *hot* tea and coffee....

E.H. Ruddock, *The Common Diseases of Women*, 6th edn., 1888, pp. 23–4.

47. From Diapers to Sanitary Towels (1880)

Dr Galabin showed the new ladies' sanitary towels manufactured by Messrs. Southall, Barclay, & Co., of Birmingham. They were extremely light and soft, and contained a pad of absorbent cotton wool. This was rendered antiseptic with boracic acid, as being less irritating than other antiseptics, and was scented with lavender. They were intended to supersede the ordinary diapers for use during the catamenia and after confinement. In addition to their lightness and softness, their great advantage was that they could be burned after use. The retail price was three shillings a dozen, and, as it was believed that they could be used longer than the ordinary diapers on account of their greater absorbent power, the cost would not greatly exceed that of washing the usual diapers. A cheaper variety could be obtained for hospital use. Dr Galabin thought that, whether or not they should come into ordinary use at catamenial periods, there could be no doubt that they would be very convenient for travelling, and also of great advantage for use after delivery, on account of their antiseptic quality....

Dr A. L. Galabin, 'Ladies Sanitary Towels', *Transactions of the Obstetrical Society of London*, Vol. 22, 1880, p. 188.

48. Improved Sanitary Towels and Cremators (1895)

Dr Galabin showed two recent improvements introduced by

Messrs. Southall in connection with the well-known sanitary towels. One was the addition of a narrower internal fold, continuous with the main mass of the towel, which rendered it more absorbent. The other was the addition of a cremator for the towels. The towel was placed in a wire cage within a cylinder, and with the aid of from one to two tablespoons of spirit it was destroyed, with little or no smoke. This would be especially valuable for travellers in foreign hotels where the rooms had no fireplaces.

Dr A. L. Galabin, 'Improved Sanitary Towels', *Transactions of the Obstetrical Society of London*, Vol. 37, 1895, p. 227.

49. An Experience of Menstruation, 1909 (1975)

I was for all practical purposes a boy until the awful thing happened. I was twelve [i.e. in 1909], still at the Dragon School, unsuspecting. I had little or no pubic hair; my breasts were ungrown and did not in fact develop until my mid-teens. And then there was blood on my blue serge knickers. I was quickly pulled out of school and I never went back. I couldn't quite understand why, only it seemed that it was something about me which was shameful and must above all never be mentioned to a school friend. It had been a complete surprise, because I had not taken in my mother's carefully veiled and no doubt physiologically inaccurate information. The process was not at all well known at that time and there were many superstitions about it and little medical help. Even for unbelievers a reading of the Old Testament (those bits of *Leviticus* probably gobbled while one was supposed to be merely taking in the bloodthirsty tribal adventures in *Kings*) with its perpetual reference to uncleanness added to one's unpleasant feelings. For many years I had monthly pain, distress and acute embarrassment; I was taken to various doctors, but, as nobody understood the physiological process, this did not help. The curse, as it was always called, was a main trouble most of my life. After all, it is only in the last twenty years or so that all this has been taken seriously and without embarrassment. In my day men knew nothing or next to nothing about it. Soon after we were married Dick told me that he had been given to understand that ladies had something in the nature of headache every month. Girls of my age were not allowed to swim at these times, which for me sometimes went on for ten days, and were discouraged from many other activities. Tampax did not come in till I was in my thirties, though at least disposables must have arrived with or soon after World War One.

It was all very discouraging and I acquiesced in it, as indeed in other discouragements, but no doubt resentments and determinations built up inside....

Naomi Mitchison, *All Change Here*, 1975, pp. 11–12, reprinted by permission of The Bodley Head.

50. Menstruation and Good Health (1915)

The girl ought to be warned that some day she will find that she has a discharge of blood, or of bloodstained fluid, from the vagina, and that this discharge may be accompanied by feelings of lassitude and heaviness, by discomfort, and perhaps by pain. She must also be told that the amount and the duration of the discharge are uncertain. In these matters each girl and woman is a law unto herself, and equally good health may be maintained whether the monthly discharge (the *period*, as it is generally called) lasts three or seven days, and whether the number of sanitary towels used daily during the first few days be two—the least demanded by decency and comfort—or three. The total number of diapers or sanitary towels that may be needed varies much, but probably any number under eight may be considered to denote scantiness, and any number over twelve profuseness of the discharge. These criteria are, of course, very rough, but they are sufficient to prevent girls who use half a dozen diapers from fearing that they are having a flooding, and, on the other hand, they would indicate to those who are using forty or more diapers that they need not desire medicine to increase the flow....

The natural interval between the periods—that is to say, the time between the commencement of one period and the commencement of the next—is twenty-eight days; that is, a lunar month, hence the word *menstruation*. But it is not to be considered abnormal or a sign of disease if there is some little deviation from this rule. The antedating or postponing of the period by two or three days does not constitute an irregularity . . . as a rule, in healthy girls under favourable circumstances neither the pain nor the discharge itself is sufficient to justify withdrawal from the usual duties and pleasures of life. The wise mother should know how to shield her child from undue exertion without making a monthly illness out of a natural function, and so setting up a false standard of health and disease in the mind of the inexperienced adolescent. . . .

Mary Scharlieb, *The Seven Ages of Woman*, 1915, pp. 12–15.

2.2 Adolescent Education

51. Adolescent Education and Hysteria (1840)

The relations of hysteria to the present modes of education are of great importance. The anxiety to render a young lady accomplished, at all hazards, has originated a system of forced mental training, which greatly increases the irritability of the brain: sedentary employments, as drawing, embroidery, &c., are followed frequently as amusements, to the exclusion of active exercise out of doors. The slow but powerful influences of music, dancing, vivid colours, and odours, on the nervous system, but especially on the reproductive system, is quite overlooked; three or four hours of severe application are occupied in the acquisition of a brilliant mechanical performance of some difficult and elaborate pieces of music on the piano-forte, which are forgotten as soon as possible after marriage when it would be least hurtful, or rather most useful. Dr. J. Johnson very justly asks, 'Is it probable that so potent an excitant as music can be daily applied for many hours to the sensitive system of female youth, without producing extraordinary effects? Is it not likely to inflame the imagination, and disorder the nerves?' and adds with great truth, that 'the stimulus of music is of a very subtle and diffusible nature, and the excitement which it produces in the nervous system is of a peculiar character, by no means generally understood.' It is well known that many mammalia, as cows, deer, horses, &c., are exceedingly fond of music; even reptiles, and perhaps insects, delight in it. Mr. Schönburgh remarks that the boys of the West Indies take advantage of the liking which a common lizard, the *anolius bullarius*, has for music, and arrest its attention by whistling to it; they can then throw a noose over its head: the Rev. L. Guilding corroborates this statement.... The baleful effects of musical studies on the mind and passions is

77

certainly not suspected at all by many excellent mothers.

Young females of the same age, and influenced by the same novel feelings towards the opposite sex, cannot associate together in public schools without serious risk of exciting the passions, and of being led to indulge in practices injurious to both body and mind.... The consequence of all this is, that the young female returns from school to her home a hysterical, wayward, capricious girl; imbecile in mind, habits, and pursuits; prone to hysteric paroxysms upon any unusual mental excitement, and yielding to them, until at last she will 'die twenty times on the poorest moment,' and, like Cleopatra, has acquired 'a facility in dying.'

The robust unmarried female, in easy circumstances, may escape many of these evils: but after the age of eighteen the reproductive organs are fully—probably largely—developed, and strong passions, indolence, and luxury, fail not to produce their effects on the system, and to develop the sthenic form of hysteria. It is to such that marriage, as recommended by Hippocrates, and his copyists, Forestus, Hoffmann, Boerhaave, Duvernay, Pinel, Esquirol, Villermay [sic], and most of our own writers, is so useful; although doubtless the asthenic forms are sometimes benefited by this procedure; the ovaria being excited to the performance of their proper function, and the cares of life dispelling the 'vapours' so apt to congregate about the idle and well-fed....

Thomas Laycock, *A Treatise on the Nervous Diseases of Women*, 1840, pp. 140–2.

52. Puberty and False Delicacy (1852)

Puberty, which gives man the knowledge of greater power, gives to woman the conviction of her dependence. Puberty is first intimated to her by an occurrence often followed by a series of disorders checquering life with infirmity; while the corresponding change seldom produces any additional chances of ill-health to man....

We also fearlessly assert that the liability to disorders incidental on the changes brought about in woman by puberty, increase daily as civilization increases ... unless prepared by professional instruction, which can be very rarely given, the best educated woman must be ignorant of many things necessary to be known, and as liable as the poorest of her sex to be guided by prejudices most injurious to health....

Far be it from our wish to diminish, even in the slightest degree, the strength of that true feeling of delicacy, which, throwing a veil over the least noble of our necessities, gives so great a charm to the relations of society. It is the boast of English women that they are particularly endowed with that feeling of delicacy,—and may its strength never be impaired by our intercourse with foreign nations!—but as it would be false delicacy for a woman in her hour of peril not to claim the assistance of a man of talent [i.e. a doctor] to save the life of herself and her child, so it would also be false delicacy in a mother not to seek to know how her daughter's health is to be managed when puberty has arrived.... Before women should appeal to the profession to set right any function, they should know whether it be rightly or wrongly performed; and as a respect for the delicate feelings of women often prevents medical men being so particular in their inquiries as is sometimes necessary, some rational notions in matrons and grown-up women would often prevent their doing what might be positively injurious....

During the crisis of puberty, and until puberty is fully confirmed, there should be a general relaxation from study, which might otherwise too forcibly engross the mind, and the energies required by the constitution to work out nature's ends. Even in man the excess of mental labour is known to produce constipation, by some prostration of nervous energy; would it not then be likely to have the same effect on girls, besides checking the critical flow which nature contemplates establishing? Nay more, even when puberty is fully confirmed, some days before, and at the time occupied by the monthly function, the head is often very much affected by pain, vertigo, drowsiness, or dulness, in which case it should be less severely taxed than usual; and those who are occupied in the education of girls should bear in mind not only this, but likewise that the same regimen cannot suit all, and that each particular pupil may require a different amount and quality of mental exertion....

Novels and romances, generally speaking, should be spurned,

as capable of calling forth emotions of the same morbid description which, when habitually indulged in, exert a disastrous influence on the nervous system, sufficient to explain that frequency of hysteria and nervous diseases which we find amongst women of the higher classes.... Without alluding to those novelists who love the confines of impurity, even the best of novels, such as the inimitable productions of Scott and many others, should only be indulged in as an occasional relaxation, for their habitual reading wastes feeling, and totally unfits women for the stern realities of life....

It will doubtless strike every mother that the daily press, which more carefully records the corruptions than the virtues of the age, should be carefully kept from the young unmarried woman. From the heart of this great empire there is daily wafted to its uttermost extremities a wave of pollution, which tinges, to a certain extent, the sentiments and thoughts of all, and leads many to act at last what they read....

E. J. Tilt, *Elements of Health and Principles of Female Hygiene*, 1852, pp. 173, 175–6, 209, 219–21.

53. Mental and Physical Exercise during Puberty (1882)

The commencement of menstruation is the borderline between childhood and womanhood, and this period of puberty is a most trying time, both as regards mental and bodily health. 'After puberty another potent sensation is added to the stimuli which move us to action. The natural love of the opposite sex will in one form an incentive to high and enobling action; in another the motive power to brutalizing indulgence. With woman this new power is even more potent. It is to one a pure sentiment leading to self-denial, to perfect subordination of self to another, and from a devoted daughter develops a perfect wife and mother. To another it is an absorbing passion, which entails loss of name, fame, family, and self-respect, and leaves the victim of it a hopeless outcast. It becomes a ruling power, and often puberty is one of the great mainsprings of human action, whose influence must never be left out of our calculations, either in estimating the sinner or the saint, and in it we will find the explanation of many an unaccountable and inconsistent action.' (J. M. Fothergill, *The Maintenance of Health*, 1874).

It is this, then, that makes it so imperative that every mother should carefully watch the effect of this wondrous change in the system of her children, and more especially of her daughters, and see that the companionships formed are of such a kind as to lessen the danger of contamination....

Now, during the monthly period, and more especially at the commencement of puberty, it should be clearly understood that the custom of making no difference in mental and physical exercises is radically wrong, and Mr Lawson Tait, an authority on these subjects, states his firm conviction that to this popular error may be often traced the existence of serious disease in young women. He is of the opinion that schoolmistresses, and all having charge of the young, should not allow them during the monthly periods to follow their music lessons, as he feels sure that the 'sitting upright on a music stool, with the back entirely unsupported, and drumming vigorously at a piano, must of necessity be detrimental, more especially as to those who are devoted to music it is a strong excitant of the emotions, while to those not so gifted, and who do not care for it, it is an intolerable and useless burden.'

Be careful, then, at these monthly periods, to take no violent exercise, to refrain from sea-bathing and cold baths, and to abstain from all iced and acid drinks. ...

The practice of taking gin and other alcoholic drinks at these periods, either for the presumed purpose of bringing on the discharge or of lessening any existing pain, is not only injudicious, but actually wrong, and it is a practice that is often the commencement of that love of spirits which is the most incurable condition into which a woman can drift.

The number of colourless, pale-complexioned, short-breathed, and sickly-looking girls that are ever to be seen, owe their condition, in nineteen cases out of twenty, to some unhealthy form of menstruation, which if not taken in time may soon land the poor creatures into a consumption, over which no medical skill can have the slightest control....

Lionel A. Weatherly, *The Young Wife's Own Book*, 1882, pp. 28–31.

54. The Reproductive System and the Brain (1892)

As puberty establishes itself, however, how great the change! The romping girl becomes shy and retiring. Her old tastes gradually disappear. New instincts, desires, and emotions, strange to her at first, take possession of her. She recognises her sexual individuality, and gradually begins to mould a new destiny for herself. . . .

Calm in the confidence which a knowledge of the truth inspires, she [science] points out the fatal perils awaiting female aspirants to intellectual fame. She points out, in the first place, that there is a decided difference between the sexes in their physical and intellectual capacity and power of endurance. This is the result of the direction which the evolution of each sex has taken. . . .

Now, there is no more important relation in the human organism than that existing between the brain and the reproductive system. In woman, on whom the greatest burden falls in connection with the reproduction of the race, this relation is a far more complex one than in man.

Think of the great disturbances marking the advent of womanhood, as well as those which occur towards the end of her reproductive life. Consider the profound changes during menstruation, during the discharge of eggs from the ovaries, during pregnancy, labour, and the nursing period. A stranger from another planet, on hearing of these great functional differences between the sexes, would certainly be filled with surprise to find that men and women do not exhibit even greater differences than exist between them.

Our present educational methods, with the attendant evils of cram and competition, both in the higher and lower walks of study, cause widespread disaster among the youths of the country. What the result will be on the girls is not hard to forsee . . . we must insist, as we have the good of the nation at heart, that no woman shall enter upon these absorbing intellectual pursuits in the critical, formative period between the advent and the full establishment of womanhood. . . .

Girls should not be allowed, at least during the first two or three years of puberty, to indulge too largely in pleasures which lead to great emotional excitement, such as dances, theatres, fashionable society life, too frequent association with the male sex. All these influences tend not only to hasten on the complete development, but to produce a condition of physical and moral instability, ill-fitted for the grave responsibilities of wifehood and motherhood....

J. C. Webster, *Puberty and the Change of Life. A Book for Women*, 1892, pp. 8, 28–31, 34.

55. Excessive Cerebral Activity in Women (1904)

Especially in the case of women is condemnation of over-culture called for, since immense mischief is done by it. We are told that the higher education, as now carried on at Girton and Newnham, is not inconsistent with maintenance of good health, and if we omit those who are obliged to desist, this appears to be true. I say advisedly 'appears to be true.' There are various degrees of what is called good health. Commonly it is alleged and admitted where no physical disturbance is manifest; but there is a wide space between this and that full health which shows itself in high spirits and overflowing energy. In women, especially, there may be maintained a health which seems good, and yet falls short of the requirements of the race. For in women, much more than in men, there is constitutionally provided a surplus vitality devoted to continuance of the species. When the system is over-taxed the portion thus set aside is considerably diminished before the portion which goes to carry on individual life is manifestly trenched upon. The cost of activity, and especially of cerebral activity, which is very costly, has to be met; and if expenditure is excessive it cannot be met without deduction from that reserve power which should go to race-maintenance. The reproductive capacity is diminished in various degrees—sometimes to the extent of inability to bear children, more frequently to the extent of inability to yield milk, and in numerous cases to a smaller extent which I must leave unspecified....

Herbert Spencer, *The Principles of Ethics*, Vol. 1, 1904, pp. 520–1.

56. Puberty and Ignorance (1909)

It [puberty] is a period for wise direction and sympathetic guidance. All the resources of physical and moral education must be brought into play to establish right habits of living, for the future woman is moulded at this time. ... All women who have the care of growing girls in the school or in the home should have an intelligent knowledge of the physiological changes going on in the developing girl. They should have the ability to teach girls in some proper way before the first menstrual period a few simple facts about reproduction, and the very little that is known about the significance of the menstrual flow.... There is little doubt that the ignorance which envelops this whole subject for the average mother and teacher, and the secrecy maintained about it, result in great harm to the mind and body of the developing girl....

The periods of the menstrual flow in the healthy girl require no marked deviation from her normal hygienic habits.... Excessive exercise should be avoided. Many women take habitually the same amount of exercise, and teachers of physical training, who do not suffer from dysmenorrhea, make no difference with their systematic exercise, apparently with no ill effects. Some healthy girls habitually rest a day or two at the menstrual period because they have been taught to do so, but unless there is marked dysmenorrhea, this is not necessary—on this question of rest during the menstrual period nothing has been added to our knowledge to vitiate the conclusion drawn by Dr Mary Putnam Jacobi in 1875 ('The Question of Rest for Women during Menstruation'). She says, 'There is nothing in the nature of menstruation to imply the necessity or even the desirability of rest for women whose nutrition is really normal. The habit of periodical rest in them might easily become injurious. Many cases of pelvic congestion developed in healthy, but indolent and luxurious, women are often due to no other cause...'.

Dr Howard A. Kelly, *Medical Gynecology*, 1909, pp. 67, 72–3.

57. Education as a Problem in Applied Biology (1912)

Safety is to be found in our recognition of elementary physiological principles. . . . The organism is a whole; it reacts not only to physical strain but to mental strain. There are parts of the world, including a country no less distinguished as a pioneer of education than Scotland, where serious mental strain is now being imposed upon girls at this very period of the dawn of womanhood, when strain of any kind is especially to be deplored. Utterly ignoring the facts of physiology, the laws and approximate dates of human development, official regulations demand that at just such ages as thirteen, fourteen, and fifteen large numbers of girls—and picked girls—shall devote themselves to the strain of preparing for various examinations, upon which much depends. Worry combines to work its effects with those of excessive mental application, excessive use of the eyes at short distances, and defective open-air amusement. The whole examination system is of course to be condemned, but most especially when its details are so devised as to press thus hardly upon girlhood at this critical and most to be protected period. Many years ago Herbert Spencer protested that we must acquaint ourselves with the laws of life, since these underlie all the activities of living beings. The time is now at hand when we shall discover that education is a problem in applied biology, and that the so-called educator, whether he works destruction from some Board of Education or elsewhere, who knows and cares nothing about the laws of the life of the being with whom he deals, is simply an ignorant and dangerous quack . . . if we desire a girl to become a woman, and not an indescribable, we must provide for her a kind of higher education which shall take into account the object at which we aim. It will be found that there are womanly concerns, of profound importance to a girl and therefore to an empire, which demand no less of the highest mental and moral qualities than any of the subjects in a man's curriculum, and the pursuit of which in reason does not compromise womanhood, but only ratifies and empowers it. . . .

C. W. Saleeby, *Woman and Womanhood*, 1912, pp. 115–7.

58. Higher Education and Perfect Health (1912)

Perfect health is incompatible with idleness. Much of the ill-health of the early Victorian matron and maid was due to the narrow 'sheltered', vegetable existence to which convention condemned the average woman ... no girl's education should stop when she leaves school, whether she requires to make her own living afterwards or not. She should go in for a 'higher' education, which will fit her to be useful, healthy and efficient.

The type of work a girl takes up must depend upon circumstances. Every woman should have a real knowledge of house-wifery, hygiene and child management, and the Domestic Science Colleges offer opportunities to many girls who may excel in this line although they are not suited by temperament and type of mind to the strenuous mental work which study for a University degree entails. The point is that girls should be efficiently trained in some definite line.

Higher education has been blamed for overstraining, mentally and physically, young girls, who are being subjected to the some-what severe curriculum of our schools and colleges. But the fact remains that the average girl is healthier as well as happier if she has to work steadily, even strenuously, than if she is allowed to lapse into the stay-at-home girl whose days are entirely filled with visiting, shopping and social recreation. Every doctor knows that a certain amount of ill-health in girlhood and womanhood can be traced to lack of occupation. Amongst the prosperous classes there are thousands of girls whose anaemia, dyspepsia, hysteria and nervous ailments generally are due simply and solely to the fact that they are living profitless, aimless lives and doing not one hour's useful work in the twenty-four....

Elizabeth S. Chesser, *Perfect Health for Women and Children*, 1912, pp. 42–3.

2.3 Chlorosis

59. Chlorosis and the Cordial Balm of Gilead (1817?)

Chlorosis, or *Green Sickness*, is an obstruction from the womb-vessels of females, when their courses begin to flow. It is attended with a sallow, pale, or greenish colour of the face, a difficulty of breathing, a sickness of the stomach at the sight of food; sometimes an unnatural desire of feeding on chalk, coals, stones, tobacco-pipes, sealing wax, and other things of an hurtful and improper nature. The stoppage of the menses is not always the cause of the distemper; as in its progress they sometimes flow regularly. According to *Etmuller*, the suppression of the menses is rather the effect, than the cause, of this disease. *Sydenham* looks upon the disease to be a species of *hysteric affection*, which is known by the paleness and discolouration of the face, and of the whole body; but it indisputably arises from stifling or suppressing the calls of nature at this vernal season, or juvenile spring of life, which is most sensibly impressed upon the whole human fabric. . . .

For this malady, which hurries thousands of amiable young females into consumption, the celebrated (Dr Solomon's) Cordial Balm of Gilead (prepared only at *Gilead House, near Liverpool*,) is the best remedy ever known; it promotes the menstrual discharge, cleanses the urinary passages, dissolves viscid humours in the blood, sharpens the appetite, stimulates the nerves, and invigorates the spirits, which in all stages of the Chlorosis are apt to be depressed. When this disorder is not very far advanced, nor obstinate, take from two teaspoonsful to a tablespoonful of the Cordial three or four times a day, in a wine-glass of cold water, for 30 or 40 days successively. . . .

Samuel Solomon, *A Guide to Health*, 66th edn., [1817?], pp. 118–20.

60. Green Sickness (1839)

... [the word chlorotic] is applied more particularly to those cases where, from a deficiency of red blood circulating through the vessels, the skin becomes pallid, and assumes a yellowish-green tint, and hence its popular appellation, the 'green sickness.' These patients complain of weariness and languor; there is disinclination to move about; a slight degree of muscular motion producing symptoms of great debility and exhaustion; the pulse is small, irritable, and frequent; the tongue pale; pains are experienced in various parts of the body, more especially in the head, chest or scrobiculus cordis.

The secretions are almost universally at fault, the appetite bad, and the bowels constipated; palpitation of the heart, difficulty of breathing, and a teasing cough, are produced upon slight exertion; the countenance exhibits most strongly a deficiency in the red particles of the blood, the cheeks becoming sallow and the lips pale; swelling of the lower limbs, especially towards evening, is also a very common symptom....

Upon a careful consideration of the symptoms just described to you, it will be evident that the non-appearance of the menstrual discharge is not *the disease*, but a mere effect, in common with many others, of an impoverished condition of the system. The indication then to be fulfilled is not to force the evacuation, but to mend the constitution, which is in too languid a condition to support its usual functions, and cannot therefore be expected to take on a new action.... The most powerful tonic remedies will next be required: amongst which the different preparations of iron have long been held in deserved repute.... The vegetable bitters sometimes are of great service, and where iron disagrees with the stomach, some one or other of these should be tried: either cascarilla, calumba, cinchona, or gentian....

Some discretion is required with regard to exercise. It is popularly believed that strong muscular efforts are of peculiar service; but this is by no means the case: it is useless, nay, it is decidedly cruel, to enforce active exertions before the constitution has in some degree recovered its tone, and when that has been effected, the female will lose the disinclination to move about, and will take as much exercise as necessary. My general advice to my patients is, that no exertion should be taken which induces fatigue....

If the view I have taken of the nature of the complaint be correct, the absence of menstruation is to be considered as a symptomatic affection, and not the original disease, the fault resting with the system at large; and, indeed, we may consider it to be a merciful provision of nature, that in such an impoverished condition of the system this drain should not be established: When recovery of the general health takes place, the uterus will perform its proper function in common with the other organs of the body.

From the natural diffidence and modesty of the female sex, the medical man is seldom applied to sufficiently early, and the opportunity thus afforded has been eagerly seized hold of by quacks and charlatans, who, by their bold and impudent assertions, and their unprincipled and flagrant violations of truth, have succeeded but too well in their attempts to deceive; and the poor, unfortunate, chlorotic, by her easy credulity, has exposed herself to months of suffering, from which she might have been relieved by proper medical advice.

In conclusion, I would observe to you that there are no cases which more strikingly evince the superiority of correct treatment than those of chlorosis. A patient applies for relief in a debilitated and emaciated condition, a trouble to herself and all around her; probably half starved, and nearly poisoned by digitalis, under the supposition of commencing phthysis. By tonic medicines and a generous diet the system becomes invigorated, and the distressing symptoms vanish. Many cases of this kind have come under my own immediate observation.

Dr Charles Waller, 'Lectures on the Function and Diseases of the Womb', *The Lancet*, 14 December 1839, pp. 426–8.

61. The Disease Called Chlorosis (1841)

Chlorosis.—Green Sickness.—Cullen most properly placed the disease called chlorosis among the adynamia, or those in which there is want of strength, or a torpid state of the vascular and lymphatic systems, and particularly as regards the uterus; and the moderns are of the same opinion, as it attacks delicate girls of pale complexion and but seldom those who reside in the country, and take active exercise in the pure open air. A sedentary life renders girls debilitated, and subject to chlorosis, as we observe in manufactories, and all situations in which they are too much confined and overworked.

The disease most commonly occurs at the age of puberty, and sometimes to married women and widows, of the lymphatic or leucophlegmatic temperament, and is generally induced by exposure to debilitating causes of whatever kind; as residence in low, damp, confined situations, want of proper and nourishing aliment, defective clothing, excessive labour, or evacuations of whatever kind; an indolent life, depressing moral affections, as grief, sadness, jealousy, disappointment in love, and privation of sexual enjoyment, all of which will tend to cause atony or want of power in the uterus. Another rare cause of the disease is absence of the womb.

Symptoms.—There is want of development of the whole body, the countenance is pale and languid, the appetite depraved, with a desire for acids, unripe fruits, chalk, earth, etc.; flatulency, and pain or spasm in the stomach and bowels, the latter habitually confined or costive; palpitations of the heart, difficult respiration at times, with a sense of oppression at the chest; headache, pains in the back, loins, and inferior extremities, the mind depressed, and the temper variable or irritable, hysteria, and absence of menstruation. There is great inaction and fatigue on slight exertion.

When the disease advances, the countenance becomes of a greenish yellow colour; the whole body is emaciated, flaccid, and wan; the feet oedematous, the respiration accelerated on the slightest exertion, the pulse becomes frequent and small, and many, if not all, the symptoms of hysteria appear. The latter disorder will be described hereafter, and is intimately connected with that under consideration, and, indeed, with most of the diseases of women. The nervous system is deranged in some cases, in which there will be severe nervous headache, palpitations of the heart or syncope, or tendency to fainting, spasmodic cough, and disorder of function in many, or in bad cases, in all the organs of the body.

Some girls complain of painful sensations in the head, neck, back, chest, loins, and upper and lower limbs; while others suffer from derangement of the senses of vision, hearing, taste, smell, and touch. It is not, however, to be expected that all the symptoms just enumerated are to be present in every case of chlorosis, as they will vary, as in every case of disease, according to the intensity of the disease, and state of constitution.

The prognosis is generally favourable in chlorosis, as a cure is usually effected.... During the use of all medicinal and dietetic remedies, the state of mind must be attended to—the *moral* as well as the *physique*, as the French term it. Amusements, parties of pleasure, travelling, resorting to chalybeate mineral waters and using them, removal to the country, change of air and scene, etc., possess their advantages.

The use of the chalybeate waters, as those of Bath, Brighton, Cheltenham, Tunbridge Wells, etc., in England; Hartfell, Peterhead in Scotland; Brownstown, Ballyspellan, Castleconnel, etc., in Ireland; Plombieres, in France; Pyrmont, Carlsbad, and Spa, in Germany; Bandola, in Italy; St. Luke's, in Naples; Buzot, in Spain; Luchalaza, in Hungary; Bigova, Sarepta, Perekop, and Naphtha, in Russia....

Dr Michael Ryan, *A Manual of Midwifery*, 4th edn., 1841, pp. 338–9.

62. The Major Causes of Chlorosis (1850)

The causes of chlorosis are thus enumerated by Dr Copland: 'The lymphatic and melancholic temperament; feeble and delicate constitutions; residence in cold, moist, and marshy localities and climates; insufficient, unwholesome, innutritious, and watery, vegetable food; inattention to the digestive functions, particularly those of the bowels; the abuse of diluents, of acid weak wines, or of spirituous liquors early in life; too great indulgence in warm bathing; prolonged sleep; tight lacing at an early age, and whatever debilitates and relaxes the system, *predispose* to this disease. The most frequent causes are sedentary occupations in crowded and ill-ventilated manufactories and towns, especially those employments which require a stooping position, and are prosecuted by females at a very early age, or before the frame is developed. The more common *exciting causes* are, longings after objects of desire, depressing passions and affections, especially unrequited love, or unfortunate or imprudent attachments; long-entertained feelings of sadness or anxiety, particularly when caused by removal from friends, and the scenes of recent happiness and affection. The influence of constipation and faecal collections in the caecum and colon in occasioning the disease cannot be questioned.'

Now, although the causes just enumerated are unquestionably competent to excite the disease, yet in the majority of instances the causes are reducible to two, viz. sedentary life and nervous depression; and of the two the latter is greatly more influential than the former. . . .

But the grand passions are not alone powerful in producing this disorder. The minor troubles of life—*les petites misères*—have the same effect. A young person, secluded from the companionship of her equals, debarred from the amusements becoming her age and condition, and subjected to over-rigid governance, easily falls into the 'green and yellow melancholy.' A young girl kept in close attendance upon the aged or infirm, and compelled to endure the fretful caprice and selfish exaction which are too frequently lavished upon those in her situation, is exceedingly prone to chlorosis; and in short, any continuous irritation, or tension, or depression, or exaltation of the mind has the same tendency. . . .

Walter Johnson, *The Morbid Emotions of Women*, 1850, pp. 49–50, 54.

63. Chlorosis as the Bane of Civilisation (1852)

The function which puberty inaugurates, to be healthily performed, should fulfil the following conditions:—

I. It should be uninterrupted; otherwise chlorosis, or green-sickness may occur.

Chlorosis, vulgarly called green-sickness, is almost exclusively met with in women; and its importance is not derived from its fatality, for it seldom of itself destroys life, but embitters it from the frequency of its occurrence and the number of its attendant infirmities to the unmarried, the married, or the pregnant.

Chlorosis seems to originate in a diminution or a perversion of that power which presides over the nutrition of all living bodies, for we can induce this complaint in vegetables; but the absence of natural colour and the tenderness of tissue, which it is so satisfactory to meet with in celery and lettuce, is a deplorable condition in a young lady.... The frequency of chlorosis is greater than is generally believed; for although we are only consulted for it in extreme cases, two-thirds of the women, of whatever class, who are seen walking about the streets of large towns, are more or less tinged with this complaint. Indeed, this state of semi-chlorosis is for woman the bane of a high state of civilization ... spinal curvature is most frequent in such subjects. Chlorosis also helps to evolve the latent seeds of consumption, and of many other complaints, and even renders young women liable to as sudden a death as apoplexy; for it is well known that perforating ulcer of the stomach, in girls of a chlorotic habit, will in a few hours cause the patient to pass from comparative health to the grave.

The great frequency of the complaint in towns, and among the higher classes, proves that it is produced by want of attention to the physical development of women, want of food, of exercise, of pure air, and tight-lacing, etc. Under the influence of these causes there is an imperfect evolution of the ovaries, which now attempt to bring about puberty....

E. J. Tilt, *Elements of Health and Principles of Female Hygiene*, 1852, pp. 229–30.

64-5. Chlorosis as a Form of Anaemia (1893)

The disease [chlorosis] is almost limited to the female sex, and to an age not far removed from that of puberty. Chlorosis is a disease largely dependent upon congenital predisposition, and frequently associated with imperfect development of the heart and narrowness of large arteries. It has also a close relation to the nervous system, for it is often characterized by the symptoms of nervous depression or irritability, and frequently owes its origin to a powerful depressing emotion, such as disappointment in love or bereavement. As regards the condition of the blood, chlorosis differs from other forms of anaemia chiefly in the fact that the deficiency in haemoglobin is far more than proportionate to the deficiency in number of the red corpuscles. This circumstance accounts for the extreme degree of the pallor of the skin, and its greenish tint.

Chlorosis may come on before the age of puberty, and give rise to primary amenorrhoea. In other cases, the commencement of menstruation is the starting-point of chlorosis, the extra demand which thus arises having proved too much for the feeble powers of the system. In more rare instances, the same effect is produced by a menstruation which in the first instance was excessive, although it becomes scanty, or is entirely interrupted, after the chlorosis is established. In general, therefore, the amenorrhoea of chlorosis is secondary to the condition of the system generally, and that of the blood. It is probable, however, that in many, if not in most, cases, the deficiency of the stimulus to nutrition furnished by ovarian development and activity contributes to the disease. Thus the tendency to the production of fat at the expense of muscular tissue, so often characteristic of ovarian torpidity, is frequently observed in chlorosis. Again, cases are not very infrequent in which the amenorrhoea appears to be primary, and to be associated at first with plethora, while anaemia and the signs of chlorosis only come on after an interval. The same inference may be drawn from the cases of chlorosis in which benefit is derived from marriage, or from direct emmenagogue treatment ... especially in chlorosis, iron is the great remedy, and in chlorosis it should be given in large doses....

Hygienic treatment is still more important than medicinal. It should comprise nourishing diet, especially an ample allowance of fresh meat, abundance of fresh air, judiciously regulated exercise (the most effectual form of which is riding on horse-back), cold fresh, or still better, salt water baths, and change of air and scene. A stay at the seaside or watering-place with chalybeate springs is especially useful. A carefully regulated gymnastic course, such as the Swedish exercises, often succeeds when other means fail....

Dr A. L. Galabin, *Diseases of Women*, 5th edn., 1893, pp. 473–6.

2.4 Hysteria

66. Hysteria as Nervous Disease in Women (1840)

The most common form of nervous disease to which females are subject, namely, *the hysteric paroxysm*, and the corporeal peculiarities of those whom it attacks, are well described by Hippocrates under the name 'strangulation of the uterus;' the ancients supposing that the disease originated in an ascent of that viscus to the diaphragm and throat, and that the dyspnoea and other symptoms were thus caused. . . .

Since that period the term, although occasionally limited to a hysterical paroxysm, has been very generally applied to almost all forms of nervous disease in women; and perhaps upon no other class of affections has more been said and written. Nor is it difficult to account for this circumstance. Their occasional singularity, their frequency, and the difficulty of distinguishing them from other and more dangerous diseases, have continually arrested the attention of the observant practitioner. Sydenham declares that few women, except such as work and fare hardly, are quite free from every species of this disorder. . . . They assume every shape, and attack every organ; now appearing as diabetes, now as ischuria; spasm at one moment, paralysis at another; every artery throbbing as if the system were labouring under intense fever, or a slow pulse, a deathlike paleness, or profound insensibility, appearing to the inexperienced observer as the immediate precursors of dissolution. . . .

First principle.—*The Nervous System the Seat of Hysteric Diseases*. . . There has been an obscure and indefinite doctrine advanced by almost every writer on the subject, which connects the nerves of the uterus in some way or other, not clearly explained, with the whole nervous system. . . [this] affords(s) no satisfactory explanation of many of the peculiar phenomena of hysteria....

Second principle.—*Hysteria is peculiar to Females...* the general rule...that it is the nervous system of women which is implicated in these affections.

Third principle.—*Women of susceptible Nervous System more liable than others....*

Fourth Principle.—*Hysteric Diseases appear only during that Period of Life in which the reproductive Organs perform their functions* ... by universal consent the nervous system of the human female is allowed to be sooner affected by all stimuli, whether corporeal or mental, than that of the male. This susceptibility of woman, and her less mental and muscular power, are known, indeed, by daily observation....

In the treatment of hysteric affections in general, it is of importance to remove all stimuli. All things and all occasions, by or in which the imagination may be excited, should be forbidden; as the society of licentious men, balls, novel-reading, much music, sentimental songs, the sight of vivid colours, &c. The patient should be required to go to bed only when sleepy, and to arise in the morning on waking; to abandon the use of tea, coffee, stimulating liquors in general, and scents, especially of the musk class, of which young women are very fond.... Exercise in the open air and occupation of the mind are sovereign remedies in hysteria....

Hysteria is often seen amongst sempstresses, lace-workers, and others of the female population of large towns, confined for many hours daily at sedentary employments, or in heated manufactories; and who, from associating in numbers, excite each other's passions. It is vain to recommend change of air and travel *to them*. Would that some influential individuals would associate to ameliorate their condition by obtaining them other employment. Designing patterns for calico-printers, paper-stainers, &c.; or waiting in the shops of booksellers, drapers, haberdashers, &c., would be suitable and profitable employment for the women of the lower classes, and much less injurious to their health and morals.

Derangement of the general health should be met by suitable remedies. Amongst the metallic tonics small doses of mercury (even to very slight ptyalism) and iron are the most efficient, combined with bitters. Of the latter, aloes, quassia, calumba, wormwood, and chamomile are most recommended. I have found very minute doses of colocynth answer remarkably well,—gr. ¼ to ⅛ every six hours. It may be observed that in general all medicines, but especially the metallic remedies, are most efficient in hysteria, when given in minute doses....

Thomas Laycock, *A Treatise on the Nervous Diseases of Women*, 1840, pp. 1–2, 6–9, 76, 209–11.

67. Hysteria: a Morbid Condition of the Uterus (1841)

Hysteria.—This disorder has long been referred to the uterus, and of late to the cerebellum, or brain. It is the general, indeed almost the universal opinion, that the disorder arises from a morbid condition of the uterus, and this has been well established by M. Mongelas, in his special researches on the origin or seat of hysteria. The phrenologists, however, refer it to the cerebellum,—but these are now very few in number.

There are few disorders whose symptoms are so numerous, and so varied, even in the same individual at different times... women seldom admit that they are hysterical, unless they suffer from convulsions, although some, or most of the other symptoms may be present. I might fill a good sized volume with cases of the various shades or species of hysteria, which have fallen under my own observation, and treatment....

The duration of hysteria varies very considerably; it may continue for months or years, or may persist during life, and then terminate in mania or epilepsy, but scarcely ever in death. It is generally cured by marriage, or pregnancy, or it may cease spontaneously, especially at the critical age, or by the effect of a strong vivid moral impression; or it may, in some few cases, excite disorganizations in the uterus and brain.... Hysteria usually commences about the age of puberty, but some of the symptoms are often observed in childhood, especially when the parents have been hypochondriacal or hysterical. The disorder is also very intense in certain cases of ovarian disease, and is then accompanied by great depression of mind, and hypochondriasis....

The most frequent causes of hysteria are an excessive sensibility, or irritability of the uterus, the abuse of venereal pleasure, strong and frequent emotions, voluptuous conversations, the perusal of licentious works, frequenting balls, theatres, dances, every thing that excites the general sensibility, and especially that of the genital organs, disorders of menstruation, masturbation, privation of sexual commerce after it had been long enjoyed, and chronic inflammation of the uterus or ovary. These diseases influence not only the brain and the uterus, but all other parts of the body....

[Treatment]... The mind should be tranquillized, and all exciting or depressing passions avoided, as well as all means which affect the nervous system. Exercise on foot, or on horseback, or in a carriage will be beneficial. The perusal of romances and other works of imagination ought to be avoided. The greatest care should be taken to prevent the perusal of licentious productions, which are of late years very often clandestinely introduced into schools and families by itinerant hawkers and others. The patient should also avoid balls, theatres, and places of public amusement, which are often grossly and shockingly indelicate; and she should retire to rest when sleep approaches, and rise on waking, so as to prevent the wanderings of the imagination, and vicious habits which result from them. She should use tea, coffee, cocoa, chocolate, spirituous or fermented liquors in moderation, or entirely abstain from them. Travelling, and the use of chalybeate, and of sulphurous thermal mineral waters, change of air and scene, and innocent diversions are valuable adjuvants.

A moral treatment ought to be adopted, when hysteria is caused by excessive organic excitement; and marriage be advised should that appear to be the object of nature....

Dr Michael Ryan, *A Manual of Midwifery*, 4th edn., 1841, pp. 400–4.

68. Hysteria and Female Emotions: the Perils of Polite Education (1850)

There exists a peculiar disease, more common among females

than males, which medical writers recognise by the name of Hysteria. It resides in great cities, and visits, though not impartially, all classes of the community. It attaches itself particularly to the noble and opulent, it is well-known among the *bourgeoisie*; and not infrequently, though far more rarely, it associates with the industrial poor. It is in some measure the barometer of national prosperity.... It is far more general and potent in woman, in whom it seems to descend from the mind into the organic frame, and to involve every fibre, every vessel, every nerve, in functional perplexity... [it is] particularly more common about the menstrual periods, and immediately after delivery, than at other times... disordered states of the functions peculiar to the female is also very frequently a cause of the disease....

But the grand cause of hysteria—that which puts out the eyes and lames the limbs, and distorts the features of the young and beautiful; that which prompts the canine bark, obstructs the breath, and wrings the brow with anguish; that which melts the women of England into powerless babes, lulls them into months of slumber, deforms the moral beauty of their souls, and shatters their intellect; what which stretches them moaning and struggling on the ground, or petrifies them into living statues; that which will sometimes freeze every faculty of soul and sense, and, by destroying reason, level them with those that chew the cud—this grand traitor and foe to humanity is Polite Education. First, the boarding-school, then the saloon, the theatre, the opera—these are the focus of infection, the very den of hysteria. At school, the unhealthy confined life, the premature tasking of the mental powers, that excessive application to music, lay a foundation which is consolidated upon the young lady's entrée into society....

Anything that gives an undue predominance to the emotions tends towards hysteria. Hence young ladies who subscribe to the circulating library, and people their brains with heroes and heroines, who weep all day over imaginary distresses, or rejoice in unreal prosperity, who are instructed alternately in superhuman virtue and satanic vice, such young ladies see always the things that surround them as superlatives, and are superlatively affected by them. They are thrown into convulsions at the aspect of a cut finger, and a tight shoe gives them ineffable agony; if a spider creep over their dress they make the welkin resound with shrieks. Should a friend notice a fault, it is a base betrayal of their friendship— malignant envy. If at a concert they hear a pretty air, they are in Elysium. With them all is limitless exaggeration. ... In a great multitude of cases, hysterical and chlorotic affections originate from excitement of the mind, from overwrought emotion. ...

Walter Johnson, *The Morbid Emotions of Women*, 1850, pp. 55, 58–9, 227, 232–3, 235, 248.

69. Hysteria: the Exaggerated Action of Female Organs (1852)

... hysterical phenomena may be produced by the monthly crisis, or be intimately connected with it; inasmuch as a fright, which at other times would be tolerated by the nervous system, sometimes produces hysteria or epilepsy when it occurs at a peculiar period of the month.

All that it is necessary for mothers to know relative to this point is, that hysteria is a disease almost entirely peculiar to women, occurring most frequently at this period of life, and depending upon the exaggerated or perverted action of the organs constituting them women, on a nervous system deteriorated by hereditary predisposition, or the usual perverse plan of education... without exaggeration, Sir B. Brodie has affirmed 'that in the upper ranks of society *four-fifths* of the women supposed to be affected with diseases of the joints, are only the victims of hysteria.'

Before concluding this subject, we must observe that nervous affections are catching; that as the vibration of one chord causes similar chords, attuned to the same note, and within a given sphere, to vibrate to the same tone; so the mysterious vibrations of the nervous system of one girl may cause that of another to vibrate in the same hysterical way. Sisters, therefore, particularly if younger, should not be allowed to witness such attacks; and in a school the sufferer should be placed in a room without any youthful companions. ...

E. J. Tilt, *Elements of Health and Principles of Female Hygiene*, 1852, pp. 252, 255.

70. The Government of the Female Passions (1855)

This disease [Hysteria]... commonly presents an exceedingly compound character, and a most diversified range of symptoms, including either the reality or the semblance of almost every possible nervous disorder; and frequently simulating the diseases of other parts and organs. It is almost confined to the female sex, although of occasional occurrence in man; and it has received the general name of Hysteria.

...there is a large class of young females, naturally of sensitive character and disposition, and prone to emotional excitement, who are said to be *hysterical*, or, vulgarly speaking, *nervous*, as a general term, and independently of any specific derangement of their health. Such persons are easily alarmed, and any trifling illness that may befall them is usually heightened by undue anxiety about its event; while its individual symptoms are increased, by emotional attention to the manner of their occurrence. Wakefulness is apt to be induced by the same causes; and this reacts upon, and increases, the general irritability of the system. Trifling symptoms, and slight sensations, that would be unheeded or forgotten by most patients, are anxiously noted by these, are maintained and aggravated by the action of the mind, and are carefully detailed to the medical attendant....

The hysteric paroxysm often furnishes a striking example of the effect of attention in guiding emotional force to some specific outlet. If several women or girls are together when alarmed, the occurrence of a fit in one of them is almost certain to be the signal for its immediate commencement in many others....

In the production either of primary or of secondary hysteria, the power of emotion must act in direct opposition to that of will; and must be strong, in exact proportion to its weakness. Perhaps, if volition were habitually cultivated, and if it were employed against emotion by turning the force into other channels of activity, hysteria might always be prevented; and certainly its occurrence would be very rare....

When once a young woman has discovered her power to produce a hysteric paroxysm at will; and has exercised it, for her own gratification, without regard to the anxiety or annoyance it may entail upon her friends, a very remarkable effect is speedily

produced upon her whole mental and moral nature. The pleasure
of receiving unwonted sympathy, once tasted, excites a desire for
it that knows no bounds.... Those who have never witnessed this
strange mental perversion, could scarcely be made to credit the
extent to which it is often carried, or the nature of the
proceedings that it will often prompt....

It is evident that, in relation to health, the government of ideas
is most important to the male sex, whose nervous diseases are
chiefly intellectual; and the government of the passions to the
female, whose nervous diseases are chiefly emotional....

Robert B. Carter, *On the Influence of Education and Training in
preventing Diseases of the Nervous System*, 1855, pp. 213-4, 216,
219, 224, 297-8.

71. The Great Malady of Hysteria (1867)

It may well be doubted whether, except under very occasional
circumstances, such a relation holds between the *uterus* and this
remarkable train of symptoms as to justify the employment of the
term Hysteria. In the large majority of cases there is no
connexion between them beyond that which the disease holds
with the other organs of the body. In the name of a disease we are
supposed to recognise its form and nature, whereas the term I
have quoted conveys to the mind no distinct idea of either one or
the other. And there is a positive objection to the resort to it, in
the fact that the word carries with it the association of a malady of
small and insignificant dimensions, while the malady itself is of
great magnitude. We associate with it the idea of 'hysterics' and
'vapours,' as they were formerly called. I wish to raise your
attention to the level of a great malady, and not of a trivial
derangement of the hour.... The disease consists in the local
evidence of some irritation or derangement of one or the other of
the nervous centres of the body, viz., the brain or the spinal
cord—at least, such is the received pathology. But the subject is
a very obscure one. ...

It is most prevalent in the young female members of the higher and
middle classes, of such as live a life of ease and luxury, those who

have limited responsibilities in life, of no compelled occupation, and who have both time and inclination to indulge in the world's pleasures—persons easily excited to mental emotion, of sensitive feeling, often delicate and refined. Such are among the mental attributes of Hysteria. But hysteric diseases are not confined to the young. I have seen many examples in females of 40 and 50 . . . I refer to the influence of anaesthetic agents, especially of opium and chloroform. In cases of Hysteria marked by local pain, relief is given by the application of opium to the affected part—a fact which does not confirm the generally entertained opinion that the local affection is dependent on irritation of the nervous centre. . . .

F. C. Skey, *Hysteria*, 1867, pp. 41–2, 54–5, 65.

72. The Hysterical Constitution and the Menstrual Epoch (1873)

. . . It may with truth be asserted that, even in the healthiest women, there is evidence of exalted nervous action under the influence of menstruation. In most instances the struggling nervous power is confined within physiological limits, or is controlled by the will. But suppose—and the case is a frequent one—the importation of a disturbing element in the form of struma, or of some subtle modification of structure derived from ancestral peculiarity; and the nervous system will react in abnormal degree and manner under the physiological stimulus.

Or take the case of obstructed or morbid menstruation. Here there will be excess of irritation, importation of the element of pain, both together tending to exhaust the nervous energy, or to scatter it in abnormal directions.

Under either of these conditions, a fit of epilepsy or of hysteria, according to the constitution of the patient, may explode. If the organic predisposition be strong, such a fit may break out under the simple irritation proceeding from the ovaries, and their appendage, the uterus. That is, it does not appear to be necessary to postulate an attendant unhealthy condition of the blood, although such condition is so frequently present at the onset of menstruation. . . .

I do not profess in this place to discuss the various theories that have been advanced as to the nature or causes of hysteria. I shall content myself with expressing the opinion that the underlying essential cause is an inherent organic condition, constituting what may be called the hysterical constitution, just as we have an epileptic constitution ... we must direct at least a large part of our remedial forces, not against the nervous disorder, the hysteria, or the neuralgia, for example, as if it were a self-supporting morbid entity, but against the accidental and removable, exciting or maintaining, causes. Where we cannot discover such causes, or where we fail to dislodge them, we may be reduced to treat the epilepsy, hysteria, or neuralgia as a disease; treating them, in fact, as we do syphilis by means of so-called specifics....

But whilst I dispute the doctrine that hysteria is an affection of the brain or of the mind, it is impossible to deny that the mind has a great influence, if not in the initiation of the disease, at any rate in provoking attacks and in aggravating them. It is, however, a grievous error to regard this influence as more than subordinate and secondary. It is rarely until the nervous system has been broken down by illness of some duration that we see those apparently perverse and perplexing mental aberrations which so often make hysteria the puzzle and opprobrium of medicine.... When the blood has become degraded and the nervous centres weakened under the protracted operation of the morbid factors, the attack is brought on by very much slighter causes than were necessary at the beginning. Hence it is that, after a while, a slight emotion, even moderate fatigue, gastric disorder, may excite an attack at almost any moment. But still the menstrual epoch is the period of greatest susceptibility....

Dr Robert Barnes, 'Lumleian Lectures on the Convulsive Diseases of Women', *The Lancet*, 26 April 1873, pp. 585–6.

73. Hysteria and the Unhealthy Womb of the Well-to-do (1882)

In nearly every case of that bane of womanhood, hysteria, you will find that menstruation is at fault. The symptoms of this complaint are too numerous for me to attempt to describe them in this book, but it is sufficient to say that the very worst of them, if taken in time, are undoubtedly curable, provided that it is possible to bring the womb, and consequently menstruation, into a healthy condition... symptoms of nervous irritability, if not carefully looked after, and attempted to be checked in their early stage, may easily merge into the more serious complaint of hysteria, and from that soon relapse into actual insanity.

This sad condition is of more or less frequent occurrence among the well-to-do female population of all countries living an indolent life, with no especial occupation, excepting that health-damaging one of a continual round of gaiety and amusement, turning night into day and day into night, forgetting all the rules of health.... On the other hand, the females of our lower, middle, and poorer classes... are seldom to be found sufferers from these nervous disorders, and thus are spared one of the worst affections of this period of woman's existence. Healthful occupation of the body, and consequently of the mind, is one of the great preventatives of this deplorable condition of ill-health.

Hysteria.—All women who are at all subject to this extraordinary and mysterious nervous affection are almost sure to suffer from an exaggerated condition of this disease (for disease it must be called), unless they make up their minds to do all in their power to prevent this truly deplorable state. By this I mean, that they should occupy themselves, and fight against the peculiar sensations and feelings which will come over them so frequently, and which are purely functional, and of no real importance, but which, if allowed to get the better of them, may soon land them into that blank, living death, insanity....

Lionel A. Weatherly, *The Young Wife's Own Book*, 1882, pp. 31, 94–6.

74. Hysteria and Hypnotism (1891–2)

The rational cure of disease depends on the removal of its cause. A woman is as much mind or brain as uterus and appendages. She is an emotional being with longings, desires, aspirations, likes, and dislikes. Love, hate, fear, envy, despair, and other emotions powerfully affect the body and its nutrition, and a chronic state of discontent is likely to lead to a chronic state of malnutrition. The child of a whining discontented woman is likely to lack contentment both by example and hereditary taint....

In treating many of these cases, I do not make vaginal examinations until I am assured that local treatment is likely to do good. I give such medicines as are likely to do good, and, after a time, if medicines and advice fail, I use local treatment if necessary; and having tried other remedies, I advise the use of hypnotism as readily as I would the use of a drug when I think it the best treatment, and far more readily than I would advise the removal of appendages.

I very frequently advise the removal of stays and all tight clothing. I often advise frequent eating and generous diet. Activity, as walking, riding, rowing, with frequent periods of rest in the recumbent position; and if the patient will reveal a mental trouble or bias, to do what I can to shake it out of her, even by hypnotism.

Dr Draper, 'Hysterical Vomiting and Other Cases Treated by Hypnotism', *The British Gynaecological Journal*, Vol. 7, 1891–2, pp. 344–5.

75. A Common Form of Girls' Hysteria (1900)

... she [Olive Maxse] is in that state that if amused and interested she becomes perfectly well at once—if with family alone and bored—or with nothing much going on she gets ill at once and will do nothing... I know it is a very common form for girls' hysteria to take—and the doctors say there need be no alarm—unless she is so bored as to fancy herself really ill—when she might create it—this makes it clear how *fatal* it is for her to be alone with us or your Mother...it has nearly worn out Leo though the novelty of it seemed a good solution at first.

Katherine Maxse to Violet Cecil, 10 August [1900], Cecil-Maxse MSS, U1599 C65/34 [Kent Archives Office].

76. Hysteria, Chlorosis and Celibacy (1904)

...Such part of the organization as is devoted to the production of offspring, can scarcely be left inert and leave the rest of the organization unaffected. The not infrequent occurrence of hysteria and chlorosis shows that women, in whom the reproductive function bears a larger ratio to the totality of the functions than it does in men, are apt to suffer grave constitutional evils from that incompleteness of life which celibacy implies: grave evils to which there probably correspond smaller and unperceived evils in numerous cases.... That the physiological effects of a completely celibate life on either sex are to some extent injurious, seems an almost necessary implication of the natural conditions....

Some effect, too, is wrought on the thinking faculties [by marriage]; not, perhaps, in their power, but in their balance. In women the intellectual activity is frequently diminished; for the antagonism between individuation and reproduction, which is in them most pronounced, tells more especially on the brain....

Herbert Spencer, *The Principles of Ethics*, Vol. 1, 1904, pp. 534, 536.

77. The Misuse of 'Hysterical' and 'Neurotic' (1913)

The entire view we take of the subject depends on what are the conditions or main symptoms to which individually we apply the term neurasthenia. Can we so sharply draw the line of differentiation between the 'psychasthenia' of Pierre Janet, the 'phrenasthenia' of Dana, and the 'neurasthenia dependent on brain fatigue' of Barker, as to regard these as distinct clinical states? Or do they not all at times merge into each other, and, for practical purposes, is it not best to regard them as constituting a clinical group in which but shadowy borderlands exist between one member of it and another, and in which it is occasionally, indeed frequently, impossible for us to delimit by any boundary line the features peculiar to any one of them? I suppose in the whole vocabulary of medicine no terms are more loosely and erroneously used than those of 'neurotic' and 'hysterical'. This is particularly true when it is a woman to whom they are applied. And if no other gain came out of this meeting than a resolution on the part of all here to discontinue their casual employment it would be sufficient to justify its being held. The misery and unhappiness that have accrued to sensitive women through the misuse of these terms cannot be computed, and is all the more serious since the ignorant lay mind has become familiar with and places an entirely wrong interpretation on them. And so the girl or woman with uncontrollable sensations and feelings is regarded as a *malade imaginaire*, as fanciful of aches and pains—and said generally to be 'nervous'—while all the time there are actual physiological anomalies of function or pathological states of the sexual organs which require to be treated and rectified....

It is only natural that, when any such exciting or depressing causes exist [as the menopause], irritability, or some erraticism of temper, demeanour, conduct, or the assumption of an unusual attitude to friends should occasionally declare itself. It is at such times that the suggestion of some slighting term as 'neurotic' becomes unjust and cruel....

Dr H. MacNaughton-Jones, 'The Relation of Puberty and the Menopause to Neurasthenia', *The Lancet*, 29 March 1913, pp. 879, 881.

2.5 'Corset-Mania'

78. The Tight-laced Maiden (1850)

There is a cause of disease in females which deserves more than a passing notice. I mean the absurd usage of tight-lacing. Whence our notion of the beauty of a wasp's waist is derived, it is difficult to discover. Certainly the Venus de Medicis does not countenance the idea; nor, in fact, would any artist of taste choose as his model the figure of a fashionable lady, or, if he did, the fashionable lady herself would be shocked at the too-faithful marble.... In truth, this habit of tight-lacing is a thing contrary to anatomy, to physiology, and even to common sense. If the fair lady could inspect, as I have inspected, the distorted chests and twisted ribs, produced by this baneful practice,—if she could see the dislocated heart, the contracted lungs, the obstructed liver, exhibited in females addicted to this habit, she would certainly shrink from its continuance; or if she persisted in complying with a ridiculous mode, aware of its consequences, I can fancy her exciting the waiting-woman's astonishment by addressing her thus: 'Lace that hole a little tighter, Mary; pull, girl; the heart must over a little further,—now, more pressure on the lungs—I breathe too freely—I speak too easily; the lungs must be diminished,' and presently, 'pinch the liver, Mary; pinch it, the unfashionable thing!' Nothing excites the bile of the conscientious physician more strongly than this silly corset-mania....

But the immediate complaints which flow from this pernicious custom sink into insignificance when compared with their ultimate effects. The tight-laced maiden in process of time becomes a tight-laced wife; and then, during the trying period of pregnancy, how are her sufferings aggravated! The abdomen, distended by its burden, encroaches upon and diminishes the capacity of the chest...the stomach, pushed by the stays from its proper situation, resents the compression exerted upon it by the enlarged womb, and that uneasiness of stomach natural to the period is exalted into incessant and dangerous vomiting. The disturbed liver is powerfully affected by the same pressure, and jaundice may ensue. The lungs, contracted from their natural size, evidence the additional contraction now produced, by cough and difficulty of breathing, and the heart in like manner becomes subject to distressing palpitation. Some of these symptoms become at times so intense, that in order to save the life of the mother, it may be necessary to procure, by artificial means, the premature expulsion of the child!...

Walter Johnson, *The Morbid Emotions of Women*, 1850, pp. 13–16.

79. Death from Tight-lacing (1871)

Sir,—Jemima H——, aged twenty (appeared to me to be twenty-four), servant, complained, on returning from an errand, of severe headache and intense feeling of cold about 2 p.m. on Dec. 21st last. Her mistress desired her to lie down for the remaining part of the afternoon; but the headache still persisting, she was permitted to retire to bed for the night. As she did not 'put in an appearance' at her usual hour the following morning, the mistress went to her room for the purpose of inquiring the cause, when she found the patient, still dressed as on the previous evening, lying on the bed, and quite incapable of being aroused. I was sent for at 7.30 a.m., and found her insensible on the bed, with all her clothes on, dressed, her face pale, pupils widely dilated, breathing stertorous, and on trying to remove her clothing, the task proved so difficult a one that I was obliged to cut them off. I then considered the symptoms due (from the meagre and faulty history) to congestion of the brain membranes, arising probably from the intense cold of the night acting on a weak heart. Some diffusible stimulant was ordered if it could be taken, and flying blisters to nape of neck and extremities. I then left. At 10 a.m., the hour of my second visit, the patient was wildly delirious, unrestrainable, and powerfully convulsed (clonic). At 2 p.m. I was informed, on again visiting her, she had died a short time previous, after a violent convulsive seizure, apparently exhausted. She was removed that night to the public mortuary to await a coroner's order for post-mortem examination. There was no history to the case, save the evidence of the mistress, given at the inquest, which went to prove that she had frequently, but unavailingly, remonstrated with the girl for her persistent folly in lacing so tightly.

Autopsy, forty-two hours after death.—Weather intensely cold; air crisp, dry; sky clear; recent snow-fall lay. Rigor mortis complete; no marks of violence; body indifferently nourished. I was at once struck with the nude configuration of the body, which was peculiar from the extraordinary amount of constriction at the loins and the 'squareness' of the shoulders, which were remarkably high for a delicately formed female; the clavicles being horizontal, straight transversely; the form of upper part of body being flat and triangular, the base being formed by the 'square' shoulders, the apex resting on the pelvis, which projected considerably, and the sides being perfectly free from contour, and sharply defined. There was little pectoral or mammal [sic] development; the lower extremities were oedematous, and the whole appearance gave me the unpleasant impression of being 'pinched'. On opening the chest, the lungs were found to fill the cavity completely; the right was adherent throughout to the chest-walls, and congested; the left congested. Pleural cavity contained some fluid, but there were no adhesions. The position of the diaphragm corresponded to that of extreme expiration. Heart very small, did not weigh four ounces, flabby, structure pale and weak; right ventricle distended with black fluid blood; left empty; valves healthy; pericardium contained about three-quarters of an ounce of fluid. Abdomen contained over a pint of serum in peritoneal cavity. Liver enormously enlarged, congested, and friable, the capsule readily tearing off; it extended completely across the abdomen, overlapping the left margin of the spleen, to which it was firmly adherent, compressing the stomach, duodenum, transverse colon, and small intestines. I should think it did not weigh less than between sixty and sixty-five ounces. Gall-bladder, distended with bile, descended an inch below superior margin of liver. Stomach very small, not larger than an infant's; walls hypertrophied; rugae considerably enlarged; it contained some dark-coloured fluid, apparently coffee. Duodenum much thickened; contained some bile and semi-digested food, as did small intestines. Spleen and kidneys intensely congested and enlarged. Brain membranes intensely congested; I do not think I have ever seen them more so, the whole surface presenting the appearance of a blackened mass, almost unrecognisable. There was an apoplectic spot on the surface of the right hemisphere posteriorly, with some effusion of lymph. The brain-substance was considerably softer than in health, and presented a 'mottled' appearance on being cut into. No fluid in ventricles. Dark-coloured fluid at base of brain. Sinuses engorged, as also vena Galeni.

I do not think the foregoing facts need any comment further than that I have never seen a case in which the viscera were so generally and to as great an extent congested, especially the brain and its membranes, and clearly points to the severe nature of the systematic torture the victim of this unnatural propensity must have submitted herself to, and for a considerable period of time evidently, to gratify a silly and wicked vanity by tight-lacing.

W. H. Sheehy, 'Death from Tight-Lacing, with Post-Mortem Results', *The Lancet*, 18 February 1871, p. 256.

80. The Girl's Supplemental Skeleton (1873)

EVILS OF STAYS.—*There must be no Corset Worn.* Aside from the evils of tight lacing, toward which there is always a temptation when stays are worn, the stays are in every way injurious. The bones which stiffen them press against the tender tissues of the growing bust, not only preventing its full development, but laying the foundation for future troubles when the girl shall become a woman and a mother. They press against the heart and retard its functions, leading to various complications of that organ which sometimes result in death. They weaken the stomach, the bowels and the lungs by checking their action, so that chronic dyspepsia, constipation and consumption may result directly and solely from their use. They are frequently an active agent in liver complaint, hindering the free action of those organs whose duty it is to secrete and dispense bile. They weaken the muscles of the entire chest, so that in time they become a necessity, and without them the girl feels as if she were 'falling to pieces.' She gets to actually believe that God and nature were not competent to create her in perfection, but that she needs a supplemental skeleton worn on the outside to complete her. The tendency of stays is to compress the internal organs and push them downward, and then there results a long train of evils, known as 'female complaints,' which unmarried women ought to be ashamed to confess to, but which are frightfully prevalent among them....

Mrs E. B. Duffey, *What Women Should Know*, 1873, pp. 40-1.

81. The Vice of Corsets and the Reformation in Dress (1885)

DRESS AND SENSUALITY.—
Let us glance at the second manner in which dress lends its influence to vice, by obstructing the normal functions of the body.
1. Fashion requires a woman to compress her waist with bands or corsets. In consequence, the circulation of the blood toward the heart is obstructed. The venous blood is crowded back into the delicate organs of generation. Congestion ensues, and with it, through reflex action, the unnatural excitement of the animal propensities. 2. The manner of wearing the clothing, suspending separate heavy garments from the hips, increases the same difficulty by bringing too large a share of clothing where it is least needed, thus generating unnatural local heat. 3. The custom of clothing the feet and limbs so thinly that they are exposed to constant chilling, by still further unbalancing the circulation, adds another element to increase the local mischief.

All of these causes combined, operating almost constantly—with others that might be mentioned—produce permanent local congestions, with ovarian and uterine derangements. The latter affections have long been recognized as the chief pathological condition in hysteria, and especially in that peculiar form of disease known as *nymphomania*, under the excitement of which a young woman, naturally chaste and modest, may be impelled to the commission of the most wanton acts. The pernicious influence of fashionable dress in occasioning this disorder cannot be doubted.

The remedy for these evils, the only way to escape them, is reformation. The dress must be so adjusted to the body that every organ will be allowed free movement. No corset, band, belt, or other means of constriction, should impede the circulation. Garments should be suspended from the shoulders by means of a waist, or proper suspenders. The limbs should be as warmly clad as any other portion of the body....

Dr J.H. Kellogg, *Plain Facts about Sexual Life*, 2nd. edn., 1885, pp. 91–2.

82. In Despair of Woman's Clothes (1909)

At the establishment of puberty with the development of the physical characteristics of the woman, the child's clothes are replaced by those of the adult. A woman's clothes are the despair of the hygienist. The dictates of fashion pay slight attention to the physiological demands of clothing. Tight collars, tight corsets, heavy skirts supported by the hips and waist, shoes too small and badly shaped, and a total disregard of the use of clothing in the maintenance of body temperature characterise the dress of the so-called 'well-dressed' woman.... While opinions as to the causal relation between the corset and pelvic congestions, movable kidney and enteroptosis [descent of the intestines] in women differ, there is no doubt, as Glénard has shown, that the corset produces artificially, while it is worn, the dislocations of the organs brought about by other causes.... As an article of dress for the girl the corset must be looked upon as distinctly prejudicial to health, and as entirely unnecessary....

Dr Howard A. Kelly, *Medical Gynecology*, 1909, p. 70.

PART 3

Marriage and Maternity

Introduction

Marriage and maternity were socially endorsed as the most important stages in the female life cycle in Victorian and Edwardian Britain. Marriage was the indispensable source of 'a social importance she [woman] could not otherwise attain'; it was the necessary 'state of subjection' (Tilt, 1852 [83]) which was the prerequisite of female domestic achievement and progeny (see 3.1). These social prescriptions took no account of the fact that the 1851 census had demonstrated the excess of females over males in the population (100 males: 104.2 females). This demographic imbalance steadily increased up to 1914, chiefly because of the higher death rates of male babies (100: 106.8 by 1911). Between 1851 and 1911 the proportion of spinsters was between 29 and 35 per cent for women aged 25 to 35, and 15 to 19 per cent for those aged 35 to 45. The more rational males could exploit this surplus of females, and become more selective about the qualities they sought in a wife (see Acton, 1865 [84]; Ruddock, 1888 [89]).

Any offer of marriage was a social opportunity in comparison with the 'few honours and small gratitude' (Hamley, 1872 [85]) of the spinster's lot, especially for women poorly endowed with money and beauty. According to Hamley's 'sensible view' of marriage, 'Sentiment is left to evolve itself gradually as man advances in refinement'. The social imperative was an efficient institution to promote reproduction, in which the private and public function of women was summed up as 'that great "Profession of a Matron"' (Cobbe, 1881 [86]). Women were socialised to accept their primary roles as wives and mothers (e.g. Mary Playne, 1882 [87]). The argument that 'Womanhood and wifehood are not co-extensive' (Anon., 1884 [88]), that women did not have to be wives, developed only gradually in the last decades of the nineteenth century, without much economic or social support. While Cicely Hamilton (1912) [90] and other feminists attacked the prevailing 'servile ideal' of marriage and maternity, there were few practical alternatives for single middle- and upper-class women. Family obligations to parents and brothers could be even more restrictive for spinsters than the demands of husband and children for married women.

While maternity was the functional high point in Victorian and Edwardian women's lives, it was also a subject surrounded by fear—fear of miscarriage, fear of childbirth, fear of puerperal fever and fear of child mortality. These fears were based on relatively high mortality rates—William Farr calculated in his *Vital Statistics* (1885) that five mothers died for every thousand live births from 1847–76. The actual maternal death rate was much higher still, since these statistics did not include deaths relating to miscarriages and stillbirths, and many other maternal deaths were not accurately recorded before the 1880s. Maternity was a real source of danger, and most women knew friends or relatives who had failed to beat the odds, or had survived with ruined health. The risks of maternal death increased significantly after the fifth child, though average family size decreased steadily from the 1860s to 1914 as birth control was more widely accepted.

Doctors and other authors of advice books for women felt it necessary to emphasise the normal and healthy features of pregnancy and childbirth (see 3.2). There was a constant refrain in the advice literature—that pregnancy 'cannot properly be called a disease' (Solomon, 1817 [91]); was 'not to be considered as a state of disease' (Conquest, 1848 [93]); and was 'a natural physiological condition' (Galabin, 1900 [96]). However, doctors still had to explain why so many women suffered or died from this natural state, as well as offering whatever relief they could, if any, for the normal symptoms of pregnancy (e.g. Drew, 1889 [94]). This was easiest for quacks like Solomon [91] who could point to the failure to imbibe his universal cure, 'Cordial Balm of Gilead'. Alternatively, 'the influence of many popular errors, which still prevail upon this subject' (Bull, 1837 [92]) could be blamed, and the remedy found in the better quality advice books providing 'Hints to Mothers'. Dr Conquest (1848) [93] and many others attacked 'the artificial and unnatural method of rearing females from their birth' which supposedly resulted in problems during pregnancy. Conquest required expectant mothers to be 'inspired with pleasing, cheerful thoughts' and uplifted by 'the beautiful prophetic language of Scripture'. Dr Mary Scharlieb (1895) [95] also castigated the effects of 'the artificial conditions of civilised life', and advocated 'a really physiological life' with plenty of exercise for the pregnant woman.

A widespread fear during pregnancy was the possibility of miscarriage: 'There is no accident befalling female health which forms a greater source of dread, anxiety, and subsequent regret to a married woman than miscarriage' (Bull, 1837 [97]). It is impossible to determine the total number of miscarriages in the Victorian and Edwardian period, since only live babies were registered before 1927. Dr Kelly (1909) [104] estimated that 'the frequency of abortion [i.e. spontaneous miscarriage] to birth at full term is from one in five or six to one in ten', and T. R. Allison calculated that 'eight women out of ten miscarry one or more times' (*A Book for Married Women*, 1894, p. 29). Dr Galabin (1900) [103] thought that 'On average, every woman who has borne children and reached the limit of the child-bearing age' had suffered at least one miscarriage or premature labour. In the century before blood transfusions and antibiotics, the primary dangers were haemorrhage or blood poisoning which could easily prove fatal (see 3.3: 'Experiences of miscarriage,' [101]). Well founded anxiety about miscarriage was undoubtedly the cause of some of the stereotyped behaviour of pregnant women, as they sensibly retired to the sofa when disturbing symptoms appeared (see Bull, 1837 [97]; Cowell-Stepney, 1886 [101(a)]). Some authors heightened anxiety rather than providing useful advice: 'The causes of [spontaneous] abortion are extremely various; there is scarcely a circumstance in life which may not induce it' (Ryan, 1841 [98]). However, most professional advisors stressed the importance of regular exercise and a normal life style for most pregnant women (e.g. Conquest, 1848 [99]), and provided increasingly specific information about the stages and problems of pregnancy as the century progressed (e.g. Scharlieb, 1895 [102]).

Childbirth for most Victorian and Edwardian women took place at home. It was a natural and usually a successful process, in which pain was perceived (until the 1850s) as a necessary prerequisite for new human life. Working-class women were usually attended by midwives but the medical profession increasingly argued for an indispensable role for doctors in middle- and upper-class childbirth (see 3.4). From the 1850s more attention was given to the medical aspects of childbirth in courses for doctors and surgeons, but training in obstetrics was at best superficial up to 1914 (see F. B. Smith, *The People's Health 1830–1910*, Chapter 1). Doctors could only play a limited role in the delivery room in any case, given their ignorance about biological functions and the few drugs available, such as ergot and digitalis. Surgical interventions like caesarian section usually resulted in death—Galabin (1900) [108] cited 'a mortality of about 84 per cent'. The woman with a normal childbirth was fortunate indeed.

The social features of childbirth concerned some doctors as much as the process of parturition. For example, the obstetrician himself 'should be distinguished for suavity of manners, politeness, delicacy, humanity, sympathy, patience, and never evince anger under any circumstance' (Ryan, 1841 [105]). Attendance of husbands at childbirth was the subject of a lively debate in *The Lancet* in 1841–2 (see 3.4 [110–115]). Dr Bull (1837) [109] had urged the necessity of restricting access to the delivery room to 'the medical man, the [female] nurse, and the patient's [married female] friend' or her mother. In the early 1840s the case against the presence of the husband at childbirth was put on the grounds of 'delicacy', 'propriety' and provincial good sense ('Country Doctor', 11 December 1841 [110]). The debate in *The Lancet* revealed a wide divergence of medical views, including expressions of sympathy for husbands wishing to attend the birth, in part because that might 'dissipate prejudices' [111] about male doctors' treatment of female patients. Prince Albert's presence in Queen Victoria's delivery room in 1841 [110] helped to popularise the attendance of husbands at childbirth among the upper-middle and upper classes [see also 117]. Several London doctors believed husbands had every right 'to whisper words of comfort' during their wives' suffering [113], but the advice books continued to press for exclusion (e.g. Conquest, 1848 [116]; Chavasse, 1889 [118]).

The doctor's value for the pregnant woman increased significantly after 1847 with the introduction of chloroform to reduce labour pain. The chloroform controversy provides a revealing case study in Victorian professional disagreements, and entrenched social and religious attitudes (see 3.5). Professor James Simpson brought a missionary zeal to his advocacy of the use of chloroform in childbirth (e.g. *The Lancet*, 13 November 1847 [119], 4 December 1847 [121]). But the initial converts (like Dr Protheroe Smith, 20 November 1847 [120]; Dr Landsdown, 19 February, 1848 [124]; and Dr Conquest, 1848 [125]) were immediately challenged by opponents like Dr George Gream (1 January 1848 [122]) and Dr Robert Lee (e.g. 24 December 1853 [127]). Gream invoked the higher power and logic of Christian theology in his defence of the 'necessary evil' of pain at childbirth, which should be considered 'even as a blessing of the Gospel' [122]. Dr Lee [127] claimed that his series of seventeen cases proved the 'injurious consequences' of chloroform during labour, opening to public scrutiny 'a systematic concealment of truth by physicians'. Dr Lee also invoked the religious justification: '"In sorrow shalt thou bring forth children" was an established law of nature—an ordinance of the Almighty, as stated in the Bible' (24 December 1853). The sensitivity and conservatism of the medical profession on this issue was exemplified in *The Lancet*'s editorial on 14 May 1853 [126] attacking the well-founded rumour that Queen Victoria had been given chloroform during labour. Yet by 1860 even the sceptical Dr Gream 'felt sure that no agent could be more safe, and none more beneficial, than chloroform in midwifery when properly administered' (22 December 1860 [128]; see also Galabin, 1900 [129]).

Puerperal fever was the most dreaded danger for Victorian and Edwardian women in the immediate aftermath of childbirth. 'Puerperal fever' was a confusing term which included almost any kind of streptococcal infection, usually causing widespread inflammation of the abdominal cavity, blood poisoning and death. Its rate steadily increased in the second half of the nineteenth century (from 1.72 per 1,000 live births for 1847–54 to 2.53 per 1,000 for 1855–94—cited by F.B. Smith, *The People's Health 1830–1910*, p.13). These figures vastly underestimated the real extent of puerperal fever because of the unsatisfactory diagnoses of causes of death and the inadequate system of registration of deaths. Deaths from puerperal fever accounted for half the total maternal mortality from 1885–94, and women who survived childbed fever were often seriously weakened for many years.

The problem for the medical profession was that 'There is no disease about which there is so much dissonance of sentiment as puerperal fever' (Ryan, 1831 [130]). Extensive and extreme lists of symptoms were presented in medical texts, and its dangers compared with the plague (see 3.6). In the 1840s, Semmelweis and Wendell Holmes independently established that it was a contagious disease but many doctors refused to accept this, especially as they were implicated in spreading the disease. *The Lancet* argued, as late as 1875, that 'there are puerperal fevers which are contagious, and there are puerperal fevers which are not so' (24 July 1875 [132]). Dr Matthews Duncan (1870) [131] concluded, more accurately, that 'Puerperal fever ... is a hotbed of insufficient and false hypotheses'. Healthy scepticism about the nature and treatment of puerperal fever increased in the 1870s, in association with research by pathologists, research chemists and others (see Priestley, 1876 [134]). The confusion surrounding its cause ended in 1879, when Pasteur published his conclusion that microbes in the lochia and blood caused the disease. The 'germ theory' approach was widely publicised in the 1880s and 1890s together with the associated antiseptic treatment (e.g. Matthews Duncan, 1880 [136]; MacDonald, 1880 [137]; Galabin, 1893 [139]), though a few doctors still clung to earlier models such as the epidemic theory (Kidd, 1884 [138]). However, even antiseptic procedures had limited success against bacterial infection, with a reduction in the death rate to 1.6 per 1,000 live births from 1905–14. Only antibiotics in the 1940s brought an effective cure, with the widespread use of penicillin.

The conventions for lying-in after childbirth, for the fortunate majority of women who survived, were also increasingly a matter of medical prescription from the Victorian period (see 3.7). Dr Conquest (1848) [141] thought that 'A most important revolution has taken place during the last half century in the management of both mother and child after delivery'. The 'revolution' involved sensible procedures to prevent 'inversion of the womb' or postpartum haemorrhage, especially horizontal posture in bed for two or three weeks after delivery (see also Bull, 1837 [140]; Galabin, 1900 [143]). The mother was expected to breast feed her baby if possible, and the value of breast feeding for both mother and child was strongly endorsed (e.g. Weatherly, 1882 [142]). The practice of wet-nursing by the rich had been under attack since the eighteenth century. The problems of raising the child could be given prominence for a brief period before the next cycle of pregnancy and childbirth began. Dr Mary Scharlieb (1895) [144] advocated a 'six months' holiday, during which she [the mother] should be neither pregnant nor suckling, when she could develop her other capabilities and gather strength.' Such a holiday was an unrealised Utopia for the great majority of Victorian and Edwardian women.

3.1 Marriage and Maternity: Women's Domestic Sphere

83. The State of Subjection (1852)

... woman, on the contrary [to man], ripening earlier into perfection, with the domestic hearth for her chief field of action, the affections of the heart for ever engrossing the chief portion of her energies, generally settles in marriage between 21 and 28 years of age. ...

But although tied by the bands of love and mutual confidence, how different is the relative position of each sex in marriage. The one gives obedience to the dominion assumed by the other, as the only principle of government capable of ensuring the peace of the family; and though the word 'obey' sounds harshly in the ears of those who often marry to be their own mistresses, the actions, and even the conversation of women, when that little word escapes their memory, show how readily they admit their state of subjection. When married, a woman cares not how much she obeys, provided she really *does* obey her husband acting for himself, and not when he is made the tool of others. ...

The general aim of English wives is practically to convince their husbands how much happier they are married than when living in bachelor solitude, or when vainly roaming after happiness; for except domestic happiness, what does man gain by marriage? A great increase of expenses, of duties, and of cares, it is true; but his experience is not augmented, nor his importance in society. Woman, on the contrary, acquires a social importance she could not otherwise attain,—it gives to youth precedence of age, a premature experience, and an *aplomb* which often creates in our minds a surprise equal to the respect it commands. But while assuming the privilege of power, women should never forget the important duties they are called upon to fulfil. In civilized nations matrons give the tone to society; for the rules of morality are placed under their safeguard....

E. J. Tilt, *Elements of Health and Principles of Female Hygiene*, 1852, pp. 258–61.

84. Features of the English Wife and Mother (1865)

CHOICE OF A WIFE.—Perhaps one of the least considered questions relating to married life, and the one on which, consequently, the most frequent and fatal errors are often made, is that which stands actually at the very threshold—What sort of person to marry....

First as to *age*; I think there should always be an interval of about ten years between a man of mature age, and his wife. Women age much more rapidly than men, and as the reproductive functions should cease in both partners about the same time, some such interval as this is evidently desirable.... As to *health*, every man should be *very* careful, and note every characteristic about any woman who attracts him which may serve as an indication of this primary requisite, or of its absence...*pale* women with colourless faces and waxy skins, even if they are tolerably strong themselves, very seldom have healthy children...(I would) urge any man who consulted me on such a subject, if he were free to choose, to select a *country* wife, especially if he be necessarily a dweller in a large town....

Let her have also the 'mens sana in corpore sano', good health and good temper; for what we call *happiness* depends very much upon the temper, and state of the digestion,—much more so, I believe, than we are generally aware of. Avoid marrying, if possible, a woman of an *hysterical* temperament....

The French say that an Englishwoman makes a better mother than she does a wife, and they have some reason for so saying; as we often see, after the first year of married life, a woman becomes a slave to the nursery duties and neglects her husband and her personal appearance; and, in fact, sinking the duties of wife into those of the mother, and often regarding the husband as an incumbrance instead of treating him as the *chief*, the real, the only one requiring her care and love.

But, after all, men must remember that women have many
sorrows and much suffering to contend with, peculiar to
themselves. The small cares and domestic troubles of life fall
largely upon them, and they require much love and affection to
enable them to bear up against the vicissitudes of life. Men are the
oak—women the ivy....

W. Acton, *The functions and disorders of the reproductive organs*,
4th. edn., 1865, pp. 84–5, 88–9.

85. Marriage: Woman's Entrance to Life (1872)

...To be married is, with perhaps the majority of women, the
entrance into life, the point they assume for carrying out their
ideas and aims; and there are not a few women in most circles
whose personal claims are not such as to promise them unlimited
choice, and who know this so well, that on receiving an offer of
marriage they recognise it as an occasion—an opportunity. If
such a clear-sighted maiden refuses a pretender to her hand
because he does not reach her social standard, she does so alive to
the alternative of a future—a life which offers her few honours
and small gratitude, in return for the sacrifice she makes to social
obligations....

Women are so made, happily for men, that gratitude, pity, the
exquisite pleasure of pleasing, the sweet surprise of finding
themselves necessary to another's happiness [or being flattered
into the notion], altogether obscure and confuse the judgment;
they either forget their ideal altogether, or think they have found
it in the very commonplace mortal who is their choice....

A woman may accept a worthy man for a husband though she is
not in love with him. The Bible nowhere bids her look about, or
even wait, for the best man. It asserts principles, and leaves them
to operate; but it regards marriage under what we will call the
sensible view—that which consolidates states and families. Sentiment is left to evolve itself gradually as man advances in refinement....

W. G. Hamley, 'Old Maids', *Blackwood's Edinburgh Magazine*,
Vol. 112, July 1872, pp. 95, 98, 108.

86. The Profession of a Matron (1881)

When it comes to the question of Married women during the years wherein they frequently become mothers, devoting themselves to any considerable extent, either to earning money for their families, or performing gratuitous out-door public service,—I must say my opinion is different. So *immense* are the claims on a Mother, physical claims on her bodily and brain vigour, and moral claims on her heart and thoughts, that she cannot, I believe, meet them all, and find any large margin beyond for other cares and work. She serves the community in the very best and highest way it is possible to do, by giving birth to healthy children, whose physical strength has not been defrauded, and to whose moral and mental nurture she can give the whole of her thoughts. This is her *Function*, Public and Private, at once,—the *Profession* which she has adopted. No higher can be found; and in my judgment it is a misfortune to all concerned when a woman, under such circumstances, is either driven by poverty or lured by any generous ambition, to add to that great 'Profession of a Matron', any other systematic work; either as breadwinner to the family, or as a philanthropist or politician. Of course all this ceases when a woman's family is complete and her children are grown up and no longer need her devotion. She may then enter, or return to public life with the immeasurable gain of rich experience of a Mother's heart. But, as I have said, till her children no longer need her, I look upon it as a mistake and a calamity if a Mother undertake any other great work to interfere with the one which would be enough to absorb the largest and noblest woman's nature ever created. . . .

Frances Power Cobbe, *The Duties of Women. A Course of Lectures*, 1881, pp. 161–2.

87. The Two Roles of Women (1882)

[on the announcement of Kate Potter's engagement]

I am truly glad you are not going to waste your life in single blessedness—I call it waste, even with a profession like yours [i.e. philanthropy and social research]. Women were made to make the men that are happy and to bring up more men who will be better specimens than the last generation.

Mary Playne to her sister, Katherine (Kate) Potter, 27 August 1882, Courtney Collection, Vol. 3, f. 121 [L.S.E.].

88. The Future for Single Women (1884)

Today blows fall thick and fast upon the old assumption that condemned every woman to be a wife and a mother, and stamped the unmarried with reproach.... It has been legitimate for them to fulfil one function alone, that of race preservation. Wifehood and motherhood... have hitherto been considered the function of *all* women.... Womanhood and wifehood are not co-extensive, but up to this time we have acted as though they were....

The moment a woman marries she is more or less the subject of every existing authority. Conventional society dictates her how, where, and in what manner it is proper for her to live. In the eyes of the law her personal liberty and her status are *nil*, her husband may lock her up and refuse her friends access to her; the guardianship of her children is not hers; again, marriage involves her in personal discomfort, suffering, and danger to life....

The mental life of a single woman is free and untrammelled by any limits except such as are to her own advantage.... We find her neither the exalted ascetic nor the nerveless inactive creature of former days. She is intellectually trained and socially successful, her physique is as sound and vigorous as her mind.... Whether it be in the direction of society, or art, or travel, or philanthropy, or public duty, or a combination of many of these, there is nothing to let or hinder her from following her own will... no restrictions but those of her own conscience and right principle. She feels that it is in no sense her duty, since it is not her choice, to devote herself to securing the happiness of some one individual, nor to add to our difficulties of over-population....

[Anon.], 'The Future for Single Women', *The Westminster Review*, Vol. 65, January 1884, pp. 152–3, 156, 158–9.

89. The Age of Marriage and the Female Constitution (1888)

Marriageable Age.—From twenty to twenty-five years of age may be stated as the proper time for contracting marriage on the part of females; and from twenty-five to twenty-eight years on that of males. Under favourable circumstances, marriage is conducive to health and longevity. As a general rule the female constitution is not sufficiently matured till the twenty-first year of age to allow of marriage without risk of injury to health and comfort.... Too early marriage often results in a broken constitution and feeble health in the mother, or in the birth of weakly children. On the other hand, too late marriage often entails much discomfort, and children born of such parents are often sickly, and die prematurely. A considerable disproportion between the ages of the husband and the wife is, for similar reasons, to be avoided....

E.H. Ruddock, *The Common Diseases of Women*, 6th edn., 1888, pp. 83–4.

90. The Trade of Marriage (1912)

Particular trades tend to develop particular types; the boy who becomes a soldier will not turn out in all respects the man he would have been had he decided to enter a stockbroker's office. In the same way the trade of marriage tends to produce its own particular type; and my contention is that woman, as we know her, is largely the product of the conditions imposed upon her by her staple industry.... Submission, suppleness, coaxing manners, a desire to please and ingratiate, tact and a capacity for hard work for which no definite return is to be expected, are the qualities encouraged in a servile or subject race by those in authority over them; and it is precisely these qualities which have been required of woman. The ordinary male ideal of a mother is a servile ideal—a person who waits on others, gives way to others, drudges for others, and only lives for the convenience of others. The ordinary male ideal of a wife is a servile ideal—a person with less brains than himself, who is pleasant to look at, makes him comfortable at home and respects his authority. And it is the unfortunate fact that she is expected to live down to this ideal—and very often does—which accounts for that frequent phenomenon, the rapid mental deterioration of the woman who has fulfilled her destiny and attained to a completeness that is synonymous with stagnation.

It is obvious that marriage—the companionship of two reasonable human beings—ought not, under natural conditions, to have a stupefying effect upon one of the parties to the arrangement; and, as far as I can see, where the woman is recognized as a responsible human being with an individuality and interests of her own, and with a right to her own opinion, it does not have that affect. The professional woman—a class which I know fairly well—is not, as a rule, less interesting and individual after marriage than before it, simply because she does not usually marry the type of man who would expect her to swamp her own ideas and personality in his; and the working woman of another class, who, as the manager and financier of the household, is obliged to keep her wits sharp, is often an extremely interesting person with a shrewd and characteristic outlook on life. It is the woman of the 'comfortable class', with narrow duties and a few petty responsibilities, who now-a-days most readily conforms to the servile type of manners and morals set up for her admiration and imitation, sinks into a nonentity or a busybody, and does her best to gratify and justify her husband's predilection for regarding her mental capacity with contempt. . . .

Cicely Hamilton, *Marriage as a Trade*, 1912, pp. vi, 73–5.

3.2 Pregnancy

91. Promoting Conception (1817?)

Pregnancy, or Child-bearing, cannot properly be called a disease, though attended with a variety of complaints which require great attention, but for the cure or alleviation of which, medical aid has hitherto proved very deficient. It is therefore in these complaints, that the Cordial Balm of Gilead exerts most extraordinary properties, and excels whatever has been hitherto offered under a medical form.

When a woman enters into the state of matrimony, she would do well to take a table-spoonful of the Cordial Balm of Gilead every morning and evening to promote conception; continue it three times a week from conception to the end of the fourth month; then it should be omitted till a fortnight before her time, when she should take a tea-spoonful or two in a wine glass of cold spring water every morning till her labour, at which time it will wonderfully strengthen her, assist her throes, facilitate the birth, promote the lochia, and carry off the after-pains. She might take it occasionally during the month, in any symptom of cold, fever or hysterics, diluted in a wine-glass of warm water, about the middle of the day....

Samuel Solomon, *A Guide to Health*, 66th edn., [1817?], p. 123.

92. Popular Errors about Pregnancy (1837)

During the period of pregnancy the happiness of a nervous and anxious woman is often completely destroyed by the influence of many popular errors, which still prevail upon this subject. And, what will be thought still worse, the effect of these prejudices on the constitution of the mother, will be found more or less to impair the health and future vigour of her offspring. . .as a subject like this has never been plainly discussed with a view to popular perusal, I find even now the sensible, and otherwise strong-minded woman, more or less under the influence of notions as absurd in themselves, as they are mischievous in their tendency. . . .

In treating this part of our subject, my principle [sic] aim is to convince the nervous and timid woman, that pregnancy is not to be looked upon as necessarily a period of deprivation and suffering; but, as it truly is, *a state demanding only a little more than ordinary care and prudence, and compatible with the enjoyment of health and comfort.*

The supposed influence of the imagination of the mother upon the child in her womb is an error still popularly current. . . . It is presumed by some that, during pregnancy, a larger proportion of food is necessary for a female than at any other time, the support and nourishment of the child demanding the extra supply. This is a great mistake, and, when acted upon, injurious to the health of both mother and offspring. . . .

There is no doubt that in some cases, in the early months of pregnancy, great and continued care is not only useful but absolutely necessary, in order to prevent miscarriage; but, that women should be encouraged to live more indolently, exercise being thought improper, unless towards the conclusion of pregnancy, when it is supposed to procure a more favourable delivery, is an error, equally injurious to mother and offspring. The fact is, a directly contrary method of proceeding is the most eligible and proper: exercise in the early months, gradually seeking a state of repose as the period of confinement approaches. . . .

Some poor women, as regularly as they become pregnant, after the second or third month go to a chemist with the request to be bled. They make a point of this, because they are impressed with the idea that pregnancy demands it. It is a remedy, however, which ought to be resorted to with the greatest precaution; and, so far from pregnancy demanding it as a necessary consequence, *it is most erroneous.* . . .

Such are the errors connected with pregnancy, which I have

thought it might be useful thus briefly to notice. . . .

Dr Thomas Bull, *Hints to Mothers for the Management of Health*, 1837, pp. 1–3, 17–18, 21–2, 24–5.

93. Pregnancy and its Complaints (1848)

. . .I would say that women, when pregnant, almost invariably become the subjects of a state of febrile excitement, which demands some attention; and thus, a condition and process intended by the great and beneficent Author of our lives to be one of comparative exemption from suffering, becomes one of almost constant and varied distress. . . . Although pregnancy is a natural alteration in the condition of the animal economy which every female seems originally intended to undergo, and therefore not to be considered as a state of disease, yet, in consequence of the artificial and unnatural method of rearing females from their birth, it does occasion, sooner or later, in most women, many distressing complaints, which evidently depend on pregnancy as a cause. . . .

. . . *mental depression*, with inquietude and restlessness, and that gloom of mind, that heavy foreboding and deep despondency . . . characterizes some women during the pregnant state, —aggravated, however, and perhaps prominently brought into activity, by tales of accidents befalling others in similar circumstances. This state is peculiar to certain women during pregnancy—in others, during suckling; but, in either case, demands care. However trifling, in a physical point of view, such a state of mind may be, and, although it is extremely probable that when the cause which has given birth to it, whether pregnancy or suckling, shall have passed away, the disease itself will vanish, nevertheless, such a condition is always important, and deserving of watchfulness. While a due care is necessary to obviate all causes of disease, and sources of distress, the mind must be inspired with pleasing, cheerful thoughts, and the prospect of a happy termination of her condition must be instilled into the convictions of the desponding female; for few things are more essential carefully to guard against, than a fearful foreboding as to the termination of pregnancy, or distrust of God's kind care and mercy and power. Everything should be done to preserve the mind in a calm and undisturbed and joyous state as the time of delivery draweth near, when new and serene and previously unknown joys will gladden the heart, now bowed down by groundless fears of suffering and danger, forgetting that, in the beautiful prophetic language of Scripture, although 'a woman when she is in travail hath sorrow, because her hour is come: as soon as she is delivered of the child, she remembereth no more the anguish, for joy that a man is born into the world,'—and this joy will more than counter-balance the antecedent sorrow....

Dr John T. Conquest, *Letters to a Mother*, 1848, pp. 23–4, 36–7.

94. An Experience of Pregnancy (1889)

... I feel how totally inadequate has been my sympathy or pity for those [women] in same circs. [i.e. pregnancy]. Back only aches occasionally but I feel horridly weak and *ill*, bad tongue, and beyond expression irritable with everybody and everything... I do so agree with Gerty in her estimate of the misery of the condition, and I think women are angels to bear it so perfectly, and wish I was more like them....

Mary [Gladstone] Drew to Catherine Gladstone, c. 5 July 1889, Mary [Gladstone] Drew Papers, BL Add. MS. 46224, fos. 175–6.

... surely surely you will come here in the course of y[ou]r fortnight ... you really can't desert me all right through these dreadful months and months. How good it is for me to realize what women have to go through. I eat now all right, in spite of the sickness wh[ich] is greatest morning and evening. But the minute I have eaten I repent as I feel perfectly stuffed up to the throat... the parents being here is better as I don't have the endless hours of

brooding solitude ... I am thin when I go to bed, but when I wake
in the early morn am fearfully fat. ...

Mary [Gladstone] Drew to Lavinia Talbot, 12 August 1889, Mary
[Gladstone] Drew Papers, BL Add. MS. 46236, fos. 300-1.

95. Pregnancy as Normal Process (1895)

Diseases of Pregnancy.—It is beyond all things desirable that
mothers, nurses, and practitioners, should remember that
pregnancy, parturition, and puerpery are normal processes, and
not in any sense diseases. At the same time the physiological
course of these states borders on the pathological, and in women
living under the artificial conditions of civilised life the dividing
line is readily transgressed. The keynote of the pregnant state is
increased tension, or to put it a little differently, *evolution*. It is a
special development affecting the generative organs primarily,
and involving the whole organism secondarily. ...

It is well to advise and encourage as much exercise as can be
borne without fatigue. The long months of pregnancy should not
be simply endured as a passive waiting for a great trial and a great
joy. It is culpably selfish for a woman to think of nothing but her
own health and the health of her expected infant. Those who give
way to selfishness and live only for themselves will not have the
same courage and energy to face their troubles as those women
who, while leading useful and active lives, caring for the welfare of
other people, are laying up stores of health and energy that will
bear good fruit later on. ...

Pregnancy is not a disease, and the pregnant woman should not
consider herself a patient, but she should be more careful than
ever to lead a really physiological life. ...

Dr Mary Scharlieb, *A Woman's Words to Women on the Care of
their Health in England and in India*, 1895, pp. 85-6, 100, 118.

96. The Hygiene of Pregnancy (1900)

Hygiene of pregnancy.—Pregnancy being a natural physiological condition, the ordinary mode of life, provided it is a healthy one, should not be too much departed from. Under normal circumstances, an increased supply of nourishing food is generally required, but it should be given in the most digestible form. It is of great importance to keep up a reasonable amount of exercise in the open air, to preserve the muscular system in good tone. Women of the labouring class, who work in the open air throughout pregnancy, pass through their confinements with much greater ease than those who lead sedentary lives. It is reasonable to expect that women who spend a great part of the day in bed, or on a sofa, will be ill-prepared for the severe muscular effort required in labour. On the other hand, excessive fatigue, strains, and the lifting or carrying heavy weights are to be avoided. Women should be protected as far as possible from any fright, mental shock, mental distress, or undue excitement. Constipation is to be guarded against by diet as far as possible, but violent purgatives should be avoided. Baths may be used according to the ordinary custom, and the genitals should be frequently washed with warm water; but some degree of caution is required as to vaginal infections. They may be used if there is leucorrhoea, but they should neither be very hot nor very cold, and the injection should not be made with much force. It is not usual to abstain from marital intercourse during pregnancy, although in this respect the lower animals set an example to the human race. Coitus is, however, a frequent cause of abortion, and much moderation is desirable, especially during the first four months. If a woman has aborted before, or if there are symptoms of threatened abortion, abstinence during at least the earlier part of pregnancy should be advised.

The dress should be such as to avoid all undue pressure. Garters should be discarded, as tending to promote varicose dilatation of the veins. Stays, if worn, should be made to expand. It is better, however, to use no stays, but have each skirt of petticoat or dress attached to a bodice, so as to hang from the shoulders. . . .

Dr A.L. Galabin, *A Manual of Midwifery*, 1900, p. 138.

3.3   Miscarriage/Abortion

97. Prevention of Miscarriage (1837)

There is no accident befalling female health which forms a greater source of dread, anxiety, and subsequent regret to a married woman than miscarriage. When this occurrence becomes habitual, there is no circumstance the consequences of which are productive of more serious injury to the constitution, blasting the fairest promises of health, and oft-times laying the first seeds of fatal disease.

The frequency of its occurrence, however, would excite little surprise, were the delicacy of attachment which exists in the early months of pregnancy between the future offspring and its parent only understood, for it would then be easily perceived with what facility this union may be destroyed...it is because the success of such a plan [to remove the disease of miscarriage] depends for the most part upon the prudence and perseverance of the female in carrying it to a happy result—for a medical man can do little to arrest a miscarriage when the process is once set up—that she ought to be fully acquainted with the means of prevention ... miscarriage occurs not unfrequently within three weeks after conception; it most frequently, however, takes place between the eighth and twelfth week....

After the patient becomes pregnant; let every cause which might excite miscarriage be avoided.... The patient must sleep alone—this is absolutely and imperatively necessary; she must be more careful and attentive than ever to her diet, and the regulation of the bowels; and, above all, guard against costiveness. Let the shower bath be still continued, and gentle exercise; but carefully avoid any fatigue. As the *period approaches*, when *miscarriage occurred before*, let vigilance and attention to rule be redoubled. The patient must now keep on the sofa nearly all day;

retire to rest early, still using a mattress, and taking care that the bed-room be airy and well ventilated. If the slightest pain or uneasiness is felt about the loins, or hips, the sofa must be immediately resorted to, and the medical attendant called in. If he approves it, a little blood should be lost, and the bowels gently acted upon. When these symptoms subside, the recumbent position must be continued, and the above directions carefully observed for six or seven weeks beyond the time miscarriage last occurred. At the expiration of that time, I might say, I believe *you safe*; gestation will go on....

... let the patient recollect when tempted to disobey the instructions she receives [from the medical man], because they may appear trifling, or a little too rigorous, that no man who enjoys her confidence would willingly lay down one rule too strict, or one injunction, the performance of which was unimportant; and remember also, that by *one* act of disobedience she may blast every hope of success....

Dr Thomas Bull, *Hints to Mothers for the Management of Health*, 1837, pp. 98–101, 114–5, 123–4.

98. 'Abortion' and its Causes (1841)

Abortions.—The expulsion of the foetus and its appendages before the uterus is sufficiently enlarged to admit of any manual operation, which is before the completion of the sixth month of pregnancy, is termed *abortion*, or *miscarriage*... It is well known that a bad miscarriage is worse and more injurious to the constitution than several natural labours at the full period. In some cases the loss of blood is scarcely perceptible, in others it is so copious as to amount to ten or twelve pints, and destroy life, unless saved by transfusion.... Abortion is most common from the second to the fifth month of pregnancy, according to my experience; and we are even seldom called to such cases, unless there is haemorrhage....

Causes.—The causes of abortion are extremely various; there is scarcely a circumstance in life which may not induce it. All mental and physical exertions may excite it.... Among the causes of abortion or premature labour may be included violent mental emotions, passions, longings, alarm or fright, dread of thunder, explosions of artillery, impression of strong or disagreeable odours, sight of disgusting objects, errors of diet, privation of sleep, rest, or food, abuse of stimulating food or drink, over exertion in walking, riding, dancing, running, jolting of carriages, raising or carrying heavy weights, frequenting crowded and heated assemblies, ball rooms, theatres, churches, etc., falls, slips, blows or wounds on the abdomen, violent coughing or laughter, the use of emetics or drastic purgatives, frequent sexual indulgence, surgical operations, even though slight, as the extraction of a tooth, irritation or pain in the genital organs, or in any part of the body....

Women in the lower class of life, who are exposed to much bodily fatigue and mental emotions, are also very liable to this disease. The disposition to abortion is so strong in some women, that the slightest cause, either moral or physical, will induce it; while, in others, the strongest moral or physical influences will not excite it. Women of full or delicate habits are liable to miscarriage....

Dr Michael Ryan, *A Manual of Midwifery*, 4th edn., 1841, pp. 306–8.

99. Exercise and the Habit of Miscarriage (1848)

One of the chief means of preserving health, is by the habitual use of out-door EXERCISE. No error can be greater than to suppose, that because a woman has become pregnant, she must necessarily lie long in bed, or recline on the sofa, and thereby deprive herself of exercise. If she has not hitherto been in the habit of taking regular exercise, let it not be neglected now. It is, in truth, one of the most powerful means of promoting health, of averting disease, and of conducing to a favourable labour. By exercise, however, is not meant violent, undue physical excitement, or over-fatigue from long walking, or late hours, and other causes. The common result of violent exercise, such as dancing, lifting heavy weights, descending rapidly from a height,—strong muscular exertion of any kind,—or of shaking or jolting of the body, to the pregnant female, more especially in the early months,—is miscarriage. This event is exceedingly frequent; but its frequency often arises from the causes above-mentioned. This evil is very seldom considered in the serious light in which it should be viewed. The habit of miscarriage thus induced becomes extremely difficult to overcome; miscarriage after miscarriage takes place, too often leading to inveterate and painful diseases of the womb, which are destructive of comfort, and embitter the after-period of life. Walking is by far the best means of taking exercise. Carriage airings are only negatively useful, inasmuch as they at least procure fresh air, and the pleasant feeling of motion; but not unfrequently they are injurious, through the jolting over rough roads, or the habits of indolence and inactivity which they encourage. The habit of taking exercise should be persevered in, even to the very day of delivery. . . .

Dr John T. Conquest, *Letters to a Mother*, 1848, pp. 6–7.

100. Miscarriage and Ignorance (1882)

Miscarriage.—This is a most serious matter, not only on account of the state of health into which it may throw the patient, not only on account of the loss of the child, but also because, as I have before mentioned, the fact of once miscarrying often means a repetition of this untimely accident. And let me here tell you that a miscarriage is very weakening indeed, in most cases more so than an ordinary confinement; and this fact cannot be too strongly impressed upon all; for I find the greatest ignorance prevails on this point, the majority of women thinking far too lightly of the immediate effects of a miscarriage, and entirely forgetting the probable after ones.

Let me first of all give you all the various *Causes of Miscarriage*.
    1. *An Accident*, such as a blow, a fall, or any sudden shock.
    2. *Over-fatigue or exertion*, such as taking too long walks, riding, a long tiring railway journey, dancing, over-reaching, lifting heavy weights, amusements which fatigue, etc.

3. *Tight-lacing.* Of this I have already written, and need say no more now. Its baneful effects upon all women must be self-evident.

4. *Strong purgative medicines.* Of these I have also warned you.

5. *A certain constitution,* such as a condition of great debility or consumption.

6. *Habit of miscarrying.* This must never be overlooked, for we continually see cases of miscarriages in women who never seem able to go their full time, however careful they may be in avoiding all the different causes of this accident....

Lionel A. Weatherly, *The Young Wife's Own Book,* 1882, pp. 57–8.

101. Experiences of Miscarriage (1886–1902)

(a) *Mary [Gladstone] Drew*

... I do hope you are staying quite in bed, or at least on a couch, till the next month is over. I know it is a fearful bore—but only think what many poor people like Blanche Kay-Shuttleworth have to do [who are given to miscarriages]. They go to bed quite at the first sign, and never get up until after the 4th month, when they rise, and have fine babies, and are none the worse for it. Shuttleworth has managed 3 in this way, after about 12 miscarriages. Not that I think you will come to this, for I do believe and pray, that if you are only careful a little longer now, it will be all right....

I *am* so wretched about you—and I *can't* wait till tomorrow to hear if it is really hopeless, or only one of those queer things people have, *without* everything being over? O, I *pray* that is what it is—I *never never* knew, till your letter came, how I had set my heart on little Sheila. My only comfort is, that if this is the end, you are sure to have some more chances.... O really Mary, I could cry with sorrow and rage—I shall never get over it, till the chance comes again.

Maggie Cowell-Stepney to Mary Drew, [August 1886], Mary [Gladstone] Drew Papers, BL Add. MS. 46249, fos. 236–7, 249.

...[Dr Dobie] made a careful examination [of Mary Drew], and found the womb was enlarged. He thinks the most probable thing is that some membranous stuff which might have to do with the afterbirth is still there, and that it will *gradually* be expelled—*slowly* he says, it is not safe to take it away with violent measures ... he said that 'region' was healthy, that her temperature was quite right, she must make up her mind to take care for a fortnight, to treat herself as if she had had a little confinement, she can lie on the sofa but not go up and downstairs ... she is taking Ergot which will help matters, and of course the syringing with Boracic Acid is continued, the nurse is careful ... patience is *the thing* required at present—it must run its course and take its own time—Dr D[obie] has known cases going on for 5 months....

Gertrude to Catherine Gladstone, 2 May 1893, Glynne-Gladstone MSS [St. Deiniol's Library, Hawarden].

(b) *Edith Lyttelton*
[19 September 1902]
... In the very middle of this letter your poor DD has had to take to her bed with a threatening of a miscarriage. I was terribly frightened at first, but as the hours go on I am less so and full of hope that it was a mere warning, and that I must be even more careful than before...it is vital to keep absolutely flat and still and not to worry....

[26 September 1902]
...I hope you think it was right to have [Dr] Croome down—the local man was not at first sure if everything had come away, and he evidently desired it—I expect it will cost something. Croome did not operate—confirmed Mathisons's opinion that from the very beginning the thing was all wrong and could never have come to a baby.... He told me I must stay in bed at least a fortnight, and that in his opinion I ought not to have another baby until I have been what they call curetted—in other words scraped ... I

seem to be very well out of this scrape for he says that if it had gone on another month or two it might have been very serious indeed...there is no reason I should not have more children—so I shall devote my energies to getting quite sound and then perhaps things may go well.... The actual night when it all happened was horrible for though I had no pain there was considerable haemorrhage. The doctor hurt me rather and I nearly fainted and frightened both myself and the nurse considerably....

Edith to Alfred Lyttelton, 19, 26 September, 1902, Chandos Papers, II, 3/11 [Churchill College, Cambridge].

102. The Dangers of Miscarriage (1895)

The subject of miscarriage is one of the greatest importance, for not only is the life of the child at stake, but in many cases that of the mother also. Even when her life is spared the mother's health is endangered by the nature of the process which, if not well managed, often causes so much bleeding that great weakness and anaemia must result. Other sources of danger to life and health arise from the internal inflammations and other morbid changes—especially blood poisoning—which are liable to occur in neglected cases, and from the mistaken idea that exists in the minds of many people that a miscarriage is not a serious accident, and does not need so much care either at the time or during convalescence, as does a confinement at the full time. It is well for all young wives to realise that a miscarriage is an accident of which no one can foretell the result; which may immediately entail a long and serious illness, and which may lay the foundation of prolonged ill-health....

... the two great immediate dangers in abortion are severity of haemorrhage, and retention of some portion of the ovum, leading to blood poisoning. Fortunately, in the earliest miscarriages, when the ovum is most likely to escape recognition, it is also most likely to be detached and cast off entire, so that nothing is left behind to decompose.

From the third month to the sixth, the process is slower, more difficult and more dangerous than the abortion of the earliest weeks, or premature confinement between the sixth month and full term.... [When the placenta is retained in] 'imperfect miscarriage,' unless carefully treated [it] entails considerable danger on the patient. So long as any part of the ovum is retained, there is danger of bleeding and of blood poisoning. So great is this danger, and so difficult is it in many cases to ascertain whether every part of the ovum has been expelled, that the services of a skilled attendant are really much more needed than they are in confinement at full term....

It cannot be too strongly impressed on the patient and on her friends that convalescence from a miscarriage needs to be more carefully watched than convalescence from confinement at full term. The popular idea that 'a slight miscarriage' is a trifling annoyance, and demands no further treatment than a few days on the sofa, is altogether unfounded and full of peril. If we consider that a miscarriage is always caused either by disease or accident, that it is never a natural process, as is delivery at term, we shall admit one convincing argument, that to heal the disease or to rectify the accident, great care will be needed. All experienced physicians (especially those who have made the diseases of women their chief study) agree that miscarriage is the most common cause of displacements, of inflammations, and other diseases of the pelvic organs of women ... it renders the patient liable to all the accidents and dangers that may attend child-birth. All the forms of puerperal blood-poisoning—the haemorrhages, inflammations, and other troubles—are as likely to occur after miscarriage as after labour. Most of these troubles can be entirely avoided by ready and skilful assistance....

Dr Mary Scharlieb, *A Woman's Words to Women on the Care of their Health in England and in India*, 1895, pp. 168, 171–2, 181–2, 188–9.

103. Spontaneous and Criminal Abortion (1900)

Premature expulsion of the ovum is one of the commonest of the morbid occurrences of pregnancy. On an average, every women who has borne children and reached the limit of the child-bearing age has had at least one abortion or premature labour. The proportion of abortions to full-term deliveries has been estimated as being as much as one to five. The attachment of the ovum to the uterine wall is less firm in the early months of pregnancy before the complete formation of the placenta. Hence it is within the first four months of pregnancy that abortions are most common. Within the first few weeks of pregnancy many abortions pass altogether unrecognised, or only suspected. A woman goes a few days or two or three weeks, beyond the expected time of menstruation; then haemorrhage occurs, resembling a menstrual period rather more profuse than usual, and an ovum may escape unobserved. If shreds of decidua are detected, these show only a slightly greater development than the shreds of menstrual decidua sometimes passed in menstruation without any conception. It is therefore impossible to estimate accurately the relative frequency of abortions within the first two months. Abortions positively diagnosed occur most frequently between the sixth and the sixteenth week....

The later the stage of pregnancy reached, the more nearly does the process resemble that of ordinary labour. In the middle months of pregnancy, after the placenta has been formed, but before the formation of that layer of open meshwork which facilitates its separation from the uterine wall, the separation of the placenta is much more difficult, and the uterine action is often insufficient to effect it completely. Hence either the whole or a portion of the placenta is liable to be retained for a longer or shorter period, unless removed artificially. It is from the 10th, and more especially from the 12th, up to about the 20th week that this specially close union exists between the placenta and the uterine wall, and hence an abortion within these limits of time is more likely to lead to grave results than either before or after....

Different women also vary immensely in the ease with which abortion can be excited. The difference depends chiefly upon the degree of irritability of the nervous system, but, to some extent also, upon the firmness of attachment of the ovum to the uterus ... with some women, any slight mental or physical disturbance, even the seeing a mouse or a spider, appears to be sufficient to cause abortion. Frequently both a predisposing and an exciting cause can be assigned; and, in the presence of a predisposing cause, the exciting cause may be of the most trivial character....

The result of incomplete abortion varies according to the firmness of attachment of the placenta to the uterus. If there is close attachment over nearly the whole surface, decomposition may be averted. There is then generally but slight haemorrhage in the first stage of the abortion.... More frequently, the union of the placenta is not close enough to preserve its vitality, decomposition occurs, and in a day or two offensive discharge begins.... When decomposition of the placenta occurs, the patient is exposed to the risk of sapraemia and septicaemia, as in the case of retention of portions of placenta after full-term delivery. The disease, however, is not usually so severe, and rarely leads to a fatal result, although sometimes death does occur. Frequently rigors come on within two or three days after the initial stage of the abortion, followed by high temperature, quick pulse, and other constitutional symptoms. Pelvic peritonitis or pelvic cellulitis not unfrequently follows, more especially the former, and often the foundation is laid for chronic uterine malady....

It is estimated by Lusk, from the statistics of deaths in New York City, that deaths from all causes after abortion are nearly as numerous in proportion as deaths from metria after delivery at full term, if it be correct to reckon one abortion to every eight to ten full term deliveries. I have known abortion in the third month not only end fatally, but form the starting-point of a series of cases of fatal puerperal septicaemia in the practice of the medical attendant. Death, however, is very rare, if abortion is treated efficiently from the outset. Abortion very frequently leaves behind it chronic uterine disease, especially subinvolution. Several causes tend to this result. First, there is frequently some already existing morbid state of the uterus, the cause of the abortion; secondly, women often disregard an abortion, and omit to take sufficient rest and care afterwards; and, thirdly, the natural stimulus of lactation in promoting the contraction and thereby the involution of the uterus is wanting.

The danger of criminal abortion is very much greater than that of spontaneous abortion. This is to be explained partly because instruments are often used by unskilled persons when the object is criminal, partly because the healthy ovum has a closer and more vascular connection with the uterine wall, so that its separation is more likely to be incomplete, or to be attended with profuse bleeding. Of cases of criminal abortion which have been made public, the women have died in not less than half. It must, however, of course be remembered that the death of the woman is generally the circumstance which leads to investigation and detection, and that many other cases remain undetected....

The drug most to be relied on to check the action of the uterus is opium. A subcutaneous injection of morphia may be given to start with; or Battley's liquor opii sedativus or nepenthe may be given in twenty minim doses for two or three doses, and afterwards in ten minim doses every four hours. If the abortion does not become inevitable, the opiate must be continued until all symptoms have completely subsided, and the patient should still be kept in bed for a week or ten days afterwards....

Dr A. L. Galabin, *A Manual of Midwifery*, 1900, pp. 385-7, 391-5.

104. The History, Statistics and Causes of Abortion (1909)

The history of abortion (i.e. spontaneous expulsion of the ovum from the uterus before the sixteenth week) reaches back to the oldest writers... I have often been astonished at the close observation of the ancients in regard to abortion. The fact that it is more dangerous than birth at full term was fully recognized by them, and Hippocrates notes the frequency with which some women abort repeatedly at the same month (Haeser's 'Geschichte der Medicin,' 1875)....

No accurate statistics in regard to the frequency with which abortion takes place can be obtained; the best which can be done is to draw what conclusions are possible from our case-books, although we at once encounter a stumbling-block in the fact that in these we have to do with sick women... All that can be said on the subject is that a consultation of the works of most authorities show them to agree that the frequency of abortion to birth at full term is from one in five or six to one in ten, and that the third month is the time when it most frequently takes place. It seems also to be generally agreed that as women grow older they are more subject to abortion, which is what would naturally be expected, as the pelvic organs become more subject to pathological changes as life advances. Stumpff gives the following figures on this point (*Münch. med. Wochenschr.*, 1892, Nos. 43 and 44):

	Per cent
Before the age of 21 years	23.6
From 21–25 years	22.5
From 26–30 years	31.0
From 31–35 years	27.1
From 36–40 years	27.5
Above 40 years	36.6

Various infections of the mother may cause death of the fetus. According to Charpentier (*Centrbl. f. Gyn.*, 1898, vol. 22, p. 198) measles was the cause of abortion twenty-three times in fifty-one cases. Scarlet fever, smallpox, typhoid-fever, pneumonia, erysipelas, appendicitis, and other febrile disorders are frequent causes, and the fact that abortions occur most frequently in them when the temperature is high, shows a relation between its occurrence and the severity of the disease. As regards the chronic infections, abortions have been attributed to tuberculosis in the mother in a few cases (Birch-Hirschfeld).

Syphilis has always played a large part as a causative factor in abortion.... Psychic disturbances and excessive cohabitation, especially when the latter takes place at a time when menstruation might otherwise be expected, are frequent causes of abortion. Acute poisoning by means of alcohol..., phosphorus, lead and other poisons is a factor in abortion.... Operative procedures during pregnancy are quite frequently a source of trouble... operations on the cervix, the vagina, the external genitalia, and the breasts are peculiarly apt to excite the uterus to contraction; and experience has shown that from twenty to thirty per cent of cases operated upon during pregnancy abort....

Dr Howard A. Kelly, *Medical Gynecology*, 1909, pp. 428–9, 431–3.

3.4 Childbirth

CHILDBIRTH AS A NATURAL PROCESS

105. Childbirth and the Medical Practitioner (1841)

Happily for humanity, the process of labour, in a vast majority of cases, is safe and free from danger, especially when women live according to nature's laws; but among the higher and middle, indeed all classes in civilized society in which these laws are frequently violated or forgotten, or when the constitution is impaired by the luxury or dissipation of modern times, the process of child-bearing is attended with more or less danger, both before and after it is completed. These observations are particularly applicable to the lower classes of society, whose customs, habits, pursuits, and intemperance, render them liable to many serious accidents during parturition, and to a vast number of inflammatory and febrile diseases after delivery....

It is, however, fortunate for suffering humanity, that the process of parturition may now be greatly accelerated, and the greatest of mortal suffering relieved by the advice and skilful exertions of the obstetrician or medical attendant, and with the most perfect safety to the parent and offspring. It is well known that even the presence of a medical practitioner will often afford relief, and hasten delivery without the performance of any manual operation whatever. The confident assurance to the patient of her safety, inspires that balmy hope, which will hasten parturition much better than any other means. It is on this account, that there are few intelligent women who do not prefer medical attendance during labour, to that of midwives. This is the case in every civilized country, as women are well aware of the superior knowledge which medical practitioners possess of their constitutions; and hence, in modern times, we observe a wise and judicious preference given to male obstetricians, and midwives are scarcely ever exclusively employed, unless among the ignorant or lower classes, who are unable to employ the former, but even this want is now supplied by our public charities.

Fruitless attempts have been made, from time to time, to calumniate medical practitioners, and to deter husbands from allowing such individuals to afford aid at the fearful and painful period of parturition. Such attempts were as wicked as fruitless, for every husband, and every man of common understanding well know, that passion and pain seldom co-exist....

What, I beg to ask, does an ignorant midwife or nurse know concerning the mechanism of human nativity, or the difficulties that attend it? I answer, about as much as an unborn babe. Is not the mortality of infants immense among all classes, unattended by medical faculty? No medical practitioner, duly educated, can deny this melancholy fact. In fine, I venture to assert, that were it practicable or prudent to address a public assembly composed of all ranks of society, I would undertake to prove, and demonstrate to the conviction of every rational individual present, the propriety, superiority, and humanity of preferring medical to other aid during the process of human parturition....

When requested to attend a parturient woman, the obstetrician should visit her as soon as possible. He should be distinguished for suavity of manners, politeness, delicacy, humanity, sympathy, patience, and never evince anger under any circumstance. He ought to possess perfect self-command and confidence, which are the characteristics of a duly educated and experienced medical obstetrician....Many women strongly object to a vaginal examination in the first stage of labour, when there are slight pains, and will not allow it; but we generally succeed in obtaining permission to make it, by not betraying the slightest conciousness of its being in any degree indelicate...

She may walk about until the discharge of the amniotic fluid, or breaking of the water, and after that occurrence she should be confined to bed, as delivery is suddenly accomplished, in most cases, but may not happen for hours or days—some say weeks, afterwards.... The function of parturition, when natural, and when the woman's health is good, requires little more attention than that of digestion, respiration, &c. But in all civilized countries, there is scarcely one woman in twenty in good health; and hence the necessity of care and caution during labour and the puerperal or child-bed condition....

Let the parturient woman place the fullest confidence in the advice of her medical attendant, who should be duly educated; strictly follow his directions, have no opinion of her own, and pay no attention to any contrary advice that may be proposed by her nurse or others....

Dr Michael Ryan, *A Manual of Midwifery*, 4th edn., 1841, pp. 167-70, 174, 185-6.

106. Childbirth as a Natural Process of Pain (1848)

Childbirth is that natural process by which the womb expels its contents, and returns to the condition in which it was previously. I call it a natural process; and, in my opinion, no sentiment is more pregnant with mischief than the opinion which almost universally prevails, that this process is inevitably one of difficulty and danger. I am well aware that some degree of suffering is connected with child-birth; and this applies equally to the whole animal creation, whether human or brute,—though the former suffer more than the latter, because the habits of brutes are less unnatural. That the suffering of women during child-birth is referable in a very great degree to their artificial habits of life, and not to their form and make, is evident from a variety of circumstances. History, in all ages of the world, establishes this position....

Still further to establish the assertion that human parturition is not necessarily a process of danger, we know that in this country servant girls who become illegitimately pregnant, very often absent themselves for an hour or two, and after giving birth to a child, return to the discharge of their household duties immediately.

It is, therefore, obvious that the difficulty and danger which so often attend child-bearing in civilised society are attributable, principally, to unnatural customs and habits of living, in which women, in this and other countries, indulge from their infancy, and which operate by preventing the constitution from acquiring its proper firmness and vigour, and by producing a weak, feeble, and irritable state of body.

But these, it must be admitted, are exceptions to the general rule, and the majority of women, in giving birth to their offspring, have to endure sufferings which often seem more than human nature can bear up under. The pains of labour sometimes convulse the whole frame, and all but destroy life by their severity; and some high and strong-minded women, even when sustained by a consciousness of Divine support and assistance, give expression by their cries and groans to agony, the intensity of which baffles all description; and not unfrequently women of the most gentle and quiet and enduring dispositions become almost wild and frantic from the intolerable anguish they suffer. With what gratitude and readiness should we, then, hail any discovery that can mitigate the violence, or lessen the duration of these heart-rending pangs. . . .

Dr John T. Conquest, *Letters to a Mother*, 1848, pp. 45, 48-9.

107. Three Stages of Labour (1882)

. . . . Be careful and never have too many people about you during your labour; the nurse and the doctor are as a rule quite sufficient, though there is no harm in having a second woman in the room if you wish it.

During the First or Premonitory Stage you need not remain in your bedroom; rather be about the house, occupying yourself with various light and simple duties connected with your household, and thus keep your mind from brooding over the immediate and inevitable future. . . .

During the Second or Dilating Stage you had better get to your room, although there is no necessity for your lying down; in fact, it is more helpful that you still continue to walk about, taking the wise precaution to lie or sit down occasionally to prevent fatigue. You must now get your clothes arranged as I have described.

It is perfectly useless during either of these two stages of labour to bear down and attempt to, as it were, 'help the pains.' This is an error many women fall into, and I cannot too strongly urge your never doing this, for it will, besides being useless, positively retard the end of the labour, by taking much of your strength. . . .

During the Third or Expelling Stage of Labour you must get on the bed, and you may now try and help your pains by gently bearing down, only doing this during the period of a pain, as at other times it is worse than useless.

Be sure and never object to your medical man making the necessary examinations; he must do so to enable him to arrive at the desirable conclusion that all is going on well, or to show him that some interference is absolutely necessary.

On the other hand, let me here remark that the idea so prevalent among the poorer women, that by a medical man examining constantly he materially helps the labour, is most erroneous....

Lionel A. Weatherly, *The Young Wife's Own Book*, 1882, pp. 62-5.

108. Caesarian Section (1900)

By Caesarian section is meant the removal of the foetus by incisions through the walls of the abdomen and the uterus. In the variety of the operation introduced by Porro it is completed by the excision of the whole of the body of the uterus....

Up to the last few years the mortality of Caesarian section had been so high as to restrict the operation to those cases in which delivery through the pelvis was either impossible or so difficult as to involve very great risk to the mother. British statistics gave a mortality of about 84 per cent. The first improvement was introduced in 1876, by Porro of Pavia, who followed up Caesarian section by the removal of the whole uterus with the ovaries in a case of pelvic contraction.... It was practised in a good many cases of pelvic contraction with a success considerably exceeding that of the old Caesarian section. The modern method of Caesarian section was first suggested by Sänger in 1882. It was perfected and simplified chiefly at Dresden and Leipzig by Leopold and other operators, and has attained such success as to displace craniotomy from a considerable portion of its field. Hitherto the operation has been performed most frequently and most successfully in Germany, where the higher degrees of pelvic contraction are commoner than in England or America. The improvements introduced by Sänger consist essentially in the adaptation of Lembert's intestinal suture for the superficial sutures of the uterine peritoneum; and in the use of a large number of sutures, deep and superficial, to secure perfect closure of the uterine wound, so that the lochial discharge is prevented from reaching the peritoneum....

Dr A. L. Galabin, *A Manual of Midwifery*, 1900, pp. 684–5.

ATTENDANTS AT CHILDBIRTH

109. Attendants at Childbirth (1837): nurse, doctor and married friend

ATTENDANTS, ETC.—At this time [the symptoms of labour approaching] the nurse should be in attendance, if possible, and every thing in the lying-in-room in order. The latter ought to be large and airy, and should have a dressing-closet attached to it.

The Friend that is to be present during the labour should be fixed upon. And it may be proper to suggest that medical men do not like unmarried females in the room; they are neither the most fit companions for the patient, nor the most useful assistants to the practitioner. Let a confidante be selected in some judicious and affectionate married friend, whose presence during the hour of trial, will ensure sympathy and yet encouragement.

During the labour the medical man, the nurse, and the patient's friend, are all the assistants the occasion demands. The lying-in-room is not the place for a crowd. A great number of persons breathing the atmosphere of the same room soon pollute it; and if there happen to be a fire, its temperature will inevitably be raised to a point which will make the patient restless and feverish,—add to her feelings of fatigue, and often, by rendering the pains irregular or ineffective, protract labour considerably.

The patient also is much disturbed by their conversation, and what is a much greater evil than this, by their imprudent remarks they frequently diminish her confidence in her own powers, or in the judgment and skill of her necessary attendants....

EXAMINATION BY MEDICAL ATTENDANT.—Soon after the arrival of the practitioner, if labour has commenced, he requests through the intervention of the friend of the patient, or the nurse, to make an examination, '*to take a pain,*' as it is termed. This is frequently objected to; and from false delicacy the patient does not consent to his wish until obliged by the severity of her pains in a more advanced stage of the labour.

Now it is highly important that in the *earliest* stage of the process, this examination should be made, for the medical attendant obtains necessary and valuable information, which regulates his conduct. Thus he ascertains whether labour has actually commenced, or if her pains are spurious or false pains only, requiring a plan of treatment for their relief, which he at once prescribes. He is enabled to determine by it whether his assistance is necessary; whereas if it is deferred he might be the means of occasioning mischief, by being an idle spectator, when he ought to be acting. And moreover it enables him to acquaint his patient not only how far she has advanced in her labour, but what is of much more importance, whether the position of the child is natural.

On the other hand there exists a vulgar prejudice that these examinations are attended with great benefit, that they materially assist the labour, and expedite the termination of the female's sufferings, and she is, therefore, naturally enough, continually looking for such supposed assistance. This is an injurious mistake, for frequent examinations are not only superfluous, but may materially retard or interrupt the process of labour...labour is a *natural* process; as such, judiciously managed, it is unattended with danger, and the amount of pain falls very far short of what is generally anticipated.

Dr Thomas Bull, *Hints to Mothers for the Management of Health*, 1837, pp. 128–30, 134–6, 141.

110. Husbands at Childbirth (1841): the example of Queen Victoria and fashionable London ladies

SIR,—The public papers at first informed us that during a late accouchement the lady [i.e. Queen Victoria] was surrounded by no less than four doctors, her husband being present in the room. In a later paper it stated that the three supernumerary doctors were in an adjoining room, and that only the accoucheur-in-chief and the husband were in the lying-in-room. However this may have been, is it right or proper for any husband to be in the room while the nurses and professional man are in attendance on the female during parturition? I bring this subject before the profession with the view of raising some discussion, and taking the sense of practitioners at large upon it. After nearly thirty years' practice I have recently been twice vexed by the intrusion of the husband into the lying-in-room. In one case I remonstrated with the female attendants, whose feelings of delicacy were somewhat outraged also, on the impropriety of the husband's coming into the room from time to time, and gave him some significant looks, intimating that his presence could be dispensed with; but I was told by the nurse that when the lady was confined in *London*, Dr.——made no objection to his remaining in the room from first to last.

In the second instance, which was a first labour, the patient being also a *London* lady, with a *London* nurse, the husband persisted in being at the bedside during the whole of the parturient process, to my great discomfiture. This may be the fashionable '*London practice of midwifery,*' but I confess it did not square with my old-fashioned notions of delicacy or propriety, and I doubt whether in either case I ought to have submitted to it....

Country Doctor, 'Husbands in Bed-Rooms During Parturition', *The Lancet*, 11 December 1841, pp. 390-1.

111. Husbands at Childbirth (1841): a matter for man and wife

SIR,—In reply to your correspondent in this week's *Lancet*, I beg to observe that I think a medical man steps very far beyond his province when he endeavours to prevent a husband being present at the accouchement of his wife. Man and wife are one, and it is a matter between themselves with which we have nothing whatever to do. I wish, indeed, that the practice were far more general, as then a husband would be able to appreciate the delicacy and decorum with which the proceedings are conducted on the part of surgeons, and thus dissipate prejudices which are, not unnaturally, sometimes entertained upon this subject. However, either from unwillingness to witness the sufferings of his wife (sometimes from indifference to them), her own objection that he should, the tittle-tattle of the women who are with her, or the black looks to which your correspondent alludes, it happens that the husband is very seldom present; but, when he desires to be so, I would caution the practitioner against joining the nurse and her coterie in wishing to throw an unnecessary mystery around the proceedings of the lying-in room. Whether the practice be, as the country surgeon states, an exclusively *London* practice, I know not; but, if so, I doubt not, eventually, by reason of the example given by the exalted and most exemplary married couple [Queen Victoria and Prince Albert] of the realm, that it will soon spread, together with the various other improvements emanating from the metropolis, even into the most remote provincial districts.

John Chatto, 'Husbands at Accouchements', *The Lancet*, 18 December 1841, p. 421.

112. Husbands at Childbirth (1841): the desire of the wife

SIR,—In reply to a letter in THE LANCET of the 11th inst., from a gentleman signing himself 'A COUNTRY DOCTOR', I beg to say that how fashionably soever the practice he mentions may be in the practice of London midwifery, it is not countenanced among the lower classes as among the higher. As to the question of delicacy or propriety, I see no reason why the accoucheur should not sanction the presence of the husband at any time during the parturient process. The manner in which everything is conducted at the present time in the lying-in room, need not offend the delicacy of the most refined or fastidious. Moreover, the husband's presence is not unfrequently urgently desired by the wife at the climax of her sufferings, and, in my own practice, this has been rarely objected to by the female friends or attendants; and I am quite sure that the presence of the husband might be more generally acquiesced in to the advantage of the accoucheur, as it would tend to disabuse the husband's mind of any false or erroneous notions that he might have entertained relative to the lying-in room, and mitigate that reserve which is sometimes felt towards the accoucheur in his future visits to the family, of which I am confident many of my professional brethren have often had cause to complain....

Dr John Bryant, 'Husbands at Accouchements', *The Lancet*, 18 December 1841, p. 421.

113. Husbands at Childbirth (1841): the beneficial effects

SIR,—"A COUNTRY DOCTOR", in your Publication of last week, wishes to take the sense of practitioners at large, as to the propriety of husbands visiting at intervals, or staying with their wives during the process of parturition: I certainly cannot mention, having had only two instances of husbands there intruding, after thirty years' experience, as my own practice within the last thirty *days* has developed more than that number, and I must confess that not in one instance have I given them notice to quit. I do not mean to advocate the propriety of husbands remaining in the apartment, as if they were the accoucheur or aged matrons to attend to the little stranger when born, but I do think that when the wife is suffering the pains of labour, and the fear and dread which are attendant upon that moment of severe trial, it is unnatural not to allow her partner in life to enter the room, and whisper words of comfort and solace. In the cases that have fallen under my care, the husband, naturally feeling for the safety of his wife, has respectfully solicited permission to enter the apartment, and give cheering hopes and assurances that all will end well and speedily, from which I think beneficial effects have been produced, particularly when the patient is of a desponding nature; and where is the heart that can censure this? I should like to ask your correspondent whether he is a married man (which I doubt), and whether, if his lady were many hours or days in suffering, he would like to be forbidden to see her on the score of delicacy. If so, what a fine sensibility he must possess, and how easily it can be shocked. Again, it often occurs that the accoucheur and nurse are the only attendants, and these may be strangers; and perhaps the doctor, honest man, may be incapable of officiating, from ignorance or other circumstances: in this case, I presume the patient is to be lost, without being able to see her husband, and state to him her fears.

B. H. W. H., 'Husbands at Accouchements', *The Lancet*, 18 December 1841, pp. 421-2.

114. Husbands at Childbirth (1842): a rare circumstance

SIR, I was somewhat surprised at reading in your Journal of the 18th December, no less than three letters on the subject of the presence of husbands in the lying-in room, and in all the writers encouraged the system. I can only say that I have been in active and extensive practice for fourteen years, and that I have not met with the circumstance of the presence of the husband during the progress of the labour more than three or four times; indeed, it is so seldom in this neighbourhood, that when it does happen it is made a subject of general remark among the gossips. I must confess that I have a great dislike to it; not because I have anything to apprehend from the observation of the husband, but *because I do not think it is delicate or decent*. We all know what offices we have to perform in the lying-in chamber, and I am sure that in forty-nine cases out of fifty the female herself does not desire the presence of her husband *till it is all over*. The husband can do no good in the room; and it surely cannot be any pleasure to him to see the progress of the labour, and watch the movements of the medical attendant. Of course, I should not *object* to the presence of the husband; but that does not imply that I should approve of it. As to any prejudices which some men may entertain on the subject, I do not believe them to be in any way general; nor am I aware of 'the reserve which is sometimes felt towards the accoucheur in his future visits to the family;' so far from that, I have ever been kindly and handsomely treated by husbands on and after such occasions. At all events, the practice alluded to is not common about here; and for the sake of decency I do not wish to see it. At the same time, I certainly should never object to the admission of the husband if the wife requested it; or if she were in imminent danger, or if the husband urgently desired it; but if the case were going on well, I think his presence would be indecent, unbecoming, and unnecessary.

W. K., 'Husbands in Lying-In Rooms', *The Lancet*, 15 January 1842, pp. 551-2.

115. Husbands at Childbirth (1842): exclusion degrading and insulting

SIR,—As a non-professional reader, I presume that it will not be quite uninteresting to give you my views of a question recently discussed in your pages, namely, 'The presence of husbands at accouchements.' I believe there are few men but are annoyed, and there are many who consider themselves to be degraded and insulted, by the exclusion which the tyrant 'custom' seems to sanction on these occasions. The moment is an anxious and depressing one, and few have the moral courage to brave the temporary odium which attaches to the disturbance of so delicate a question; but the question must arise, 'Why am I to be so delicate as to absent myself at such a time, when so many others, even of the *modest* sex, whom necessity and curiosity bring to the room, claim to dispense with this feeling?' And it may be argued thus, 'Does not my wife feel confidence enough in me to believe that any supposed indelicacy to which she is obliged to submit, would never lower the standard of my feelings with respect either to her person or her morals?' Which is most likely to affect a man's feelings; to exaggerate the proceedings of the lying-in chamber into something that is revolting even to the imagination; or, his presence and knowledge of what is really necessary to be done there, leaving nothing for the mind to dwell on afterwards? May these duties be performed by a man to a woman whom he has perhaps never before seen,—can they be witnessed by other women who have not the excuse of absolute necessity for their attendance, and yet a father and a husband is forbid by delicacy to be present at the birth of his own child? It would seem preposterous, but that a clue to the inconsistency is obtained in the fact that it is not the wife's feelings or decency that is consulted, but the objecting accoucheur, and the gossips who surround him. The idea of a woman's submitting, in the presence of persons of both sexes, to what she would not submit to before her husband, is to place a wife's confidence and affection in a very false view. Husbands may appear *voluntarily* to withdraw themselves, but there are few who like to be treated like children, loitering at a distance, and pretending that they feel the propriety of all that is dictated by those who usurp their proper place at a wife's side, to cheer her in the intervals of pain, and to watch with kind and anxious interest her progress. Appeals to notions of delicacy at such times are unworthy of a liberal profession. I have been present at two accouchements with my wife. Everything was both decorous and courteous, and I think I should be doing the accoucheur injustice to say that he would have felt more at ease if I had been absent.

'F', 'Husbands at Accouchements', *The Lancet,* 26 February 1842, pp. 759-60.

116. Attendants at Childbirth and After (1848)

Wherever practicable, it is always advisable that the nurse should be in the house some days before the anticipated event, because, although, in first confinements, there is generally sufficient warning and sufficient time to summon both attendants [i.e. the nurse and the doctor], yet all subsequent labours may proceed so rapidly as to leave her destitute of assistance and to place both the mother and the child in jeopardy. It is also always advisable to send for the medical attendant, not only because his services *may* be required to combat accidental complications, but because the very fact of his being at hand consoles the female and inspires her with confidence. It may scarcely be necessary to advise the female to have her bed and dress properly prepared for the coming event; but as both these duties are often left unattended to, these circumstances must not be forgotten; the nurse, or female friend, who should be a married female of light and easy mind, cheering in her disposition, and acquainted with the routine of the lying-in chamber, will attend to the former....

It is highly important that in this process the seclusion which all animals naturally seek should be permitted to the human female. Besides the usual attendants, one friend is abundantly sufficient, and if the mind of the woman be firm, she, also, may usefully be dispensed with. The greater the number of people, the more conversation, the greater restlessness and agitation of mind, the greater diminution of confidence,—the more disturbance, and the less naturally is the process conducted. Quietness and seclusion are indeed natural, and whatever is opposed to these circumstances, is opposed to the simplicity, and safety, and natural termination of the event....

...[the delivery room] should be kept cool and well ventilated, and free from intruding, talkative friends,—a caution even more important now than heretofore. In truth, the ill-judged, and tedious, and troublesome attentions of visitors at this period, are pregnant with great danger, and many women have lost their lives through neglecting to secure to themselves silence, solitude, and comparative darkness during the forty-eight hours which succeed delivery. That the intrusion of relatives at this time is unnecessary may be assumed by the calm, quiet, and grateful serenity of mind which so naturally fills the heart of the mother after so great a deliverance....

Dr John T. Conquest, *Letters to a Mother*, 1848, pp. 38-9, 44, 73.

117. Attendants at Childbirth (1853, 1857): nurse, doctor and husband

(From the *Court Circular*)

BUCKINGHAM PALACE, APRIL 7.

At 10 minutes past 1 o'clock this day the Queen was safely delivered of a Prince.

There were present on the occasion in Her Majesty's room— His Royal Highness Prince Albert, Dr. Locock, Dr. Snow, and Mrs. Lilly, the monthly nurse. In the adjoining apartments, besides the other medical attendants (Sir James Clark and Dr. Ferguson) were her Royal Highness the Duchess of Kent, the Lady in Waiting on the Queen, and the following Officers of State and Lords of the Privy Council, viz., the Earl of Aberdeen, First Lord of the Treasury; Earl Granville, Lord President of Council; the Duke of Norfolk, Lord Steward; the Duke of Wellington, Master of the Horse; the Duke of Newcastle, Secretary of State for the Colonies; the Marquis of Lansdowne, the Marquis of Breadalbane, Lord Chamberlain; the Duke of Argyll, Lord Privy Seal; Viscount Palmerston, Secretary of State for the Home Department. . . .

The Times, 8 April 1853, p.5.

BIRTH OF A PRINCESS
(From the *Court Circular*)

BUCKINGHAM PALACE, APRIL 14 [1857]
At 15 minutes before 2 o'clock p.m. this day the Queen was safely delivered of a Princess.

There were present on the occasion in Her Majesty's room His Royal Highness Prince Albert, Dr. Locock, Dr. Snow, and Mrs. Lilly, the monthly nurse. In the adjoining apartments, besides the other medical attendants (Sir James Clark and Dr. Ferguson), were the Mistress of the Robes, the Lady in Waiting on the Queen, and the following officers of State and Lords of the Privy Council—viz., his Royal Highness the Duke of Cambridge, the Lord Chancellor, Viscount Palmerston, Sir George Grey, Earl of Clarendon, Mr. Secretary Labouchere, Lord Panmure, Sir Charles Wood, the Bishop of London, and the Marquis of Breadalbane. . . .

The Times, 15 April 1857, p.7.

118. Husbands at Childbirth (1889): absence and cleanliness

Should the husband be present during the labour? Certainly not; but as soon as the labour is over, and all the soiled clothes have been put out of the way, let him instantly see his wife for a few minutes, to whisper in her ear words of affection, of gratitude, and consolation....

Pye Henry Chavasse, *Advice to a wife on the management of her own health*, 13th. edn., 1889, p. 214.

3.5. The Chloroform Controversy

119. A New Agent to Prevent Pain in Obstetric Practice (1847)

At the first winter meeting of the Medico-Chirurgical Society of Edinburgh, held on the 10th of November last, I had an opportunity of directing the attention of the members to a new agent which I had been using for some time previously, for the purpose of producing insensibility to pain in surgical and obstetric practice.

This new anaesthetic agent is chloroform, chloroformyle, or perchloride of formyle. Its composition is expressed by the chemical formula $C_2H Cl_3$. . . . It possesses an agreeable, fragrant, fruit-like odour, and a saccharine, pleasant taste.

As an inhaled anaesthetic agent, it possesses, I believe, all the advantages of sulphuric ether, without its principal disadvantages. . . .

I have had an opportunity of using chloroform with perfect success in several surgical operations, (removal of tumours, of necrosed bone, partial amputation of the great toe,) and in tooth-drawing, opening abscesses, for annulling the pain of dys-mennorrhoea and of neuralgia, in two or three cases where I was using deep and otherwise very painful galvano-puncture for the treatment of ovarian dropsy, and in removing a very large fibrous tumour from the posterior wall of the uterus by enucleation, &c.

I have employed it also in obstetric practice, with entire success. The lady to whom it was first exhibited during parturition had been previously delivered in the country by perforation of the head of the infant, after a labour of three days' duration. In this, her second confinement, pains supervened a fortnight before the full time. Three hours and a half after they commenced, ere the dilatation of the os uteri was completed, I placed her under the influence of the chloroform, by moistening, with half a teaspoonful of the liquid, a pocket-handkerchief, rolled up in a funnel shape, and with the broad or open end of the funnel placed over her mouth and nostrils. In consequence of the evaporation of the fluid, it was once more renewed in about ten or twelve minutes. The child was expelled in about twenty-five minutes after the inhalation was begun. The mother subsequently remained longer soporose than commonly happens after ether. The squalling of the child did not, as usual, rouse her; and some minutes elapsed after the placenta was expelled, and after the child was removed by the nurse into another room, before the patient awoke. She then turned round, and observed to me that she had 'enjoyed a very comfortable sleep, and, indeed, required it, as she was so tired, but would now be more able for the work before her.' I evaded entering into conversation with her, believing, as I have already stated, that the most complete possible quietude forms one of the principal secrets for the successful employment of either ether or chloroform. In a little time, she again remarked, that she was afraid her 'sleep had stopped the pains.' Shortly afterwards, her infant was brought in by the nurse from the adjoining room, and it was a matter of no small difficulty to convince the astonished mother that the labour was entirely over, and that the child presented to her was really her 'own living baby.'

Perhaps I may be excused from adding, that since publishing on the subject of ether inhalation in midwifery, seven or eight months ago, and then for the first time directing the attention of the profession to its great use and importance in natural and morbid parturition, I have employed it, with few and rare exceptions, in every case of labour that I have attended, and with the most delightful results. And I have no doubt whatever, that some years hence the practice will be general. Obstetricians may oppose it, but I believe our patients themselves will force the use of it upon the profession. I have never had the pleasure of watching over a series of better and more rapid recoveries, nor once witnessed any disagreeable result follow to either mother or child, whilst I have now seen an immense amount of maternal pain and agony saved by its employment. And I most conscientiously believe, that the proud mission of the physician is distinctly twofold—namely, to alleviate human suffering, as well as preserve human life. . . .

Professor J. Y. Simpson, M.D., 'On a New Anaesthetic Agent, More Efficient than Sulphuric Ether', *The Lancet,* 13 November 1847, pp. 549-50.

120. Simpson's Success with Chloroform (1847)

. . . Powerful, however, as ether is as an anaesthetic agent, I have now to state that it is very inferior to the perchloride of formyle, or chloroform, which has just been introduced into the practice of midwifery and surgery by Professor Simpson, of Edinburgh.

The advantages which chloroform possesses over ether are—
1. The smaller quantity required; thus rendering it more portable. Half a drachm or a drachm of chloroform will almost always succeed in producing perfect narcotism.
2. The absence of the stage of excitement or stimulation, which almost invariably attends ether, and sometimes to an inconvenient extent.
3. The greater rapidity and certainty with which the patient is brought under its influence.
4. The more complete and longer-continued state of perfect insensibility produced.
5. Chloroform does not leave any disagreeable odour about the breath or clothes of either patient or operator; in fact, chloroform has a very pleasant, fruit-like, though transient smell.
6. No headache or other unpleasant effects are left behind.

On learning Professor Simpson's success with chloroform, I determined to try its effects on midwifery, and now beg to transmit to you the history of a case—the first, I believe, in England—in which this agent has been exhibited. The experience of seven months had convinced me of the great value of anaesthetic agents in obstetric practice, and I had no hesitation in substituting chloroform for sulphuric ether, as I was supported by the statements in Dr Simpson's recently published pamphlet,

and by the result of four cases (healthy persons) in which I had
exhibited chloroform....

Dr Protheroe Smith, 'On the Use of Chloroform in Midwifery
Practice', *The Lancet,* 20 November 1847, p. 572.

121. Anaesthesia and the Agony of Labour (1847)

'The distress and pain' (observes Denman) 'which women often
endure while struggling through a *difficult* labour, are beyond all
description, and seem to be more than human nature would be
able to bear under any other circumstances'. But even the amount
of agony endured in most cases of common, or *natural* labour, is
enormously great. It is, I believe, education and custom, and
perhaps the idea of its inevitable necessity, which have made the
profession in general look upon the degree of maternal pain and
physical suffering attendant upon natural parturition as less
deserving of consideration than in reality it is. They have, in a
great measure, blinded us as to its actual amount and intensity and
importance....

Is it *right* for the physician to interfere with these fearful
sufferings and agonies, in order to save and shield his patients
from the endurance of them? Is it *proper* for him to exercise the
skill of his art, so as to moderate and remove these 'maximos et
fere intolerabiles dolores'? Would it be *fit* and *meet* in him to use
human means to assuage the pangs and anguish attendant upon
the process of parturition in the human mother?

These questions, and questions like these, I have often, during
the currency of the present year, heard complacently put by
medical men—men, too, whose opinions and actions, in other
matters and in other respects, were fully and truly actuated by
that great principle of emotion which both impels us to feel
sympathy at the sight of suffering in any fellow-creature, and at
the same time imparts to us delight and gratification in the
exercise of any power by which we can mitigate and alleviate that
suffering. Such questions, I repeat, are seriously asked by
physicians and surgeons, the professed object of whose whole

science and art is the relief of human disease and human suffering.
They are questions propounded with all imaginable gravity and
seriousness by individuals who (in a mere abstract point of view)
would, no doubt, strongly object to being considered as anxious
to patronize and abet the continuance of pain, or traffic in the
perpetuation of human sufferings of any kind. Nay, probably at
this date there is not one in twenty, perhaps not one in a hundred,
of the physicians and surgeons of Great Britain, who have, as yet,
thought seriously upon the propriety of annulling the tortures
attendant on human parturition, or who have acknowledged to
their own minds the propriety of bestirring themselves, so as to
be able, in the exercise of their profession, to secure for their
patients an immunity from the throes and agonies of childbirth.

Perhaps, as an apology for their indolence and apathy, some
may be ready to argue, that the pain and suffering attendant on
parturition is not dangerous and destructive in its results,
however agonizing and distressing it may be to the patient during
its continuance. But the argument is fundamentally unsound. All
pain is, *per se*, and especially when in excess, destructive, and may
be even fatal in its action and effects. It 'exhausts' (says Mr
Travers) 'the principle of life.' 'It exhausts' (says Mr Burns, of
Glasgow) 'both the system and the part.' 'Mere pain' (observed
the late Dr Gooch) 'can destroy life'. And the great pain
accompanying human parturition is no exception to this general
pathological law; for, in fact, the maternal mortality attendant
upon parturition regularly increases in a ratio progressive with
the increased duration of the woman's sufferings. The statistical
data published by Dr Collins, in his excellent report of the Dublin
Lying-in Hospital, affords ample proof of this as a general
principle, with regard to the effect of pain in protracted
parturition. For, according to calculations which I have made
from Dr Collins' data, while in the women delivered in the
Dublin Hospital, and whose sufferings were terminated within
two hours, only one in 320 of the mothers died; where the labour
varied in duration from two to six hours, one in 145 of the
mothers died; in those in whom it continued from seven to twelve
hours, one in eighty died; where it endured from twelve to
twenty-four hours, one in twenty-six died; where it lasted from
twenty-four to thirty-six hours, one in seventeen died; and out of
all those whose parturient sufferings were prolonged beyond

thirty-six hours, one in every six perished....

Now, if experience betimes goes fully to prove to us the safety with which ether may, under proper precautions and management, be employed in the course of parturition, then, looking to the facts of the case, and considering the actual amount of pain usually endured, I believe that the question will require to be quite changed in its character. For, instead of determining, in relation to it, whether we shall be 'justified' in using this agent under the circumstances named, it will become, on the other hand, necessary to determine whether, on any grounds, moral or medical, a professional man could deem himself 'justified' in withholding and *not* using any such safe means, (as we at present presuppose this to be,) provided he had the power, by it, of assuaging the pangs—and anguish of the last stage of natural labour, and thus counteracting what Velpeau describes as 'those piercing cries, that agitation so lively, those excessive efforts, those inexpressible agonies, and those pains apparently intolerable,' which accompany the termination of natural parturition in the human mother.

Since the latter end of January I have employed etherization, with few and rare exceptions, in every case of labour which has been under my care. And the results, as I already stated in THE LANCET two weeks ago, have been, indeed, most happy and gratifying. I never had the pleasure of watching over a series of more perfect or more rapid recoveries; nor have I once witnessed any disagreeable result to either mother or child. I do not remember a single patient to have taken it who has not afterwards declared her sincere gratitude for its employment, and her indubitable determination to have recourse again to similar means under similar circumstances. Most have subsequently set out, like zealous missionaries, to persuade other friends to avail themselves of the same measure in their hour of suffering. And a number of my most esteemed professional brethren in Edinburgh have adopted it with success and results equal to my own. At the same time, I most sincerely believe that we are, all of us, called upon to employ it, by every principle of true humanity, as well as by every principle of true religion. Medical men may oppose, for a time, the superinduction of anaesthesia in parturition, but they will oppose it in vain; for certainly our patients themselves and their friends will force the use of it upon the profession. The whole question is, I believe, even now, one merely of time. It is not—Shall the practice come to be generally adopted? but—When shall it be generally adopted?...

Professor J. Y. Simpson, M.D., 'Cases of the Employment of Chloroform in Midwifery, With Remarks', *The Lancet*, 4 December 1847, pp. 625–6.

122. The Pain of Childbirth as a Gospel Blessing (1848)

... Why, if no impediment was thrown in the way of inhalation in surgical operations, should it be anticipated in midwifery, unless there are cogent reasons against its employment in the one, which did not militate against it in the other?—reasons, however, totally disregarded by Dr. Simpson, who considers, that in the few instances in which he has exhibited chloroform he has been enabled to gain such experience as will allow him to publish to the world that it may be employed with impunity in all cases of natural as well as artificial delivery.

In the operations of surgery anaesthesia has been fairly tested; its utility has been proved, and few operations are now performed without it. How much is learnt from this! Within a fortnight of its introduction it was employed with due care by the most eminent surgeons in London. Their testimony was favourable to its employment, and from that time it has gained ground in the estimation of all. Not so, however, in midwifery: the most strenuous efforts have been made to enforce its use; exaggerated reports have been published; births under its influence have actually been advertised; means most unprofessional have been employed to bring it into use; but its reception by those really able to judge as to the propriety of employing it has been decidedly unfavourable, and instead of progressing it has declined in their estimation.

By common observation, therefore, it becomes evident that some insurmountable impediment exists to the use of chloroform in midwifery; but how much is this strengthened by the conduct of those who uphold the principle of it? How great must be the resistance offered to it by medical opinion, and by the conscientious convictions of parturient women, when it is considered necessary to make such extraordinary exertions to keep it before the public, and when a physician finds it incumbent upon him to publish a pamphlet expressly for the purpose of overthrowing the religious objections urged against it!—a circumstance proving distinctly the validity of the objections, for had they not been based on a valid foundation, so many vague arguments as are contained in that pamphlet would not have been thought necessary to overthrow them.

It occurs, if women are willing to suffer pain rather than act against their convictions, why should such strenuous endeavours be made to overcome them? If inhalation produced any other benefit than that of allaying pain,—if it ensured the patient's safety, or expedited delivery, it then would be possible to understand the motive of any one who was himself convinced of its efficacy in these respects for strongly urging his objections to the religious feelings entertained against it. But when we know, that since the time of Eve, pains of labour have been endured by women—that the most severe suffering for hours does not necessarily endanger life—that women express their dislike to the use of it, and are willing to suffer pain, is it not unjustifiable that such efforts should be made to coerce them to act contrary to their inclinations?

Erroneous arguments, however, have been put forward, to prove that life is preserved by the use of anaesthetic agents in midwifery, and Mr. Travers has been quoted as an authority for affirming that women die from the prolonged pains of labour. That women *will* die from their effect, no one will deny, and that they *have* done so is certainly true; but to esteem this as a proof of the usefulness of anaesthesia is showing an ignorance of the means always at the command of those who scientifically practise midwifery, which, if properly employed, will, in all cases, effectually prevent the occurrence of death from the prolonged pains of labour. . . .

But Dr. Simpson's estimation of pain is not in accordance with that of much more able judges. They do not consider that in all instances it is to be allayed—that it is to be avoided at a sacrifice and the risk of life; and this is their feeling even regarding suffering from disease. How much more strongly, therefore, does their estimation of pain attendant upon the natural process of parturition differ from that of Dr. Simpson. 'Christians,' says a theologian, perhaps unequalled in learning, 'may bear to look at it without undue apprehension, for the very infliction which touches the heart and imagination has been invested by Almighty God with a new and comfortable light, as being the medium of his choicest mercies towards us; pain is no longer a curse with us—a necessary evil to be undergone with a dry submission or passive endurance, but may be considered even as a blessing of the Gospel, and being a blessing, admits of being met well or ill.'

There are many circumstances that could be named which would be barriers in the estimation of conscientious men to coercing the employment of inhalation in midwifery; but I am borne out by numberless opinions, formed from the most extensive experience in London practice, in saying, that a feeling of aversion, to use no stronger term, pervades the minds of females of rank and education in this country, almost without exception, to the use of it; and it will be a difficult matter, except in an occasional instance, where fallacious promises of its effects captivate the weak-minded, to find any woman seeking an intoxication that renders her, of all people, ignorant of the birth of her child, until told by her medical attendant (its effeminacy would better have suited the nurse) that what she sees is 'her own live baby'.

By the great advocates of anaesthesia in midwifery, all considerations not according with their own are considered futile; they have not hesitated to risk human life in using agents which, for anything they knew to the contrary, might have made their patients victims to their hardihood; they regard not as warnings the several deaths that have already resulted from them; but they designate as immoral the caution and judgment exercised by others less reckless than themselves. . . .

Very many instances might be recorded of the ill effects of anaesthesia, and although concealed with great precaution, all by degrees are becoming known, to the discomfiture of the promoters of its reckless employment. . . . My endeavour has been to point to the danger that must ensue from the too ready belief of all that has been said of anaesthesia in the reports of its prejudiced supporters; but I in no way recommend its hasty abolition in midwifery; for in some few cases it may by time prove highly beneficial, particularly in those requiring artificial delivery; but as yet it is in its infancy,—its effects, both immediate and ultimate, are unknown, and under any circumstances its exhibition requires the utmost consideration; for the experience of one or two practitioners does not prove its efficacy; and when evidence is before us that a one-sided view has been taken in describing its effects, we can only wait until others more to be depended on give their authorized and really substantial decision regarding it. . . .

G. T. Gream, M.R.C.S.E., 'Observations on Anaesthesia in Midwifery', *The Lancet*, 1 January 1848, pp. 228–9.

123. Experiences of Chloroform (1848)

[Lady Stanley of Alderley to her son's wife, Mrs Henrietta Stanley, 3 February 1848]:
. . . I went to see Emma Mainwaring yesterday who was full of her intention to be delivered without knowing it. She has been collecting information from many quarters & been encouraged by several medical men as well as by Mrs. Middleton Biddulph who has practised it with the greatest success. Mrs. Russell is another. I think in her case she *appeared* to suffer, & screamed, but had no recollection of anything afterwards & recovered particularly well—but in general people wake in about 10 minutes after all is over in perfect ease & comfort.

Mr. Dean & Mr. Harrison of Chester who have both attended Emma in her confinements strongly advise her to try & I think she told me that Dr. Locock either had made use of chloroform or had expressed approbation of it as a boon not to be rejected. She has large children & always suffers very much in her labours. She expects in a fortnight, & had an alarm lately that it was all over, but by lying up hopes to go on. . . .

[Lady Stanley to Mrs Henrietta Stanley, 24 February 1848]:
I do not like chloroform for teeth, I have heard of several cases where the experiment has been a very disagreeable one for the

bystanders, & Alice's preserving a sort of consciousness throughout & being alive enough to *talk* rather makes me believe more than I had done in the account we read of some Edinburgh *experiences*, where the young lady calls her dear Charles to come to her arms—& elsewhere I have heard that it is very desirable every body should have a friend with them & one who *may* hear anything that *may* come out during these trances. I think it a *cowardly* thing to use it for tooth drawing only, & dangerous perhaps for nervous people. I think you certainly should not allow Blanche to try it. It is a very curious discovery & most valuable in some cases, & doubtless there will be a great improvement both in the preparation of the chloroform & the manner of applying it. I think the most extraordinary part of the business is this partial consciousness, & Uncle confirmed it by an instance he knew of amputation, where a man talked of the operation all the time, like one looking on, yet felt no pain.

Emma Mainwaring was delivered yesterday *without* chlo: & had the best & shortest labour she ever knew. She had been dissuaded from trying it—had she done so how they would have given all the credit of her good time to that. . . .

Nancy Mitford (ed.), *The Ladies of Alderley*, 1938, pp. 151–2, 155.

124. The Great Boon of Chloroform (1848)

The recent discovery, by Professor Simpson, of the anaesthetic effects produced by the inhalation of chloroform, will no doubt prove a great boon, not only to the public generally, but especially to those medical men who may think fit to apply its use practically. For my own part, I consider myself much indebted to the Professor, not merely for the discovery he has made, but also for his great kindness in so early forwarding to me an account of it.

I did not fail to take the first opportunity afforded me of testing its qualities, and I have found that the experience of my own practice fully bears out its properties, as described by Professor Simpson, and the advantages of the chloroform over ether. . . .

I have used it several times to relieve pain in natural labour, in operations, and in tooth-drawing; also for the reduction of strangulated hernia, and in a case of delirium tremens. Each time I have used it I have found the effects produced more suddenly than they can be with the ether, and that the state of sleep can be continued for a much longer period without a renewal of the inhalation, should such be desired, as in performing operations about the mouth, when a renewal of the vapour may be impracticable. It is also by many considered exceedingly pleasant in taste. This, added to the peculiar state of quietude or happiness which some experience during the period they are under its influence, renders its inhalation a thing to be desired rather than to be dreaded, or, at the best, to be taken as the alternative against the suffering of pain. . . .

The rapidity with which it takes effect renders it peculiarly applicable to obstetric practice. I find in such cases the patient is insensible with the chloroform in ten seconds; while with ether the usual average is twenty-five seconds. Thus it being more speedy in its action, a less quantity is required to be taken previously to the pain coming on with its full force, after it has given the patient the warning of its approach, thereby allowing her to be insensible to pain before the time arrives for her to cry out; whereas, when inhaling the ether, should the action of the uterus assume its full force before insensibility is produced, the patient will sometimes cry out instead of continuing to inhale. . . .

Since I commenced practice in 1828, I have seldom gone to a labour without my tincture of ergot in my pocket; not with the intention of using it during the labour,—a mode of practice which, when employed indiscriminately, by way of hurrying the labour, cannot, I think, be too much condemned,—but for the purpose of suppressing haemorrhage after the expulsion of the placenta, should such occur. I have now quite forsaken my little bottle for the ether, which in its turn must make way for the chloroform. But the state of the perinaeum is a thing which has forcibly struck me while using the ether; that has invariably relaxed before the head has come to bear upon it, thereby not requiring the pressure of the head to force it open and to lacerate it, as was frequently the case when left to itself in the old mode of practice. This advantageous quality I have not observed while using the chloroform, the parts under its use continuing unaffected by it; neither have I ever found the action of the uterus, when in a sluggish state, induced by the chloroform as it is by the ether....

J. G. Lansdown, M.R.C.S.E., 'On the Use of Ether and Chloroform in Surgery and Midwifery', *The Lancet*, 19 February 1848, pp. 10–11.

125. Chloroform, Opium and the Alleviation of Suffering (1848)

... what high delight is imparted to the medical man who may have it in his power to bring science and art to bear on the alleviation and removal of sufferings which he has hitherto been compelled to witness, without the ability to do much more than give expression to his sympathy, in common with those relatives and friends who endure, mentally, almost equal suffering with the agonized patient; and how much greater is the delight of every humane practitioner, should he be able *not only to alleviate the pains, but even to diminish the perils*, of labour. Yet all this, and even more, has been accomplished by the employment of a medical agent,

CHLOROFORM,—a fragrant volatile fluid, obtained by the distillation of spirits of wine over powdered Chloride of Lime, the vapour of which, if inspired from a hollow-shaped sponge or pocket-handkerchief, on which a tea-spoonful has been sprinkled, will sometimes, in less than a minute, produce unconsciousness, of some duration. It has recently been introduced into the practice of midwifery by Dr Simpson, of Edinburgh, whose untiring efforts in the cause of science and humanity have done more to entitle him to the grateful homage of his fellow-creatures than most men of the present day. By his calm and dispassionate and conclusive reasonings, and by the accumulation of facts which he has published, he has quieted the passions and prejudices of many who most violently opposed the use of this inestimable and wonder-working agent; so that now the most formidable and agonizing operations are performed without the consciousness of the patient, and women may pass through 'the hour of nature's sorrow' without apparent suffering. My own experience fully substantiates all his statements, and confirms the accuracy of all his deductions. . . .

Nothing can be more injudicious than the too prevalent custom of exhibiting large and repeated doses of *opium* to a woman after delivery. She may be exhausted and irritable, and therefore require a single and moderate dose of this article; but the frequent repetition of it is decidedly injurious, not only by producing the ordinary unpleasant effects of opium, but more especially by putting a stop to those natural and voluntary, although painful, secondary contractions of the womb, termed *after-pains*, by which the organ is restored to its ordinary size and situation. After-pains are usually least severe after a first labour, and must not give rise to alarm. . . .

Dr John T. Conquest, *Letters to a Mother*, 1848, pp. 49–50, 77–8.

126. Chloroform and Queen Victoria (1853)

A very extraordinary report has obtained general circulation connected with the recent accouchement [7 April 1853] of her most gracious Majesty Queen Victoria. It has always been understood by the profession that the births of the Royal children in all instances have been unattended by any peculiar or untoward circumstances. Intense astonishment, therefore, has been excited throughout the profession by the rumour that her Majesty during her last labour was placed under the influence of chloroform, an agent which has unquestionably caused instantaneous death in a considerable number of cases. Doubts on this subject cannot exist. In several of the fatal examples persons in their usual health expired while the process of inhalation was proceeding, and the deplorable catastrophes were clearly and indisputably referrible to the poisonous action of chloroform, and to that cause alone.

These facts being perfectly well known to the medical world, we could not imagine that any one had incurred the awful responsibility of advising the administration of chloroform to her Majesty during a perfectly natural labour with a seventh child. On inquiry, therefore, we were not at all surprised to learn that in her late confinement the Queen was not rendered insensible by chloroform or by any other anaesthetic agent. We state this with feelings of the highest satisfaction. In no case could it be justifiable to administer chloroform in perfectly ordinary labour; but the responsibility of advocating such a proceeding in the case of the Sovereign of these realms would, indeed, be tremendous. Probably some officious meddlers about the Court so far overruled her Majesty's responsible professional advisers as to lead to the pretence of administering chloroform, but we believe the obstetric physicians to whose ability the safety of our illustrious Queen is confided do not sanction the use of chloroform in natural labour. Let it not be supposed that we would undervalue the immense importance of chloroform in surgical operations. We know that an incalculable amount of agony is averted by its employment. On thousands of occasions it has been given without injury, but inasmuch as it has destroyed life in a considerable number of instances, its *unnecessary* inhalation involves, in our opinion, an amount of responsibility which words cannot adequately describe.

We have felt irresistibly impelled to make the foregoing observations, fearing the consequences of allowing such a rumour respecting a dangerous practice in one of our national palaces to pass unrefuted. Royal examples are followed with extraordinary readiness by a certain class of society in this country.

The Lancet, 14 May 1853, p. 453.

127. The Injurious Consequences of Chloroform? (1853)

In these seventeen cases the author traced a series of injurious consequences to the employment of chloroform during labour. Thus, in Cases 1 and 2, the contractions of the uterus were arrested by the chloroform, and delivery was completed by craniotomy. In Cases 3, 4, 5, 10, 14, 15 and 16, insanity and great disturbance of the brain followed its use. The necessity for delivery by the forceps was attributed to its employment in Cases

6, 8, 11, 12 and 13. Dangerous or fatal peritonitis or phlebitis ensued after the exhibition of chloroform in Cases 7, 8, 11 and 13. Epilepsy occurred in Case 14; and dangerous fits of syncope arose from its use in Case 17. The reports of friends had confided many more analogous cases, and public rumour swelled the list still further, but he was desirous of confining attention to those which came directly under his own observation. He thought that a contemplation of the subtle action of this poison on the nervous system would have induced caution in its application to practice, but, on the contrary, the greatest levity had characterized its employment. Very soon after the discovery of its physiological effects the author was astonished and counfounded by the announcement of its application to midwifery; and it was not difficult for him to forsee that rashness in its application and use would lead to most deplorable results, and he regretted to find that in this he had not been mistaken. It was not wonderful that women doomed to bring forth their offspring in pain and sorrow should seek to escape from the troubles of our race by means of this treacherous gift of science; neither could we feel surprised that the instances of women who were saved from the grievous pains of child-bearing, without bad consequences, should have for a time reduced to silence those unwelcome monitors who pointed to the possible evils of this new agent; but it did seem strange to the author that, amidst so widespread an experience as now existed of the noxious and dangerous effects of chloroform, it should be necessary for him to assemble the proofs of the havoc it had made. The two most serious effects produced by chloroform on women in labour were, a languid and deficient contraction of the uterus, and a greater susceptibility to the risks that arise from inflammation and fever. With regard to the first, the direct testimony of his own senses convinced him that the action of chloroform did very manifestly slacken the uterine contractions, and in some cases had put a stop to them altogether. Of the second class of effects, the risks of the puerperal condition were much complicated; for to inflammation and fever must be added severe cerebral and nervous disorders. He had no doubt that the use of this noxious agent ought to be expelled from the practice of midwifery. In conclusion, the author observed that, though his opinions had been confirmed by conversation with the most discreet and experienced practitioners, yet he entertained grave doubts of the result of the present appeal to the good sense of the profession, when he considered the arts used to propagate a faith in this practice. It had become almost an extra-professional question. There was a systematic concealment of truth by physicians; appeals were made to the natural timidity of women, and the most fallacious promises of perfect safety were boldly held out. Conceited or ignorant women of fashion made a pastime of this as of other quackeries, and the cause of science and humanity was placed in the hands of the most presumptuous and frivolous part of the community, while young and inexperienced mothers were decoyed to their destruction. If he had helped to rescue the medical profession from the dominion of a great and dangerous error, and had placed some restraint on an ignominious and disgraceful practice, the author would rest satisfied that this essay had not been written in vain.

DR. SNOW said that the expressions in the latter part of Dr. Lee's paper were to be regretted. He had great respect for Dr. Lee, and for the manner in which he carried out his views, but he could not agree with him as to the connexion between the chloroform and the unfavourable symptoms which had been met with in the cases just related. As regarded the two cases in which the uterine action was said to have been altogether stopped by the chloroform, he could only say that he had never seen such a result from its use, and he considered that it must be extremely rare, if it ever occurred, when the agent was properly administered. In the fifth case headache and various symptoms of hysteria, which appeared on the third day after delivery, were attributed to the chloroform, but it was contrary to all that had been observed of this agent, whether administered in surgical operations, or in medical or obstetric cases, that any kind of illness from its use could come on two or three days afterwards. The effects of chloroform subsided much more rapidly than those of the older and less volatile medicines. A patient was generally as free from the influence of this medicine in an hour as from an ordinary dose of opium in twenty-four hours. . . .

. . .it should be remembered that this agent was in most cases administered during labour at the particular desire of the patient, who had a more than usual dread of pain. These patients often had an unusual excitability of the nervous system, and might possibly be more liable to mania, under any circumstances, than others....

It should be remembered that no death from chloroform had occurred in midwifery, and he only knew of one case where the patient was in danger, and that arose from gross mismanagement, for the husband was giving the chloroform, and looking another way. With regard to the use of chloroform in surgical operations, he believed more lives had been saved than lost by it....

[Dr. LEE] in forceps cases, (continued Dr. Lee,) and in all the great operations of midwifery, chloroform could produce nothing but mischief, for in all these cases consciousness was the great safeguard of the patient. No forceps cases—and he had had as many as any person in that Society—were so unmanageable as those in which the consciousness was lost from puerperal convulsions, where the patient could not be held in the same position for any length of time. In uterine haemorrhage, and in all cases of protracted labour, from whatever cause, nothing but mischief could result from the use of that narcotic poison. The exhibition of chloroform in labour he held to be contrary to the sound principles of physiology and morality. 'In sorrow shalt thou bring forth children,' was an established law of nature—an ordinance of the Almighty, as stated in the Bible, and it was in vain to attempt to abrogate that law. There could not be a doubt that it was a most unnatural practice to destroy the consciousness of women during labour, the pains and sorrows of which exerted a most powerful and salutary influence upon their religious and moral character, and upon all their future relations in life. But he might put aside all these physiological and moral considerations, and rest his objection to the use of chloroform in labour upon the danger of introducing a subtle narcotic poison into the system at such a time. When only one drachm was given, who could be certain that it should not instantaneously be followed by the death of the person to whom it was administered? Upon this point the whole question might be allowed to hinge.

Dr Robert Lee, 'An Account of Seventeen Cases of Parturition in which Chloroform was inhaled with pernicious effects' [and discussion by Royal Medical and Chirurgical Society members], *The Lancet*, 24 December 1853, pp. 608–11.

128. The General Use of Chloroform in Midwifery (1860)

In obstetric practice, the instances where the author has found the inhalation of ether or chloroform to be called for in an especial degree, and where anaesthetic aid has proved decidedly useful, have been cases of version, forceps, twins, convulsions, and crotchet operations. He has known chloroform used in puerperal mania, but its apparent effect is perhaps a coincidence, and not of a curative nature.... There have been no accidents from chloroform in about 30,000 cases of midwifery conducted with the aid of these agents. The mode of applying chloroform in the lying-in chamber recommended was that which is adopted now by all the chief obstetric practitioners in Europe and America with whom the author has personally communicated on the subject....

In tedious labour, the agony and pain will not permit the poor woman to sleep. Even opium is followed but by a tedious intoxication, without sleep, for hours; but chloroform is not an intoxicant, and acts at once and quite as safely. A patient in ordinary anaesthesia may be said to be doubly asleep. This is what is wanted for a short time in this class of labours, as thus reflex, sensorial, and muscular power are renewed. Emotion, also, is removed out of the way by chloroform sleep; and by a confident, cheerful demeanour on the part of the accoucheur, he may effect as much in two or three hours by chloroform as he might in almost as many days by delay, and opium, and waiting for nature.... Chloroform is invaluable where there is exhaustion, debility, or shock, the result of great or long-continued pain; where there is loss of nerve force, or convulsions from excess of reflex irritability or pain, or mental emotion or excitement, &c. But chloroform is of less importance, as even wine, bark, iron, ammonia, &c., are of less use, where there is exhaustion the result of haemorrhage, hectic, diarrhoea, exhausting suppuration, &c....

Dr.TANNER stated that he made it a rule always to take chloroform with him to every case of labour. When the pains became bad, he explains to the patient—provided he finds no objection to the employment of an anaesthetic—that he can relieve her of all suffering, if she wishes it, by means of chloroform. Many patients are anxious to inhale; a few decline. During the present year, Dr. Tanner had only had one case in his private practice which had caused him much anxiety; and in this the dangerous symptoms arose, as he believed, from the formation of a clot in the right side of the heart. This lady did not take chloroform. Dr. Tanner observed that he was careful only to give this anaesthetic during each labour pain, taking away the handkerchief or inhaler directly the pain went off. Stating the results of his experience briefly, he might say that he had never found chloroform do harm, but, on the contrary, much good; while it shortened the afterperiod of convalescence. He was careful, in cases where he feared haemorrhage, to give a large dose of ergot towards the close of the labour; but he did not object to the use of chloroform as well. In operative midwifery anaesthetics were invaluable....

Dr. GREAM said that, from some observations which had been made, it might be inferred that chloroform was but little used in midwifery in London; but he was sure that in no place was it more extensively employed, and he could positively state that amongst the upper classes it was almost universally employed, but with a general feeling of abhorrence of anything like intense insensibility. Surprise had been expressed by Dr. Barnes at the statement that so large a number of cases had occurred in which chloroform had been used in midwifery without accident; but there appeared to be no difficulty in understanding this, for it should be remembered that it was never right, nor was it required, to carry insensibility so far as in surgery; and he (Dr. Gream) was sure that all the fatality which had attended the exhibition of chloroform in midwifery had arisen from some little want of care, or from a want of appreciation of its power. When anaesthesia was first introduced he had opposed, with others, the indiscriminate use of it, for he thought that at that time it was recklessly employed; and he believed that the present safe and efficient manner in which it was exhibited in London was the result, in a great measure, of the opposition offered to its former indiscreet and dangerous employment. It was a fact that no death from chloroform in midwifery had occurred in London; but allusion having been made to two authorities 'beyond the Tweed,' it was right to state that *there* the same immunity from calamity had not been enjoyed; yet he felt sure that no agent could be more safe, and none more beneficial, than chloroform in midwifery when properly administered. He thought the author of the paper had unintentionally exaggerated the ill effects (if there were any), and also the good effects, of chloroform. For three reasons he (Dr. Gream) thought chloroform most beneficial in labour: it removed pain, it rendered turning more easy, and it facilitated recovery... in instrumental delivery of every kind it was most advantageous, and he had seen fewer cases of haemorrhage since he employed chloroform, indeed he had exhibited it to patients who had habitually been subject to this occurrence without haemorrhage supervening—a fact worthy the attention of theorists, but nevertheless a fact....

Dr Charles Kidd, 'On the value of anaesthetic aid in midwifery' [and discussion by Obstetrical Society of London members], *The Lancet*, 22 December 1860, pp. 613–4.

129. Chloroform Risk-free in Normal Labour (1900)

USE OF ANAESTHETICS IN LABOUR.—In the great majority of cases of labour where an anaesthetic is required, chloroform is the one to be chosen. Even when it is necessary to give it to the full surgical extent, as in obstetric operations, it does not appear to involve the same increased risk, as compared with other anaesthetics, such as ether, which it does in ordinary cases....

If given to the partial extent which alone is ever necessary in normal labour, chloroform may be regarded as entirely free from risk. Ether is more disagreeable to the patient than chloroform, and has not the same satisfactory effect of deadening pain when given in partial degree. Most of the objections formerly made to the use of chloroform in normal labour have not now to be considered; and, as a rule, it may always be given whenever the pains are felt acutely, or the patient is desirous to take it. Its use is a distinct advantage, putting aside the question of relief of pain, in those cases in which the pains are too violent, or occur at too short intervals. There are, however, two drawbacks to its use;

first, that it tends to diminish the vigour of the pains, and so is apt somewhat to increase the duration of labour; secondly, that it increases the risk of post-partum haemorrhage in patients predisposed to that accident. These disadvantages may be avoided to a great extent by not giving the chloroform too freely. When, however, there is manifest inertia of the uterus or a history of post-partum haemorrhage on former occasions, it is better to avoid it entirely, or give it only in inifinitesimal degree. Thus, when a patient is very anxious to take chloroform, and its effect appears undesirable, a very little chloroform may be mixed with Eau-de-Cologne.

Anodynes in the first stage of labour.—As a rule chloroform should not be given until the pains of the expulsive stage begin....

Dr A. L. Galabin, *A Manual of Midwifery*, 1900, p. 221.

3.6 Puerperal Fever

130. The Nature of Fatal Child-bed Fever (1831)

PUERPERAL FEVER—FATAL CHILD-BED FEVER.
It has become fashionable of late years to question the opinions of our predecessors, and in no instance more remarkably so than on the nature of the disease under consideration. There is no disease about which there is so much dissonance of sentiment as puerperal fever; many of the most eminent obstetricians in Europe and America entertain discordant opinions as to the pathology of the disease.... The approach of the disease is often so obscure as to elude detection.

When the disease is inflammatory, copious depletion is the remedy; when epidemic, it defies all treatment. The greatest caution must be observed in using the lancet. Leeches and cupping are often valuable adjuvants....

This disease commences from one to eight days after delivery, the patient complains loudly of the severity of the after-pains, and refers all her suffering to the region of the pubis and uterus. The disease is ushered in with much shivering or rigors, the pulse varying from 120 to 160. There is great prostration of mind and body, and a sense of undescribable oppression about the praecordia, and often an utter carelessness about the infant. There is always intense pain in the head. Sometimes the skin is hot and dry, face flushed, and indicative of great distress of mind. Respiration anxious and profound, as if performed with a sigh. Pain in the uterine region aggravated by pressure (metro-peritonitis), which is first confined, but soon extends to the whole abdomen. There is much restlessness and jactitation, the abdomen rapidly becomes distended as large as before delivery, the pain sometimes diminishes or ceases. Nausea, or vomiting, at first of bilious, and at length of a coffee-coloured matter occurs;

sometimes there is diarrhoea or constipation, the face is peculiarly ghastly, and becomes pale, circle about the eyes livid, lips dry, headache, tinnitus aurium, tongue pallid or red, secretion of milk suppressed lochia continued, but may be suppressed, according to Dr. John Clarke; urine sparing and high coloured, bowels confined. The eyes become dull, the pupils dilated; the nose sharpened, the cheeks hectic or pale, the lips purple, or the face livid, as in the last stage of typhus; the forehead and chest are covered with cold perspiration. The patient lies on her back, with the lower limbs drawn up, to relieve her respiration, which is much impeded by the tumefaction of the abdomen from gas or effusion; the tongue becomes black, mouth aphthous, teeth covered with sordes, the breath cadaverous, vomiting of a brown pitchy fetid matter, involuntary alvine evacuations of black colour, with fetid odour; the abdomen becomes less swelled, the countenance is inanimate, the alae nasi are tremulous, the respiration becoming more and more panting. The patient speaks incoherently, mutters to herself, or is delirious and attempts to get out of bed. The pulse is so rapid as not to be reckoned, the perspiration is cold and clammy; there is subsultus tendinum, and death soon closes the scene. Dr. W. Hunter stated in his Lectures, 'treat the disease as you will, three out of four will die...'.

This disease attacks every temperament and constitution, the strong and weak; the young and middle aged, the poor and rich; but is more common among the poor and middle classes, and from the age of puberty to thirty-five, than at any other period. It occurs most frequently within the first eight days after delivery. It is one of the most fatal diseases.... It is most rapid in its fatal career, often terminating in forty-eight or thirty-six hours —nearly as rapid as the plague....

Dr Michael Ryan, *A Manual of Midwifery*, 3rd edn., 1831, pp. 635–7, 639–41.

131. Non-epidemic 'Puerperal Fever' (1870)

Puerperal fever, or metria, is, to me, a hotbed of insufficient and false hypotheses. I do not believe there is any such single disease. The term includes a variety of diseases, and a variety of modifications and terminations of diseases.... It is described universally as occurring in epidemics; not merely as endemic. I feel certain, and believe I can prove, that an epidemic of puerperal fever never occurred.... Both doctors and people seem ignorant of the fact that there is a regular and practically constant mortality from puerperal fever all around them...puerperal fever causes nearly as much havoc in private practice as in hospitals—at least in those that are pretty well arranged and managed....

Dr J. Matthews Duncan, 'On Puerperal Fever in Hospital and in Private Practice', *The Lancet*, 1870, pp. 765–6.

132. Puerperal Fever not a Constant Entity (1875)

There must, then, for practical purposes be some conventional or provisional name which shall embrace all the febrile conditions to which the lying-in woman is liable. What name so convenient as 'puerperal fever'?—one consecrated by custom, and possessing the inestimable advantage of not committing the physician to any absolute theory? Struggle as you may, prove to demonstration that there is no such entity as puerperal fever, this or some equivalent general term will be imposed upon you by the irresistible logic of facts. Nor will it help us much to adopt Dr Farre's term, 'post-partum fever.' This is only shifting the difficulty....

...there are puerperal fevers which are contagious, and there are puerperal fevers which are not so. It might be stated generally, bearing in mind that the rule is not absolute, that the heterogenetic class contains the contagious forms, and that the autogenetic forms include those which are not contagious. The great point to remember is that puerperal fever is not a constant entity; that it may be one thing or another distinct thing; and that it may therefore present various characters. In the presence of this difficulty and of the unsettled opinions upon the whole subject, it becomes simply impossible and absurd to lend any countenance to the popular belief that puerperal fever is a disease always communicated to the patient....

... our facts are probably defective. It may still be wise to wait for fresh material. Will the final, the solving evidence come from the bedside or the laboratory? Hitherto the chemist pure has done little. Will the man who combines chemistry with a profound knowledge of histology and the changes wrought in the body by disease, aided by experimental inquiries, do more? There is greater hope in this direction. In the meantime the clinical physician will not be tempted out of his path by the golden promise of bacteria.

'The Discussion on Puerperal Fever', *The Lancet*, 24 July 1875, pp. 133–5.

133. 'Puerperal Fever': an Almost Inextricable Confusion (1875)

... Dr. PLAYFAIR.—If there is one fact to be gathered from this discussion, it is, I think, how remarkably little reliable knowledge we have about the subject on which we are talking. It seems to me that there is a lesson really of the greatest importance; because I cannot but fancy that a great part of the almost inextricable confusion that surrounds the whole matter has arisen from the non-recognition of that fact; from the circumstance that systematically writers upon the subject have thought it necessary to give a complete and fully rounded history of puerperal fever without recognising, as I hope they will do after this discussion, that we are only at the threshold of the inquiry, and that we have to build up all our knowledge by unprejudiced and patient clinical investigation.

... my belief about puerperal fever is very much what I understand to be that of several other speakers. I do not believe that there is any specific condition justifying the name of puerperal fever; nor do I believe that there is any special miasm arising from the puerperal patient capable of being conveyed to another patient; nor do I think that there is any evidence whatever to show that there has ever been an epidemic of puerperal fever in the strict sense of the word, although we all know how fatally endemic it has been in our large lying-in hospitals. In the second place, I believe that the theory which considers the so-called puerperal fever to be practically the same disease as surgical septicaemia or pyaemia, or whatever we choose to call it, is the one which is most consonant with the facts of the case; that it arises from the contact of septic matter, with lesions of continuity in the generative track, such as exist in every parturient woman; that there are channels of diffusion through the lymphatics, or possibly the veins; and that there are, just as there are in surgical pyaemia, secondary general and local results of great consequence, rendered in the puerperal patient particularly intense and virulent, on account of the peculiar condition existing after delivery.... But, sir, the moment that that theory is stated, a great number of difficulties and objections naturally present themselves....

'Relation of Puerperal Fever to the Infective Diseases and Pyaemia', *Transactions of the Obstetrical Society of London*, Vol. 17, 1875, pp. 200–1.

134. Several Puerperal Fevers and Diverse Causes (1876)

... The event of the session has been the discussion on puerperal fever.... The acute forms of illness which occur after delivery, and often end fatally, are especially cruel affections; attacking women, as they commonly do, during the very flower of their age, just at the dawn of fresh hopes, and at the time of their greatest usefulness in life. The anxiety of mind caused to the medical man when such cases occur in his practice, and the damage which, rightly or wrongly, results to his professional reputation, can only be appreciated by those who have had the painful experience. The mental anguish so engendered is reported, indeed, sometimes to have culminated in mental aberration.

Dr. Farr, of the Registrar-General's office, estimates the mortality after childbirth in this country as 1 in 190 women delivered; but Dr. J. Matthews Duncan, in his address at

Norwich, in 1874, regards this as much too low a rate, and after careful computation, states the mortality, within four weeks after delivery, to be 1 in 120; while, if the time be extended beyond four weeks, he believes that the number of puerperal deaths reaches as high as 1 in 100.... Moreover, the number of ascertained deaths does not express all the mischief done. Many of those who survive the attack are greatly hindered in recovery, are exposed to much suffering, and possibly remain permanently enfeebled or maimed for life. If reason were required, therefore, for the interest manifested in the late discussion, it is sufficiently forthcoming in the above statistics, and more especially as in and out of the profession there is a growing impression that these deaths are in a great measure preventable....

... so high an authority as Dr. Arthur Farre...has defined puerperal fever to be 'a continued fever, communicable by contagion occurring in women after childbirth, and often associated with extensive local lesions, especially of the uterine system.'... Taking, then, the outcome of the discussion in this Society, and the evidence from other sources, it may be stated that puerperal fever, or fevers which are attended by high temperature, and are commonly associated with extensive local lesions, are due to the inception of a morbid poison which vitiates the blood, and which produces a great variety of symptoms in accordance with the nature and intensity of the virus, the amount of the dose absorbed, the state of the patient when attacked, and a diversity of other conditions, which have been alluded to more or less fully by the various speakers....

There seems to be literal truth in the remark made by Dr. West, that 'there is not one single solitary cause to which we can refer the symptoms of puerperal fever; that it occurs now from one cause, now from another.' With equal truth, also, it may probably be asserted that there is not one puerperal fever, but several, arising from a diversity of causes. The term puerperal fever has been somewhat loosely but habitually applied to all diseases of lying-in women which are attended by febrile symptoms and tend to a fatal termination. In attempting a more accurate pathology, it is well to bear in mind that fever is only a symptom of disease; and that we have to find out what is the underlying disease, of which the fever is but the indication....

The influence of a vitiated atmosphere in overcrowded

hospitals in producing an endemic form of the disease is only too well confirmed. Whenever a number of lying-in women are aggregated together, there is danger that a miasm may be generated which will develop puerperal fever, and it is by no means easy to define the amount of ventilation and isolation which are necessary to prevent these untoward consequences. Hence a feeling has been gradually growing up that, notwithstanding the economic and educational advantages of lying-in hospitals, poor women are more safely confined at their own homes.... At King's College Hospital we had a notable instance of the very serious results provoked in puerperal women by their being confined under the same roof with patients in general medical and surgical wards. The mortality in the lying-in wards gradually increased year by year, until at length it reached the fearful maximum of nearly one in every thirteen women delivered, and then it was determined to close the midwifery department altogether....

For a long time, the contagiousness of puerperal fever was disputed, and in Paris writers and practitioners remained unconvinced of its contagiousness long after it had been conceded elsewhere. In our day, the direct proofs of its contagious quality have accumulated to such an extent, that to disregard them in practice would amount, on the part of a medical practitioner, to a plain dereliction of duty... of the several ways in which the subtle poison may be conveyed to the lying-in woman, none is more certainly proved than that it may be conveyed by the hands of the practitioner in making vaginal examinations. But this is not the only way. It may probably be communicated through the clothes, instruments, respiration, or even the secretions of the medical practitioner, midwife, or nurse....

I quite concur in what has fallen from the several speakers concerning the relation of bacteria and other allied forms to puerperal diseases. We are obviously only on the threshold of that important inquiry; and although the researches of Klebs, of Waldeyer, of Mayrhofer, of Lister, of Sanderson, of Heiberg, and Orth have established a nearly connecting link between bacteria or other allied organic forms and pyaemic processes, the field of investigation is rather one for the pathologist and microscopic observer than the obstetrician. The gynaecologist would, nevertheless, thankfully receive any information which would enable him to cope successfully with these terrible maladies, either in the way of prevention or cure.... It is certainly better to err on the side of over-caution than of over-laxity. The method, therefore, to be pursued for guarding the lying-in woman from noxious influences, consists of all those measures which prevent the formation of poisonous materials in her own system, and which secure her isolation from all contagion from without....

Dr William O. Priestley, 'Annual Address', *Transactions of the Obstetrical Society of London*, Vol. 18, 1876, pp. 29–32, 36–7, 44, 46–7, 50–1.

135. The Germ Theory of Puerperal Diseases (1878)

The very name of the disease, 'puerperal fever,' is so vague and unscientific as to convict those who use it of vague and indefinite ideas regarding its real nature. That a woman should be occasionally feverish in the puerperal state goes, as the French say, without telling; but to say that she has puerperal fever tells us nothing of the nature of that fever, of its etiology, pathology, mode of propagation or development. To encounter such a formidable malady with any prospect of success we ought to have the most precise ideas of its true nature; and, further, since experience tells us that, in the great majority of cases, all treatment is of no avail—such profound changes in the vital fluids having taken place as to preclude all hope that the structures can maintain their integrity,—we are thrown back upon merely preventive measures as our only means of safety, the only means whereby we can hope to satisfy the public demand for exemption from the ravages of a malady so unamenable to curative efforts.

It has been my lot to be called in consultation, within a comparatively brief period, to some fifteen or sixteen of these sad cases, three only of which terminated in recovery. Occurring as they do every now and then in series of cases, then being altogether absent for long periods, happening as often, or more often, amongst the higher classes as amongst the lower, the consternation they occasion in provincial society is at once detrimental to the medical man in whose practice they occur, and destructive of public confidence in the resources of our art.... Now, although I do not affirm that what is called the germ theory of these diseases is sufficient to explain *all* their phenomena satisfactorily, it is certain that that theory is alone capable of explaining *any* of the symptoms to our satisfaction....

What a farce does it not seem to us to see nurses and attendants placing a little Condy's fluid in saucers about the room of a woman lying ill of puerperal septicaemia! The disinfectants are wanted in the vagina and uterus—even in the blood itself; and all other modes of using them are but a delusion and a snare, which may result in the most fatal consequences. The great desideratum undoubtedly is some subtance which, introduced into the patient's blood, would kill the poisonous germs without also killing the blood itself. Such a substance is not yet known, but there is no reason, theoretically speaking, why it may not be discovered. Salicylic acid, or the new disinfectants thymol and carvol, should have a fair trial; and we may hope that some other germicide may be discovered which, whilst tolerated by the blood, may be destructive of the poison in it. Meantime, as I set out with observing, until the happy discovery of some such *curative*, we must pay all the more attention to *prevention*....

Dr William Strange, 'On Puerperal Septicaemia', *The Lancet*, 20 July, 27 July, 1878, pp. 80, 116.

136. Treatments of Today and Yesterday (1880)

Although only a few years ago it was far otherwise, the remark may now pass unchallenged, that there is no such disease as 'puerperal fever,' whose treatment is yet my subject for this evening. That name has been for a century in constant use, and indicates, though with deplorable lack of precision, a group of diseases for whose designation it may meantime be, for convenience sake, retained. Whatever designation we may adopt, we experience no difficulty in recognising the diseases meant, and there is no hesitation in ascribing to them the highest place in importance to lying-in women who suffer and die, as well as to medical men who observe and treat. Their baneful influences, including their mortality, exceed those of any other group of diseases of childbed. It is truly said that childbearing proves fatal to every hundredth mother, and it may be added that, of this fatality, the far greater part is due to these diseases. How enthusiastic does the study of them become when we contemplate the reduplicated danger of mothers who have just borne a first child; how grave and awful when we regard the rapidly increasing perils of mothers who count their children by numbers that rise higher and higher into the physiologically excessive.

It is misleading to estimate the importance of puerperal fever by death alone.... In many cases so-called recovery is anything rather than restoration to health; it is merely an escape, more or less narrow, from early death. The escape is generally into paths which lead to health ultimately; often it is into paths which lead to death more or less directly, more or less slowly, and after a lapse of months or even years....

A good deal of undesirable mystery and much of positive error has been propagated in this subject by the long-continued and still persistent practice—a mere practice, now, without any rational basis—of regarding puerperal fever as occurring chiefly in epidemics. In its prevalence it has a seasonal variation, which Buchan and Mitchell have traced, and which closely resembles that of erysipelas; but it has no periods of epidemic raging; or, rather, none have been demonstrated.... The group of diseases called puerperal fever is ever with us, its frequency varying slightly, never rising very high, never sinking very low, always governed by an average....

A great old obsolete plan of treatment is not to be regarded as erroneous or bad, and so contrasted with ours. Such plans were not the fruits of caprice, nor the *ipse dixits* of great and famous physicians, but represented the knowledge and wisdom of their times. I have lived long enough to see the gradual decadence of the antiphlogistic treatment of Gordon, with its venesection and leeching and blistering.... Indeed, since the days of antiphlogistics, no great therapeutical plan has been common, for no great medical doctrine has prevailed. The profession has relied much on special drugs in the hope of curing rather than treating the disease whatever it might be; and latterly many have devoted themselves to treating symptoms....

Living among great physicians, and, as a young practitioner, willingly submitting myself to them, I have seen several changes of treatment. In my earliest days, as a hospital resident and for some time subsequently, while bleeding was a decaying treatment, the great remedy was calomel and opium.... Gradually the calomel disappeared, because it almost always produced painful and debilitating diarrhoea, and it was replaced by blue-pill. Then the mercurial disappeared entirely; and, under the influence of the teaching of Graves, opium alone became the great resort; and this medicine still keeps its place as a valuable adjuvant in treatment. While its great utility is incontestable, I feel bound to record that I have often seen it act injuriously from its being used in far too large doses. The last treatment which had a passing pre-eminence was the copious administration of food and alcohol....

The search for 'cures' is, as yet at least, a wild-goose chase. We have a long course to pursue in acquiring intelligence regarding the disease to be cured before we can hope even for a well-established plan of treatment.... Heroic treatment may be required to reach the remotest part of the genital tract in search for decomposing matter, or to ascertain that there is nothing but putrid lochia in the case. Mere vaginal washing may suffice, or intra-uterine washing, or the volsella may be passed into the uterus to grope for the decomposing structure, or with the same view a finger or fingers may be passed, or even the whole hand; and it may be necessary to dilate the cervix preliminarily. Most of this may be done without an anaesthetic, but where the hand is to be introduced into the vagina, the previous induction of anaesthesia is desirable....

Though these washings have been described by the ancient authors, and though they were recommended by Harvey and by Baudelocque, it is well known to you that no such practice was in use among us till the antiseptic theory of treatment was promulgated. Yet they are not covered by an antiseptic theory, for you know it was based on the presence of bacteria which passed into the blood, and the antiseptic treatment was planned to destroy them or prevent them reaching the wounded surface. Here we use antiseptics not with these views, but to remove and arrest putrefaction, with a view to stopping the supply of a chemical, not a living, poison, the product of putrefaction, which enters the blood and endangers the constitution....

There has always, indeed, been a tendency to regard puerperal fever as desperate, or almost certainly fatal. I can remember well the saying of an eminent physician, with whose retrospective diagnosis many agreed, that if a case recovered it was not one of real puerperal fever. Probably he did not mean his words to be held as strictly true, but to express his sense of the hopelessness of such cases. This disheartening opinion should not be entertained, for it is not based on ascertained truth, and it induces despondency and feebleness in treatment which are prejudicial to the thorough management of a case.... The word treatment implies too high an estimate of the physician's powers; or if not too high, at least a too definite view of them. We cannot arrest or even moderate the storm, but we may guide the bark through it. When the organisms producing these diseases are in the blood we cannot kill them, nor do we know any means of certainly controlling their growth. But we may wisely consider the constitutional and local circumstances of the patient, and judiciously interfere to modify them with a view to the patient's survival....

The use of stimulants requires a little more discussion. At present the favourites are brandy and champagne, and I adhere to the general voice in preferring them—on one condition, that they be really good. At the same time I make no objection to other wines and spirits. Brandy and champagne are common and simple, and, for me at least, it would be only an affectation of refinement to appraise the merits of different wines and different vintages. But I am sure that, in regard to all stimulants, our aim should be to use as little as possible....

Such, gentlemen, is an outline of the treatment of a group of terrible diseases. How imperfect it is no one can feel more strongly than I do. It is not a fixed treatment, but the treatment of to-day. Were I the wisest therapeutist and had I the best rhetoric, my description would still be imperfect, for no one can describe, with a near approach to perfection, what is imperfectly known and very dimly understood. But the variations of health and constitution, of complications, and of other conditions, are so numerous that a perfect theory or system of treatment would not carry with it directions for every individual case. Boundless scope, after all, would be left for intelligent interference of the practitioner warmed into zeal by a kindly sympathising heart.

Meeting with these puerperal diseases, the practitioner dare not fold his hands in apathy and inaction on account of the incompleteness of his knowledge. No one would listen to him were he to proclaim that all our experience and all our laboriously acquired information had yielded no fruit for the benefit of suffering women. . . .

Dr J. Matthews Duncan, 'An Address on the Treatment of Puerperal Fever', *The Lancet*, 30 October, 6 November 1880, pp. 683–4, 721–3.

137. Puerperal Fever as Septicaemia (1880)

. . . it may safely be asserted that as a result of careful investigation of the phenomena involved, modern opinion is now very nearly at one in regarding puerperal fever as in all cases a septicaemia.

The essential element in our idea of this hitherto rather vaguely defined ailment is, that it is always due to the absorption through or from a wounded surface of some septic material by which the blood becomes poisoned. It is therefore in all cases a true septic intoxication—a fever of resorption—and differs essentially in no wise from surgical fever. . . .

The observations of Mayrhofer, Orth, Heiberg, Haussmann, Spillmann, Pasteur, Doleris, and others, have within the last ten years accumulated such an amount of evidence, that it seems to me next to impossible to refuse credence to the belief that the septic changes which take place in the lying-in woman are dependent upon the action of certain micrococci, which can always be detected in the fluids of the dead, and usually also in the blood of the living who are affected with puerperal septicaemia. . . . Thus, if we regard the micrococci as causing the disease directly, to destroy the micrococci is to prevent the disease. . . .

The investigations of Lister in this country, of Koch, etc., in Germany, the experiments of Dr. Alexander Ogston of Aberdeen, have combined to advance our knowledge a very long way in this department, and have given us a footing on which we can with a considerable degree of assurance rest our therapeutic or rather prophylactic action in dealing with puerperal septicaemia....

It would thus appear that a solution of carbolic acid, which will not injure the hands of the physician, is sufficient to destroy the minute organisms on which, according to the modern idea, the poison of puerperal septicaemia depends for its existence and activity.

I therefore believe that we have now arrived at the time when we are able to state that, with the employment of extreme care and cleanliness, coupled with the use of proper antiseptic precautions, we may, without danger, attend patients suffering from puerperal fever, and do all that is required of us as doctors, without the slightest risk of communicating the disease to our other patients....

The principle of thorough, rapid, and complete disinfection ought also to be practised by nurses and midwives. If such measures were intelligently adopted, we should find less need to place nurses on a lenthened period of probation after attending a case of septicaemia than we do at present....

Dr Angus MacDonald, 'The communicability of puerperal fever by the medical attendant,' *The British Medical Journal*, 13 November 1880, pp. 772–3.

138. The Epidemic Theory Revived (1884)

Here, then, is a disease which approaches gradually; which suddenly acquires such force as to make the mortality of an hospital nearly tenfold; which, at its onset, caused the death of all who were attacked by it; which affected the city at large; which manifested itself sometimes within three hours of the patient's delivery; and which gradually exhausted its violence and ceased. Is not this the history of an epidemic? Does it not remind one of the history of cholera, or of smallpox, epidemics of which are also characterised by their gradual approach marked by sporadic cases, their furious onslaught, and their gradual subsidence indicated by diminished violence and the increased number of recoveries?

Epidemic diseases vary as to the mode of their commencement. Generally their advent is heralded by the occurrence of isolated cases at varying intervals. It was thus in the epidemic of 1854–5, of which we have been speaking, and in that of 1826, described by Dr. Collins. In the epidemic of 1845, also described by Dr. M'Clintock, there were no indications of its approach. Its invasion was sudden and unexpected. It sometimes disappears abruptly....

The mortality of lying-in hospitals may be taken as depending on the extent to which puerperal fever prevails. For short periods, when fever is absent, the average is low; but, when the observation extends over a longer term, the average is equalised.... Epidemics of other diseases, small-pox for example, sometimes subside as completely as did that of puerperal fever in 1826; but they more frequently linger on, the epidemic influence getting less and less active, till a new wave approaches and overlaps that which was disappearing. This seems to have been the case in the epidemics of 1845 and 1854....

Epidemic disease is defined to be 'a disease prevalent among a people or a community at a special time, and produced by some special cause or causes not naturally or generally present in the affected locality, as distinguished from an endemic disease.' The facts now mentioned seem to me to prove that there is a large group of puerperal cases that come strictly within this definition, and that the epidemic thus constituted is a specific disease.... the history of great hospitals, such as that of Dublin or Vienna, shows that puerperal fever will prevail and cause sad mortality at times, and disappear again, and that the conditions governing its movements have not yet been discovered....

Dr George H. Kidd, 'Address in Obstetric Medicine: On Puerperal Fever', *The British Medical Journal*, 2 August 1884, pp. 219–21.

139. The Antiseptic Transformation (1893)

The nature of the disease known as puerperal fever has been the subject of much controversy. The view that it is a specific zymotic disease, analogous to small-pox or scarlatina, but liable only to affect puerperal women, has been generally abandoned. The modern view is that the affections which have been included under the title of puerperal fever or metria are analogous to the febrile disturbances which may follow surgical wounds, and are due, for the most part, to absorption at some surface, either that of the placental separation, or at lacerations of the cervix, vagina, perineum, or vulva.

That puerperal fever, in its severe forms, is a highly contagious disease there can be no doubt. This is proved both by the records of lying-in hospitals and by those of private practice. In consequence of this disease, the death-rate of some lying-in hospitals has, over a considerable interval, been as high as 15, 20, or even 30 per cent. In many instances such hospitals have had to be closed in consequence of its prevalence, and, in some, when the closing has been too long deferred, almost every puerperal patient has died. On the other hand, recent experience in lying-in hospitals has shown that, with careful use of modern antiseptic precautions against the possibility of contagion being conveyed, mortality may be as low, or lower, in lying-in hospitals than in private practice. The contagious character of puerperal fever is equally proved in private practice by the unfortunate instances in which a single case of the disease is followed by a series of severe or fatal cases among the patients attended by the same person, a series arrested only by his entirely giving up midwifery practice for some time....

The transformation, by which lying-in hospitals, not only in Britain but on the Continent, have now been transformed from the most dangerous into the safest places for a lying-in woman, appears to depend mainly upon the use of perchloride of mercury as an antiseptic. Taking the General Lying-in Hospital as an example, the death-rate has been reduced from 10 or more to less than 4 per 1,000; the death-rate from septicaemia or pelvic inflammation to 1.5 per 1,000; and cases of septic pyrexia, including slight and transient ones, from 40.0 to 2.5 per cent.

These results have followed from the following use of antiseptic agents. Perchloride of mercury, 1 in 1,000, is used to disinfect hands and non-metallic instruments by everyone who touches the patients. A douche is employed before labour, but this has varied in its character without affecting the results. A douche of perchloride of mercury, 1 in 2,000, is used after labour. The same antiseptic is used for washing and douching the patient regularly throughout the puerpery; for the first three days, of a strength of 1 in 2,000, afterwards 1 in 4,000. Horsehair mattresses are employed, and are disinfected by heat only when an unfavourable case has occurred. A separate irrigator is provided for each bed, having a vaginal tube of glass....

Dr A.L. Galabin, *A Manual of Midwifery*, 3rd edn., 1893, pp. 759, 792.

3.7 Lying-in

140. Hints for Lying-in (1837)

The medical attendant having retired from the [delivery] room, it will frequently happen that the nurse proposes to make her mistress comfortable [after childbirth]...she will perhaps lift her off the bed, or if not, place her in an *erect* or *sitting posture*, upon it. Nothing can be so improper, or more likely to induce serious consequences ... *the horizontal position is to be strictly preserved....*

Immediately the infant is dressed, many nurses are in the habit of dosing it with castor oil, or honey of roses and almond oil. It is objectionable on many accounts.... The infant should be put quietly to sleep, and allowed to repose for four or five hours, when the mother having also obtained some sleep, it is proper to place the child to the breast. This should always be done within the first four and twenty hours....

The suckling should be performed at regular intervals of about four hours, during the night as well as day. And during sleep, the nipple ought not to be allowed to remain in the infant's mouth, as is too often the case; nor during the day, the child put to the breast every time it cries, to quiet and soothe it. Both much interfere with the health of the infant, the stomach is kept constantly loaded, and unable therefore to digest its contents,—time must be given for this purpose, and an interval of four hours is not too much. A child thus nursed will be found less troublesome and fractious than one that is hushed by the breast at every cry, and will awaken with great regularity as the time for its meal approaches....

· ... I [do not] consider the lying-in room, a sick room, or approve of a very usual plan of treatment. For it is a frequent but very injurious practice for nurses, for several days after delivery, to keep the bed-room curtains drawn-close—to increase the number of blankets,—and to be continually giving everything as hot as it can be swallowed, deluging the patient's stomach with water-gruel and slops with a view to promote perspiration, and prevent her taking cold. This is the most direct way to produce the evil so much dreaded, for it follows as a natural consequence, that by these means, she is rendered more than ever susceptible to the impression of cold,—is sure to be much debilitated, and a troublesome species of fever will be induced, which it may be found difficult to remove....

Indeed for *three weeks* after delivery an almost constant compliance with the latter direction [to keep the horizontal position] is highly important. Among the poorer classes of society, who get up very soon after delivery, and undergo much fatigue, '*the falling down of the womb*' is a very common and distressing complaint. It is the effect, simply, of their not being able to keep the recumbent posture long enough. I cannot too strongly endeavour to impress upon the recollection of a female the importance of this hint, the more especially as some nurses are the first to induce the lying-in patients to break it....

It is never safe for her to join her family before the expiration of the third week,—and the *month* from her delivery having terminated, she gradually resumes her accustomed domestic duties....

Dr Thomas Bull, *Hints to Mothers for the Management of Health*, 1837, pp. 144–5, 147–8, 152, 155–8.

141. A Post-delivery Revolution (1848)

A most important revolution has taken place during the last half century in the management of both mother and child after delivery; so that the treatment of lying-in women is now as natural and prudent as it was formerly irrational and injurious.

It was customary in bygone days to adopt a highly injudicious mode of management. Immediately after delivery a sheep was killed, where the expense could be sustained, and the skin, reeking hot, was applied over the abdomen. On the second day a sear cloth with a Galbanum plaster was substituted. In some cases the warm bath was used, and the parts concerned in labour were fomented and fumigated. A load of bed-clothes were heaped on the patient, and the key-hole, and every crevice of the lying-in room, were most assiduously closed, and the temperature of the apartment kept high. All fluids and every article of food were taken hot, and heated still more by spices....

Presuming that no unusual circumstances requires it for a longer time, the mother must remain whilst the infant is being dressed, or for at least half an hour, in the same situation as when delivered, after which she is to be gently moved up in the bed, by one assistant at the shoulders and another at the feet. The patient, during these operations, must remain perfectly passive and in the horizontal posture, because disagreeable accidents are liable to ensue from a neglect of this salutary advice, such as bleeding, fainting, falling down or inversion of the womb....

Many women suffer during the remainder of their lives from the very general and reprehensible custom of indulging too early in an upright position; and even those who are solicitous to remain longer than is necessary in bed, often do themselves much mischief by a half-recumbent posture, presuming that if the lower limbs be kept horizontal, the position of the rest of the body is unimportant. This practice is so manifestly injurious, that it is to be wondered how it is so prevalent. The most severe consequences arise from this error. But, although the horizontal posture is necessary for a fortnight or three weeks after delivery, yet it is not necessary that that position should be maintained under the bed-clothes; it may be more comfortably and more rationally obtained by rest on a sofa or on the bed....

Dr John T. Conquest, *Letters to a Mother*, 1848, pp. 71–2, 84–5.

142. Breast-feeding an Absolute Duty (1882)

If the mother is healthy, and if the breasts have secreted milk, nothing should prevent the mother suckling her infants. The mother's milk is the proper food for her babe, and it is beyond doubt that the rate of infant mortality among those who are nursed by the mother is less than among those suckled by a wet-nurse, and far less than among those who are weaned from birth ... every mother should consider it her absolute duty, unless her health is delicate, and her medical man's opinion is against her so doing, to suckle her infant for at least six months. It must be best for her infant, and it can but be productive of good to her in the large majority of cases. Fashion has lately stepped in among a certain class of women in an iniquitous manner, in her curious and inscrutable way, and has attempted to prevent this true mother's mission from being accomplished; and lazy mothers are glad, for the sake of getting rid of to them an inconvenient and troublesome process, to pander to this inexcusable fashionable heartlessness. I cannot speak too strongly concerning this frivolous and unmotherly habit; and I can only hope and trust that medical men will on all possible occasions speak out their minds against this inhumane and truly wicked practice.

If the mother should not have enough milk in her breasts to feed her babe entirely, or if through force of circumstances she is away from her babe during the day, there is no reason why she should give up suckling altogether; for it is an erroneous idea that cow's milk and the mother's milk, given at different times in the day, are sure to disagree with the baby....

Among those of the poor who are unable to suckle their babe, it is no uncommon thing to find that the almost entire dietary of the infant consists of boiled bread and water. It may, I grant, be often due to sheer ignorance, but in many cases it is due to the difficulty the poor have of getting milk, besides the difficulty from a pecuniary point of view. It stands to reason that on such a dietary no infant can be expected to live; and now we have such good condensed milk, and sold at such a reasonable price, we ought to seldom hear, as we have so much of late, of death carrying off so many children, simply because of improper and insufficient nourishment....

PROPER TIMES FOR SUCKLING.—This is most important, and all mothers must fully understand that they cannot expect their little ones to keep well unless they feed them with systematic regularity.

For the first month the infant should be fed every hour; during the next month the interval might be increased to two hours, and gradually from this to four hours, as the child grows older. Once

208   *Marriage and Maternity*

get the child into this regular and proper way of taking the breast, and you will have saved yourself an immense amount of trouble. Overfeeding is the cause of many an infant's death. Never by any chance give the child the breast at irregular hours simply because it cries, and never be so foolish as to allow the babe to drag at your breasts the greater part of the night through, for this is detrimental to yourself and the child in more ways than one. To you it gives a restless night, and maybe a sore nipple; and to the little one it not only gets it into bad habits, but probably produces all those intestinal disturbances so often fatal....

Lionel A. Weatherly, *The Young Wife's Own Book*, 1882, pp. 117-9, 129-30, 82.

143. Post-partum Haemorrhage and Lying-in (1900)

Haemorrhage after delivery may come from various sources. Haemorrhage from the placental site is, however, so much the most frequent and most important, that this is regarded as post-partum haemorrhage *par excellence*. The subject is one of immense importance, for post-partum haemorrhage is not only one of the most dangerous complications, but is a relatively common complication of parturition. It may occur after the most perfectly normal labour, and a household may thus be unexpectedly plunged into grief by the sudden death of the patient. Nor is there any emergency in which so much depends upon the care and skill of the physician. The occurrence of haemorrhage at all may generally be prevented by a careful and correct management of the third stage of labour. When haemorrhage does occur, the life of the patient will generally depend upon the promptitude and vigour of the treatment.

FREQUENCY.—The frequency of post-partum haemorrhage varies so much, both according to the circumstances and social position of the patients and the skill of the accoucheur, that no estimate can be given....

If possible, the patient should keep her bed for ten days, or for a longer time, if the discharge is still sanguineous, and she should return to it, if getting up brings on again a red discharge. On first leaving it, she should spend much of her time reclining on a sofa, and should not return completely to her ordinary mode of life, or undertake severe exertion, till the end of six weeks, at which time involution ought to be fairly complete. In the case of a primipara, when there has been much laceration, or bruising of soft parts, it is often desirable for the recumbent position to be maintained, for the most part, for three or even four weeks....

Dr A.L. Galabin, *A Manual of Midwifery*, 1900, pp. 741, 282.

144. Sexual Abstinence after Confinement (1895)

If we could persuade men and women to regulate their lives in a strictly physiological model, much suffering might be saved, and the race would become more vigorous and healthy.... Marriage is not the legalisation of unbounded desires, and no man worthy of the name would interfere with his wife's recovery of health and strength, nor with her duty towards their helpless babe... a separate life should be led for, at any rate, three months after childbirth. Again, if the mother is doing her simple duty by the child in suckling it, it is greatly to be desired that she should run no risk of pregnancy....

The late Dr. Matthews Duncan, who made a careful study of Fertility, Fecundity, and Sterility, thought that the physiological arrangement was for a woman to bear a child once in two years. Lactation should not be prolonged more than nine months, and if to this is added the nine months' pregnancy with the next child, each woman would have six months' holiday, during which she should be neither pregnant nor suckling, when she could develop her other capabilities and gather strength. Women would save their health, their temper, and their good looks by such an arrangement....

The same authority, Dr. Matthews Duncan, was also of opinion that the risk to women in childbirth increased greatly after the sixth or seventh pregnancy, because they were so exhausted generally and locally, that the risk from flooding, etc., became great. This risk would be much lessened if a reasonable interval occurred between each birth....

Dr Mary Scharlieb, *A Woman's Words to Women on the Care of their Health in England and in India*, 1895, pp. 162–5.

PART 4
Female Sexuality

Introduction

The history of nineteenth-century bourgeois sexuality has been undergoing extensive and fundamental revision in recent years, in general approach, perspective and detailed analysis. In the first volume of his *The History of Sexuality* (1979) Michel Foucault emphasised that sexuality should be interpreted as a specific historical construct rather than a universal and a-historical condition, a social construct which was especially linked with relations of power. Peter Gay is aiming to integrate psycho-analysis with history in his multi-volume study of *The Bourgeois Experience: Victoria to Freud*. Volume one, 'Education of the Senses' (1984), examines the sensual life of the bourgeoisie in America and Europe from the 1830s, and rejects the stereotypes of repression and hypocrisy which have prevailed in much of the literature. Jeffrey Weeks has provided a pioneering study of *Sex, Politics and Society: The regulation of sexuality since 1800* (1981) for Great Britain, which also emphasises the specific historical character of British sexuality. At the same time, detailed studies of particular aspects of bourgeois sexuality have been published, such as Judith Walkowitz's *Prostitution and Victorian Society: Women, Class and the State* (1980).

These books and others point to the need to open up bourgeois sexuality for reassessment. As Jeff Weeks notes, 'Historians still have before them the difficult task of charting the area before they can properly explore its hidden riches' (pp. 15–16). Female sexuality is a much more complex area to chart than male sexuality, in part because the majority of texts were written by males, and because the social convention was that female sexual experiences and ideas were a private matter, even more so than for males. As Peter Gay argues, 'The bourgeois

213

century made Woman problematic' (p. 145) and female sexuality was the most problematic and sensitive territory of all. This part of our book will document some of the prescriptions and assumptions about female sexuality which were developed in Victorian and Edwardian 'non-fictional' literature. The emphasis is once again on the preoccupations of medical and other advisers—the ways in which the medical profession became involved in the definition of 'healthy' and 'unhealthy' female sexuality, and how they dealt with enthusiasts for sexual surgery. The final section is concerned with the separation of sexuality from reproduction with the increasing popularisation of birth control. There was no single orthodoxy about female sexuality in Victorian and Edwardian England, in spite of attempts by some writers to simplify the issues and create a common sexual consciousness.

Female sexuality was usually confined within the biological model of the female life cycle, to the period from menstruation to menopause. The social framework for sexuality was established by a set of major assumptions: by its supposed integral relationship with reproduction, by the moral standards of nineteenth-century Anglican Christianity, and by the social conventions of privacy and selective ignorance for women. The subject of sex education for young girls was supposedly non-existent for most Victorians, because it was a violation of the accepted code of secrecy, a questioning of what should be unquestioned (see 4.1). However, medical and moralist authors dealt at length with the subject of female sexuality and female sexual knowledge for professional and parental readers, especially from the late nineteenth century. The initial point of attack was the necessity for more information on their sexual duties for women about to be married, in order to prevent incomplete unions (e.g. Acton, 1865 [145]), or to check the spread of 'special diseases' (Tait, 1877 [146]). 'False modesty', 'ignorance' and 'false ideas' about female physiology were portrayed as dangerous to health and domestic happiness, since 'instinct' could not guarantee satisfactory 'sexual congress' or health.

The task of sex education for young girls was usually assigned to their mothers (e.g. Tait, 1877 [146]; Hawksley, 1894 [148]). But there was increasing recognition that mothers were also bound by 'the old, old confusion between innocence and ignorance' (Hawksley [148]); and appeals for more information and guidance on sexual questions were made to 'physicians of the body, who have, as a class, too long shirked their public responsibilities concerning it [sexual morality]' (E.M.S., 1895 [149]). By the 1890s there was considerable support among enlightened middle- and upper-class women for girls to 'be taught some necessary physical facts' (Balfour, 1898 [150]); some even believed that 'education will more and more concern itself with sex questions' (Johnson, 1899 [151]).

However, the content of that education remained the difficult and controversial question. The Reverend Edward Lyttelton (1900) [152] was quite clear that more sex education was needed, but felt that girls required less information than boys about 'the fact of maternity'; for most girls it would be enough for the parent to advise that 'the seed of life is entrusted by God to the father in a very wonderful way, and that after marriage he is allowed to give it to his wife...'. Effie Johnson (1899) [151] also accepted that education should emphasise the spiritual quality of physical relations, but argued that the 'failure of love's attractive power on either plane [the animal and the spiritual], must mean disaster in the long run'. The problem was that sex education was inextricably linked with different views about female sexual character and the religious emphasis on moral restraint. Laurence Housman (1911) [153] argued strenuously for more sex instruction for girls, but concluded that it was 'very generally characteristic of girl-nature to remain less conscious than boy-nature of the inducement of sex'. Elizabeth Chesser (1913) [154] justified 'direct teaching in sex hygiene' on the moral ground that the right kind of sexual knowledge would help to prevent vice, as well as preserving health and providing a sound preparation for motherhood. Her endorsement of 'instructed innocence' was an illustration of the way in which sexuality was given second place even by exponents of sex education.

There were two broadly opposed views about female sexuality in nineteenth-century Britain, and also in Europe and North America. Some authors argued that women were only capable of a limited or negligible sexual response (e.g. Acton, 1865 [159]). But a positive view of female sexuality was maintained by many writers on human passions (see 4.2). Puberty was defined as the beginning of sexuality for both genders: 'All healthy persons, at the time of puberty, must certainly feel the passion of physical love...the most delightful of all the passions' (Ryan, 1831 [157]). Dr Ryan and Richard Carlile (1838) [158], for example, generally emphasised the equality of female and male passions, and Carlile strongly attacked the hypocrisy of prevailing views on the necessity for female repression. Priscilla Barker (1888) [160] argued for 'the passion of lust' being stronger in the female sex, an interpretation at least as old as the story of Adam and Eve. Dr Kellogg (1885) [147] also accepted the reality of 'excited passions' in both sexes, but blamed an overly stimulating diet, tobacco and reading novels for the excessive 'storms of passion' which disturbed both girls and boys.

William Acton (1865) [159] was the most renowned advocate of the absence of sexuality in women: 'the majority of women (happily for them) are not very much troubled with sexual feeling of any kind'. This was moral prescription rather than physical description. Acton wanted to restrict women to the useful areas of domestic life: 'The best mothers, wives and managers of households, know little or nothing of sexual indulgence. Love of home, children, and domestic duties are the only passions they feel'. Acton's comments provide some insight into his mind and values, but they were not a reliable guide to female behaviour or opinion. Edwardian advisers continued to emphasise the presence of adolescent erotic curiosity (Chesser, 1913 [161]) and 'sexual feeling' (Scharlieb, 1915 [155]) in women as well as men. The moralists' concern was usually to restrain female sexuality by the proper 'sense of moral responsibility', rather than to deny its existence. Mary Scharlieb [155] favoured equal self-control by men and women as a solution to their common problem. The suffragettes went one step further and advocated 'votes for women and chastity for men'.

One of the most revealing avenues for investigating educated Victorian and Edwardian attitudes to female sexuality is the obsession with masturbation (see 4.3), and the proposed cures for what was identified as a 'disease'. The most extreme 'cures' for women were ovariotomy, or surgical removal of the ovaries, and clitoridectomy, or surgical removal of the clitoris (see 4.4). Masturbation was usually referred to in more popular literature by euphemisms like 'secret evil habits', 'secret vice' (Duffey, 1873 [162]) or 'the secret sin of Self-abuse' (Barker, 1888 [165]).

Recognition of its existence was an acknowledgement of female sexuality, but of a particularly threatening kind—because it was autonomous and divorced from reproduction. A real problem of diagnosis faced Victorian parents and doctors because of the difficulty of establishing reliable 'symptoms', and there were a wide range of possible moral, physical, mechanical and surgical treatments (see 4.3). Some specialists argued that 'masturbation is very common amongst boys, and comparatively rare amongst girls' (Tait, 1877 [163]), on the basis of an Actonian view of a weak sexual instinct in women. But leading members of the British Gynaecological Society were convinced of a widespread female 'habit', often acquired at school, and they searched with concentrated attention for physical 'symptoms or the signs of this habit' (Routh, 1886–7 [164]; see also Savage and Smith, 1890–1 [166]), extending even to the 'curly character' of the pubic hair. And so 'this learned mania spread across the civilized landscape' (Gay, p. 297), and advice books for women translated the 'secret sin' into even more terrifying pictures of female self-consumption (e.g. Barker, 1888 [165]).

Morality rather than medical science was the real issue in the spread of masturbation mania. Dr Kelly (1909) [168] explicitly argued that 'The physician is the moral sanitarium directly responsible' for the patient's moral welfare, and 'that there is on us the troublous duty of moral prophylaxis'. While recognising that 'The physical results of self-abuse…seem to be surprisingly small', Dr Kelly spoke in the name of 'our ideal of purity' in suggesting curative treatment. Dr Elizabeth Blackwell (1902) [167] similarly emphasised the moral consequences of masturbation, as a threat to 'individual self-control, the highest distinctive mark of the human being'. But doctors could do more than take on the moral role of the priest—in extreme cases they could intervene surgically to remove the physical cause of the moral problem. This mentality led directly to one of the most scandalous and horrific controversies in nineteenth-century medicine—the Baker Brown affair.

Isaac Baker Brown was known as one of the best Victorian surgeons, and in 1865 was elected President of the Medical Society of London. He was not distinguished from his fellow doctors either by his advocacy of surgery in treating appropriate women's illnesses (Brown, 1854 [170]), or by his belief in the curative power of clitoridectomy [171ff.]. Brown's misfortune was that he publicised his cure and the activities of his London Surgical Home; he performed too many clitoridectomies and did so in semi-public by welcoming professional visitors to his operations; and he failed to obtain permission from his patients for this specific operation. Baker Brown had numerous supporters among the medical profession (e.g. Granville Bantock and Pickop, 14 July 1866 [173–4]), but even more critics once the clitoridectomy debate got under way in *The Lancet* and other medical journals in 1866 [172–9]. The debate was notable for its diversity and confusion of views about female physiology and sexuality. As the leader writer in the *British Medical Journal* concluded in December 1866, referring to an Obstetrical Society meeting on 5 December, 'Very little was urged on scientific grounds for or against the proposal of Mr Baker Brown'—'It is a dirty subject' [178]. Baker Brown's expulsion from the Obstetrical Society of London in April 1867 was not based on outrage at unnecessary mutilation and its consequence, nor on a scientific refutation of the value of clitoridectomy. Rather, the issue was his failure to inform and obtain the consent of the patient or her husband, and the 'public scandal' which resulted. The most revealing comment was made by the President of the Society: 'It is the manner in which the operation is performed, not the operation itself, which we have met to consider. It is the ethical question' [180]. Baker Brown's expulsion did not mean the end of clitoridectomy, and certainly not the end of the moral attitudes and medical ignorance which made the operation possible (see 'The British Gynaecological Journal' discussion of 8 December 1886 [181]).

Nineteenth- and early twentieth-century bourgeois writing on birth control provides another revealing source for attitudes towards female sexuality and social roles. Effective birth control broke the link between sexuality and reproduction, and created the possibility of greater sexual freedom for women, as well as helping to reduce family size. Birth control was another key topic increasingly appropriated by the medical profession, who combined moral prescriptions with incomplete and inaccurate knowledge of reproductive functions. Medical opposition to birth control was expressed in a mixture of warnings about the injurious consequences for health and the associated moral decline (e.g. Routh, 1879 [184]). The medical profession was striving for respectability and joined the clergy in remaining aloof from such an indelicate subject. Dr Scharlieb (1915) [187] emphasised the more subtle injuries supposedly caused by birth control, but the ultimate sanction was that it was 'a real sin when a young married woman refuses to bear a family'. Medical conservatism was illustrated when H. A. Allbutt was struck off the medical register for publicising birth-control methods in his popular *The Wife's Handbook* in 1887.

However, against the harbingers of doom, there were strong public advocates of birth control and the right of women to choose whether and when they had children. Radicals like Francis Place and Richard Carlile popularised methods of contraception in the 1820s. Carlile's *Every Woman's Book* (1838: first published 1826 [183]) explicitly justified contraception for women on the grounds that it increased their freedom of choice and 'neither lessens the pleasure of the female nor injures her health.' The publicity surrounding the Bradlaugh-Besant trial in 1876 was a major boost to the birth-control cause, and opponents of birth control in the middle and upper classes felt increasingly surrounded by the 'evil in our midst'. Mary Drew (1886) [191], for example, wrote to her father, W. E. Gladstone, that '[I] have found myself almost alone amongst my friends and contemporaries in the line I have taken' against birth control, in spite of the support of medical authorities like Matthews Duncan and Paget (see also Drew, 1911 [193]; Asquith, 1925 [189]). This subjective impression was supported by the population statistics, with a declining birthrate from the last quarter of the nineteenth century (from about 6 live births per family about 1880 to 2.2 live births by 1925–9).

The 'real revolt' against the 'The curse of Eve' (MacFadyen, 1907 [186]) occurred in the bedrooms of the middle and upper classes before 1914, rather than in books and magazines. Ironically, the 1911 census [see 188] indicated that doctors and clergymen had among the smallest families of all occupational groups (Stopes, 1918), though they did not alter their public stance on contraception until the inter-war years. The historical record from the interior of the pre-war British bedroom is sparse, but evidence from private letters [e.g. 190, 194] and diaries suggests that some husbands and wives, engaged couples and sisters could discuss intimate details of contraceptive practice with honesty and affection. There was anxiety, but contraception could also be integrated into the erotic framework of close relationships. The changing idea of the family, with conscious decisions to limit family size, led to the maintenance or improvement of living standards, and created new role possibilities for middle- and upper-class women.

4.1 Sex Education for Females

145. Ignorance and False Ideas about Sexual Congress (1865)

We now come, after these preliminaries, to the consideration of the matter-of-fact duties [i.e. sexual intercourse] of married life. It is but seldom, and then incidentally, that these matters are treated of in books. Nevertheless, ignorance, or false ideas respecting them, has caused much evil and much domestic misery. It is, I believe, generally assumed that instinct teaches adults how sexual congress should take place. But from several cases that have come under my notice, I should say that many would be entirely ignorant, but for previously incontinent habits, or such notions as they pick up from watching the practices of animals.

IGNORANCE AMONG MARRIED PEOPLE ON SEXUAL SUBJECTS.—For instance, a short time ago, I attended a member of the Society of Friends, who had been married some years. The marriage had never been consummated, and I believe that the almost incredible ignorance displayed in this case, as to the duties of matrimony, was not in the least assumed. So common is this ignorance that it is far from seldom that I meet with cases in which the hymen has never been ruptured. . . .

W. Acton, *The functions and disorders of the reproductive organs*, 4th. edn., 1865, p. 89.

146. False Modesty on Physical Subjects (1877)

By the time a male arrives at the age of marriage, he will have learnt, from the education which all men go through soon after puberty, whether or not he has marital capacity; and if he finds that he has not, he will not attempt to enter married life. But the majority of women enter the married state with but a very hazy notion of what its functions are, a misfortune to which a large proportion of their special diseases may be attributed. If a mal-formed male, therefore, should be brought up as a woman, he may enter, and in very many instances actually has entered, the state of marriage, utterly unaware of his misfortune....

It would be a great blessing to women about to be married if their mothers would give them a little advice based on their own experience; but there is a false modesty on these subjects ingrained in our English life which has to be paid for in much suffering amongst women....

Robert L. Tait, *Diseases of Women*, 1877, pp. 36, 42.

147. From Disturbing Diet to Dissoluteness (1885)

DIET vs. CHASTITY.—From earliest infancy to impotent old age, there is a constant antagonism between diet and purity. Sometimes—rarely we hope—the helpless infant imbibes the essence of libidinous desires with its mother's milk, and thence receives upon its forming brain the stamp of vice. When old enough to take food in the ordinary way, the infant's tender organs of digestion are plied with highly seasoned viands, stimulating sauces, animal food, sweetmeats, and dainty tidbits in endless variety. Soon, tea and coffee are added to the list.... Flesh, condiments, eggs, tea, coffee, chocolate, and all stimulants, have a powerful influence directly upon the reproductive organs. They increase the local supply of blood; and through nervous sympathy with the brain, the passions are aroused.

Overeating, eating between meals, hasty eating, eating indigestible articles of food, late suppers, react upon the sexual organs with the utmost certainty. Any disturbance of the digestive function deteriorates the quality of the blood. Poor blood, filled with crude, unelaborated material, is irritating to the nervous system, and especially to those extremely delicate nerves which govern the reproductive function. Irritation provokes congestion; congestion excites sexual desires; excited passions increase the local disturbance; and thus each reacts upon the other, ever increasing the injury and the liability to future damage.

Thus these exciting causes continue their insidious work through youth and more mature years. Right under the eyes of fathers and mothers they work the ruin of their children, exciting such storms of passion as are absolutely uncontrollable. . . .

TOBACCO AND VICE.—Few are aware of the influence upon morals exerted by that filthy habit, tobacco-using. When acquired early, it excites the undeveloped organs, arouses the passions, and in a few years converts the once chaste and pure youth into a veritable volcano of lust, belching out from its inner fires of passion torrents of obscenity and the sulphurous fumes of lasciviousness. If long-continued, the final effect of tobacco is emasculation; but this is only the necessary consequence of previous super-excitation. The lecherous daydreams in which smokers constantly indulge, are a species of fornication for which even a brute ought to blush, if such a crime were possible for a brute. . . .

[BAD BOOKS] The works of our standard authors in literature abound in lubricity. Popular novels have doubtless done more to arouse a prurient curiosity in the young, and to excite and foster passion and immorality, than even the obscene literature so bravely warred against by Mr. Comstock. The more exquisitely painted the scenes of vice, the more dangerously enticing. Novel-reading has led thousands to lives of dissoluteness. . . .

Dr J.H. Kellogg, *Plain Facts about Sexual Life*, 2nd. edn., 1885, pp. 83–5, 88.

148. Sex Education for Girls: the Mother's Task (1894)

Girls are to-day constantly married without any idea of what matrimony implies than has been imparted by the prurient, whispered gossip of an impure-minded schoolfellow; and frequently—especially, as I have said, in the case of members of high-born families—without even the modicum of enlightenment. This condition of things, moreover, is regarded by many a satisfied matron as proving the perfection of watchful guardianship upon her own part and of sweet pliability upon that of her child.

And why?

Men, we are told, like to perform their own initiation. Men, it is constantly and truly said, prefer girls of innocent mind. In which latter statement, by the by, crops up the old, old confusion between innocence and ignorance....

When, before they stand at the altar, girls know to what they will be yielding themselves; when they understand the distinction, the huge distinction, between lust and love, animalism and affection, carnality and comradeship; when they possess the liberty of a comprehending, voluntary choice—then, and not until then, will they have their right.

A girl, four or five days before her marriage, went to her mother and implored to be told what that was which lay before her, to which her vows would commit her. She had heard much that to her seemed horrible to incredulity, repellent beyond words. She was half frantic with a vague dread, worse than any certainty. And she craved to know. But she was laughed at and refused. Why? A bride upon her husband's first approach believed him mad, and in her dread tried to reach a bell and summon help. Why?... Because men will to have it so, and mothers shrink from the task—truly a terrible task—involved. Perhaps they forget their own past suffering....

The matter remains with the mothers—mothers not merely in the carnal, but also in the moral and spiritual sense—those elder women, in fact, in whose hands rest the education of the rising generation. The preservation of true innocence, that horribly maligned but most beautiful word; the dispelling of a blinding mist of misconception; the prevention of untold suffering; all hang upon their decision....

Mrs W.M.A. Hawksley, 'A Young Woman's Right: Knowledge', *The Westminster Review*, Vol. 142, September 1894, pp. 316–8.

149. Chastity and the Physician's Silence (1895)

We find, therefore, that knowledge of the history of marriage—of its evolution out of unchecked animal instincts to the ordered systems now prevailing, and also a study of the physiological problems to which the laws of sex give rise amid the complexities of highly civilised life, are both necessary to the formation of any adequate conclusions respecting the basis on which to found sexual morality.

It must be universally acknowledged that no such basis has yet been arrived at. The physiological difficulties of the situation cannot be overrated, and much difference of opinion exists among those best qualified to judge—viz., the medical profession—as to the physical advisability or moral obligation of chastity. This uncertainty is of paramount importance when we consider that the question how far chastity ought to be regarded as equally binding upon both sexes is one of the turning-points of the whole subject of sexual morality. Any decision on this grave question must rest ultimately with physicians of the body, who have, as a class, too long shirked their public responsibilities concerning it, and, by their silence and inaction, left its difficulties to the well-meant but often inefficient handling of physicians of the soul.

E.M.S. [Elizabeth Missing Sewell?], 'Some Modern Ideas about Marriage', *The Westminster Review*, Vol. 143, May 1895, p. 521.

150. The Teaching of Necessary Physical Facts (1898)

...The present and future generations will as a rule do better I trust—at least they will mostly be taught some necessary physical facts which in my generation it was considered immoral to allow girls to have even a suspicion of—it was of course false delicacy & false modesty but it takes time to divest yourself of prejudices and lines of thought which are impressed upon you when you are quite young ... now-a-days girls are better prepared for their duties as mothers than they used to be....

Mrs Balfour to her daughter, Edith Lyttelton, 8 January 1898, Chandos Papers, I, 5/2 [Churchill College, Cambridge].

151. More Education about Sex Questions (1899)

Indeed, history is so faithful in recording the abnormal and exaggerated customs and acts that have obtained with regard to sex-relations—showing established polygamy in this country, prevalent polyandry in that, intermarriage of blood relations here, pillage of wives and perfect promiscuity there,—that custom justice reduces the student of sociology to say thoughtfully and unprejudicedly now in modern times: 'Bring all the knowledge you can to this debatable controversy, that we may see what issues compel to Progressive conclusions, since we in our own day have nothing better to show than that terrible growth, prostitution, linked with a miscalled Monogamy, which admits a one-sided licentiousness *under monogamic laws* truly appalling to contemplate'....

The advocate who pleads only for variety and excess in sex-exercise, stands convicted of immorality by Nature herself, in the guerdon she gives as his deserts—imbecility, disease, and death. The slave of sexual excess can never pose as reformer, since his own creed loses for him his very foothold in the evolutionary race itself....

Once having raised pure Monogamy, then, as the standard of morals,—having grasped the permanent as the principal and most necessary principle in the sex-tie,—having exterminated unfairness from the legal marriage basis,—it will doubtless follow that education will more and more concern itself with sex questions.

Instead of bemoaning the fact that happy wholesome Marriage is rare, and that disgracefully mercenary and cowardly and debased Marriage is frequent, education will instruct children that a constant duality of the animal and the spiritual exist in their natures; and point out that no affinity called forth only on the one side should deserve to experience, the culmination which sex-union constitutes; since failure of Love's attractive power on either plane, must mean disaster in the long run to the life which constantly makes calls upon it from both! This knowledge might save many from the casual indulgence of mere animal passion, and prevent many more unhappy unions!...

When it shall be universally acknowledged, then, that sex-relations afford the greatest spiritual lever to be found in life and human experience; destined to conduct from the physical to the spiritual; capable of producing that which will endure in spite of Death itself—Spiritual Love, is it likely that futurity, in its highest progressive moral code, will become again enamoured of the promiscuity which is the distinctive characteristic of the streets?...

Effie Johnson, 'Marriage or Free Love', *The Westminster Review*, Vol. 152, July 1899, pp. 92–3, 97–8.

152. A Difficulty in Teaching Girl Children (1900)

At some time between eight and eleven years of age, in any case before a child leaves home, the fact of maternity should be explained.... It will be felt by some that as to paternity there is a difficulty in teaching on the subject at so early an age as under eleven years. Possibly, also, the difficulty would be felt to be more acute in the case of girls....

... on reaching the point where the beginning of conception in the mother is explained ... the parent can perfectly well add that the seed of life is entrusted by God to the father in a very wonderful way, and that after marriage he is allowed to give it to his wife, this being on his part an act of the love which first made him marry her. Seldom, I should fancy very seldom, would more than that be required in the case of girl children....

Rev. The Hon. E. Lyttelton, *Training of the Young in Laws of Sex*, 1900, pp. 79–81, 85–6.

153. The Woman's Right to Knowledge of Sex (1911)

... it seems, as far as I can gather, to be very generally characteristic of girl-nature to remain less conscious than boy-nature of the inducement of sex, and, up to a certain age, to assimilate such instruction as is given to it in a curiously impersonal and unfleshly form ... now that passionless quality in the life of girlhood is used sometimes as an argument against the course of instruction [sex training] which I am advocating, because it seems under normal conditions to hold her so far removed from the need for such knowledge; yet that very passionless experience may be the ground of false confidence, from which she steps into danger, and finds too late that her own nature has sprung itself upon her in a totally new aspect and left her defenceless. . . .

And it comes back to my memory still, as a thing for wrath and shame, that when in my own youth, I discovered how girls were sent ignorant through life into marriage, and pleaded that they, like men, had a right to know themselves and what was the nature of the contract to which they were giving themselves for life—then I remember I was told by one, who herself had the care of daughters, that that ignorance formed too valuable an addition to the virginal charm of womanhood in the marriage market. 'We cannot afford to do without it,' I was told; 'it makes them more attractive'. . . .

I admit the difficulty of initiating the untried virginal mind of girlhood in these matters, without making it unduly introspective and self-conscious. We are very untrained in meeting that difficulty, but it has got to be met. The conditions which surround the lives of women are changing, and their training must change with the conditions.

The only real surrender of love from woman to man that is worth having is the free and conscious surrender which knows the meaning and the value of what it is giving. . .it is the woman's right. . . .

Laurence Housman, *The Immoral Effects of Ignorance in Sex Relations*, 1911, pp. 32–5, 41–2.

154. Direct Teaching in Sex Hygiene (1913)

SEX HYGIENE.—Definite teaching in hygiene and physiology would give the new generation of mothers knowledge which would go a long way to preserve their own health and ensure the welfare of their children. Education for parenthood must necessarily include direct teaching in sex hygiene. Such instruction, if included in the school curriculum, would have to be very carefully given, either by teachers who possessed the right sort of knowledge themselves, or, better still, by men and women doctors respectively to boys and girls. But it must be given, because ignorance or perverted knowledge is a fundamental factor in the causation of vice. Sex is everywhere, and sex ought not to be, indeed it cannot be, ignored.

'Whatever is worth being is worth knowing,' said Bacon, and what is worth knowing is worth teaching by right methods.... Much depends on the character of the teaching. Mere instruction in physiology is not enough, but 'instructed innocence,' as Margaret Stephens so aptly says in 'Woman and Marriage,' is far preferable to the old method of permitting children to discover, generally in undesirable ways, the meaning of sex and parenthood. Knowledge must be so imparted that it will appeal to the child's reverent imagination. We must create in the child respect for love and sexual selection, instil the idea that just as 'love' is the source of all beauty in life, so this same sex instinct perverted, misused, misdirected, is the source of sorrow and suffering, disease and death.

The sex troubles of modern life are largely the result of our false attitude towards sex truths. Whilst ignorance is dangerous, perverted and irreverent knowledge is fatal.... Opinion on this subject [of direct teaching in sex hygiene] is not by any means unanimous; many people believing that sex instruction should be not the task of the teacher but of the parent, the mother. In this respect motherhood has failed lamentably. How many mothers tell even their daughters the meaning of sex? How many give any warning of the potential dangers which the most sheltered girl may have to face in the world? The fallacy that to keep a girl innocent it is necessary to leave her ignorant, uninstructed concerning the most important question which faces girlhood, is responsible for a great deal of unhappiness and not a few tragedies.

But it is folly to blame the women who have never been educated for motherhood, who have not the language nor the requisite knowledge to explain the great mysteries of life and birth. Our educational system fosters a silly prudery, a false and dangerous modesty, a sense of shame concerning all questions relating to maternity. When girls are educated for motherhood the mother will be able to face these questions simply and bravely. She will not lie to her children and dishonour her motherhood by silly sentimentalities about stars and rose bushes. Whilst she should answer questions, the subject ought not, of course, to be dilated upon, nor should unasked information be supplied. It will be the task of the teacher later to impart definite knowledge, to teach elementary physiology, the principles of eugenics, the care and right conduct of the sexual life. The whole school training should indirectly prepare for motherhood by a sound physical, mental and moral education. . . .

Elizabeth Chesser, *Woman, Marriage and Motherhood*, 1913, pp. 230–3.

155. Education for Continence, Modesty and Discretion (1915)

It may be conceded that a man's passions are stronger than a woman's, but it is an open question whether this additional strength of passion is not the result of education. Girls are taught from childhood that any exhibition of sexual feeling is un-womanly and intolerable; they also learn from an early age that if a woman makes a mistake it is upon her and upon her alone that social punishment will descend; consequently for generations, ever since the civilisation of society, women have perforce been habitually continent, and more than continent—modest and discreet.

Society has condoned incontinence in men, but has visited incontinence in women with severe condemnation. The time, however, has now come in which a higher morality and a better instructed regard for the true interests of the race have led to the demand that a man's life should be under as strict discipline as is that of a woman. If this demand is to be made and carried into effect, mothers will have to begin to teach their little boys self-control just in the same way as they have always taught it to their little girls. Not only must impurity and absolute wrongdoing be checked, but the lesson of self-control and self-reverence must be taught to all children alike....

Mary Scharlieb, *The Seven Ages of Woman*, 1915, pp. 75–6.

4.2 Puberty and the Passions

156. The Natural Impulse of Puberty

Girls of this age [at puberty] have much need of surveillance. For then in particular they feel a natural impulse to make usage of the sexual faculties that are developing in them; so that unless they guard against any further impulse beyond that inevitable one which their bodily development of itself supplies, even in the case of those who abstain altogether from passionate indulgence, they contract habits which are apt to continue into later life. For girls who give way to wantonness grow more and more wanton; and the same is true of boys, unless they be safeguarded from one temptation and another; for the passages become dilated and set up a local flux or running, and besides this the recollection of pleasure associated with former indulgence creates a longing for its repetition....

Aristotle, *History of Animals*, 581a, *The Works of Aristotle*, ed. J.A. Smith and W.D. Ross, Vol. 4, Book VII. 1, Oxford 1910.

157. Puberty and the Passion of Physical Love (1831)

At the epoch of puberty, in both sexes, a lively sensation, irresistible, and hitherto unknown, breaks forth; leads to a union of the sexes, and inclines them to copulation. This sensation has hitherto been attributed to the genital organs, until Gall has made it one of the faculties of the soul, and asserts it is placed in the cerebellum, as old men and very young boys have sexual desire. At this time man is endowed with more principles of life than are necessary for his body; and this superabundance is intended for the perpetuation of his species....

The sensation of desire in females, causes a congestion in all the erectile parts of the vulva and vagina, the approach of the other sex, and particularly the introduction of the penis, throws her into a voluptuous orgasm, which sometimes causes cramp or convulsions, and terminates by a secretion, more or less considerable, from the mucous membrane of the vagina, which is succeeded by a total prostration that is far from being void of pleasure....

In order to have coition effectual, there is a mutual relation necessary—a union in mind and pleasurable enjoyment as well as in body, and unless this union of love be mutual, conception will seldom, if ever happen; for it has been long observed, that frigidity and reserve in either party will defeat procreation—a want of love being a certain cause of barrenness....

All healthy persons, at the time of puberty, must certainly feel the passion of physical love. It is a part of their health, and as natural a consequence as hunger or thirst. It is the most delightful of all the passions, and makes the greater part of human happiness....

Dr Michael Ryan, *A Manual of Midwifery*, 3rd. edn., 1831, pp. 50–2, 58, 60.

158. Equality of the Passions (1838)

It is a barbarous custom that forbids the maid to make advances in love, or that confines these advances to the eye, the fingers, the gesture, the motion, the manner. It is equally absurd and ridiculous. Why should not the female state her passion to the male, as well as the male to the female?... Equality and the right to make advances, in all the affairs of genuine love, are claimed for the female. The hypocrisy, the cruelty, that would stifle or disguise a passion, whether in the male or in the female, is wicked, and should be exposed, reprobated, and detested....

The desire for this [sexual] intercourse is a principle which must always exist, and will always seek to be gratified.... No reasoning, no caution, no consequence, will operate against it [the passion for intercourse] ... the idea, that the species of chastity which consists of a constrained absence from sexual commerce is a virtue, whatever may be the evils which follow it, and that the indulgence of choice in all cases is a vice, is absurd. ...

Richard Carlile, *Every Woman's Book or What is Love?*, 1838, pp. 8, 26-7, 34.

159. Limited or Absent Sexual Feeling in the Female (1865)

... I should say that the majority of women (happily for them) are not very much troubled with sexual feeling of any kind. What men are habitually, women are only exceptionally ... [sexual feeling in the female] requires positive and considerable excitement to be roused at all; and even if roused (which in many instances it never can be) is very moderate compared with that of the male. ...

There are many females who never feel any sexual excitement whatever. Others, again, immediately after each period, do become, to a limited degree, capable of experiencing it; but this capacity is often temporary, and will cease entirely till the next menstrual period. The best mothers, wives, and managers of households, know little or nothing of sexual indulgences. Love of home, children, and domestic duties are the only passions they feel.

As a general rule, a modest woman seldom desires any sexual gratification for herself. She submits to her husband, but only to please him; and, but for the desire of maternity, would far rather be relieved from his attentions. No nervous or feeble young man need, therefore, be deterred from marriage by any exaggerated notion of the duties required from him. The married woman has no wish to be treated on the footing of a mistress. ...

W. Acton, *The functions and disorders of the reproductive organs*, 4th. edn., 1865, pp. 112-3.

160. The Passion of Lust in the Female (1888)

The passion of lust is the most important of all others, especially in the female sex. The study of anatomy, physiology, and natural philosophy, teaches us that the genital organs are, so to speak, the physical centre of the female organism, the metropolis of her whole economy. Rebellion in the metropolis then spreads injury throughout everywhere else. How serious, therefore, becomes the rebellion of lustful passions. The steam engine is a useful and valuable means of conveyance when kept well in hand by proper control; let the control be lost however, and you send forth a veritable demon of destruction....

Priscilla Barker, *The Secret Book...for women and young girls*, 1888, p. 13.

161. Sexual Abstinence before Marriage (1913)

Social reformers, parents, clergy, employers, must be alive to the need of influencing young people on the lines of promoting a higher moral tone in their relationship with each other and their regard for sex questions. It is for fathers and mothers together to instil the sense of moral responsibility into the young generation, to reckon with the erotic curiosity which may have disastrous effects if inculcation of self-control is absent. Mothers, equally with fathers, should be alive to the danger of 'quack' literature, leaflets and pamphlets which, whilst not legally coming into the category of the obscene, are yet full of dangerous suggestions, clothed in insincere 'moral' language, which tend to alarm boys regarding innocent physiological functions and to stimulate sex perversions.

Whatever medical teaching may have been in the past, physiologists of the newer school consider that sexual abstinence until maturity in both sexes is a gain to the organism. Men have handed down from generation to generation the teaching that sexual lapses are harmless, necessary, even beneficial. The best modern medical teaching is entirely opposed to this idea ... Sir James Paget emphatically declared, in a lecture to medical students, that 'chastity does not harm body or mind, its discipline is excellent, marriage can safely be waited for.'. . .

We must reckon with the natural desire of the boy and girl for amusement and recreation. Whilst excess of pleasure and excitement is not desirable, young people must have an outlet for natural energy as well as interesting occupation to satisfy the restlessness and desire for change associated with adolescence. Properly supervised clubs for girls [e.g. the Girl Guide movement] and boys should be established in every town. In seeking to protect girls, let us not forget the needs also of the boy. If we are to cure the social evil, we must begin with the boy. Here again we have this question associated with the mother as the educator and nurturer of the child. Let the ideal of a chaste fatherhood be held before the new generation of boys. The ideal is harder for the boy than for the girl, but yet not impossible, and this must be recognised by the mother in training her sons and her daughters. . . .

Elizabeth Chesser, *Woman, Marriage and Motherhood*, 1913, pp. 218–9, 221.

4.3 'The Secret Sin of Self-abuse'

162. The Disease of Secret, Evil Habits (1873)

What shall a mother say to a daughter whom she suspects of being addicted to secret evil habits? Nothing, until she is certain beyond mistake; for it would be the height of cruelty to wound the feelings of an innocent girl by hinting at any doubt of her guiltlessness in this respect. But when there is no longer room for doubt, the mother must do more than give general instruction and exert watchfulness, though neither of these should be omitted. . . .

She [a daughter] must be shown how a persistence in secret vice will undermine her health, prostrate her nervous system, weaken her mental powers and degrade her morally. She must be told that, to a certain degree, it will render her unfit to fulfill the functions of her sex, to which fulfillment, in the course of nature, she will probably be called. She must be reminded that her own feelings will be, should she ever become the wife of an honorable and virtuous man, in remembering that there is one act or series of acts in her life which she can never confess to him except with burning shame. Her full confidence must be invited and secured, and the mother must offer to be her aid in the correction of her evil habit. It should seem to be regarded more as a disease than as a crime. If all efforts fail in effecting a cure, then, still in the spirit of kindness and pity, the girl should be told that a physician will have to be consulted to devise a means of cure. If she have any shame left, this threat, offered not as a threat, however, ought to be sufficient. . . .

Sedentary employments should be abandoned as much as possible, and active labor substituted in their stead. The girl should be forbidden all reading of an imaginative character. She should be left alone as little as possible during the day, and some responsible person should sleep with her at night. If with all these cautions the habit seems uncontrollable, medical advice should be sought. It may be possible that there is abnormal development of the generative organs which requires medical or surgical treatment. If so serious measures as these do not seem necessary, an application of caustic might be made to the affected parts, which would effectually prevent their being touched....

Mrs E.B. Duffey, *What Women Should Know*, 1873, pp. 53–5.

163. Physical Delinquency and the Weak Female Sexual Instinct (1877)

No reference to this organ [the clitoris] would be complete without a discussion of the practice of masturbation, of which it is the chief seat. This painful subject is usually involved in such mystery, and spoken of so seldom and so incompletely by medical authorities, that it is by no means easy to determine to what extent it prevails, how to discriminate its victims, or how to suggest a remedy. When discovered in a school or in a family, it strikes everybody with such horror that it is at once concealed and hushed up, instead of being treated, as it always ought to be, as a disease; and the unfortunate children who are discovered in the practice are regarded by their discoverers as having sunk to the lowest moral depths. It is a sad misfortune that all sexual questions are so completely hidden from children at puberty that they are driven to make discoveries for themselves, often with disastrous results.... The female organism has always been merely the vehicle for the maturation of the ovum, and for the reception of the fertilizing influence of the male; being, in fact, what we may call the passive factor in the reproductive act. For her part of the process, then, only enough of sexual passion or instinct is required to indicate to the male the stage at which his share may be effectually performed ... in the human race the sexual instinct is very powerful in man and comparatively weak in woman ... [thus] it is not surprising that masturbation is very common amongst boys, and comparatively rare amongst girls ... and that it is generally the result of direct contamination....

The most pernicious effects are met with when the

contamination reaches a congregation of young women, as in a girls' school. I have been consulted concerning endemics of this kind in both boys' and girls' schools, and have always found the chief difficulty to be that of persuading those having charge of the schools that the practice was a physical delinquency rather than a moral evil; and that the best remedy was not to tell the poor children that they were damning their souls, but to tell them that they might seriously hurt their bodies, and to explain to them the nature and purport of the functions they were abusing. In one instance, the head of a very large girls' school took my advice on this subject with the best results.

The evil effects of masturbation have been greatly overrated, thanks to a reticence on the part of those who know all about it, and this has permitted a disagreeable subject to fall into the hands of those who live by trading on the ignorance and misfortunes of their fellow-beings. In the case of men, it may and often does result in serious mischief, especially to those of weakly constitution. In women, I believe it is not often carried to such an extreme as to do any harm, though I have met with cases where serious injury has resulted; and I am quite certain that girls may almost always be induced to give the practice up when a reasonable explanation is afforded to them of the risks attached to it. . . .

In young children, masturbation is often associated with defective mental development, and it should always be a ground for placing them under special care. . . I think it possible that in some inveterate cases clitoridectomy might be beneficial, but I have never tried it. . . .

Robert L. Tait, *Diseases of Women*, 1877, pp. 48–52.

164. Symptoms of Imprudent Habits (1886)

[Dr C.H.F. Routh]
It may be stated and admitted as a fact beyond doubt that this condition [i.e. the imprudent habit of masturbation] cannot always be made out in very young women; but past the age of 26, if the habit has been continued for a long period of years, the

symptoms or the signs of this habit will be very clear. In the first place we notice that the internal labia are extremely developed, projecting considerably beyond the external. Sometimes one internal labium projects extremely, generally of the side to which they are handed—i.e. the left in left-handed persons and the right in right-handed persons—and I have known a labium so long as to hang like the tongue of some of those bulldogs where it is considered a sign of good breed.... The clitoris is generally swollen and enlarged, or hard and small, and it cannot be pressed upon without making the woman jump, which is a symptom of its extreme sensibility...while the hairs for the most part have lost their curly character....

Dr. FENTON JONES considered that it was a matter open to discussion as to whether long pendulous labia minora were not more often the cause rather than the effect of masturbation in the female. By harbouring sebaceous secretions undoubtedly the natural local sensitiveness of the parts was increased, and a constant irritation maintained, which in the neurotic subject frequently led to the thoughts and imagination being diverted into a prurient channel.

In cases where both nymphae were equally large and pendulous it would be very unfair to set down a woman as a victim of this unfortunate practice. On the other hand, if one labium minus was largely developed and the other not, the inference became very strong that the patient had given way to the habit.

Dr. Fenton Jones had had several ladies under his care who had frankly confessed to him that they had contracted the habit and indulged in it frequently, yet on inspection it turned out that there was no hypertrophy of nymphae, either one or both, nor was there any alteration of the appearance of the clitoris.

[Dr Bantock]

It was very much to be deplored that the foundation of this habit [of masturbation] was so often laid in our private schools. While it was very difficult to declare from external local signs that at an early age, say under 20, a given patient was addicted to this habit, it was usually quite easy at a more advanced age....

Dr C. H. F. Routh, 'On the Etiology and Diagnosis, considered specially from a Medico-legal Point of View, of those Cases of

Nymphomania which lead Women to make False Charges against their Medical Attendants', and discussion, *The British Gynaecological Journal*, Vol. 2 (1886–7), pp. 493–4, 503, 506.

165. The Secret Sin of Self-abuse (1888)

... this specific sin of Self-abuse is related to a whole set of sinful corruptions, impurity of thought and imagination leading the way into the beastial realm of impure literature, art, and the whole science of sin. Impure literature is eagerly, ravenously seized, secreted, revelled in. Impure pictures are gloated over in private and sought after in public. Thus Satan undermines the citadel of womanhood; working insidiously in secret; but none the less bringing about destruction. He only waits till the undermining is complete, to bring along the battering ram and have the building levelled with the dust....

I tell you, in plain woman's words, your body cannot be abused without injury to the life forces, which will bring in its train all kinds of complaints and diseases. Even now, I have in my mind's eye a young woman who is thought to be in consumption, whilst all the time it is the secret sin of Self-abuse that is sapping the vital strength and bodily vigour.... The face loses its colour, and the eye grows dull, heavy, and weak, the hands feel soft and clammy, and often the smell of the feet is unbearable. Inwardly the ravages are even more serious, nervous exhaustion and hysteria, loss of energy, memory, &c. These are only the heralds of more terrible things to come, such as epilepsy, insanity, and a mighty host of innumerable evils, all of them paving the way too sadly, and too surely, to a premature grave. I am not exaggerating, girls, for there is no habit which is so exhausting, or so shamefully absorbing as Self-abuse. Neither is there any gratification which is so shortlived and costly, both as regards the outlay of body and mind.

Case 1.—Three years ago I engaged a servant by letters. The first moment I looked at her, I felt that I had before me a fearful victim to Self-abuse. The next morning when I came down from my room, I expected to find things nice and tidy, but to my utter astonishment she told me that 'she could never work until she had had her breakfast.' What was the cause of this? The answer is that in secret she weakened all her vital forces by abusing her body, and until she had partaken of food, she was utterly useless, and run down. When I found that such were her habits, I felt that she was too dangerous an element among my family of boys. Upon enquiry I found that her friends were all tired of her, and eventually she had to go into a home, where her habits could be looked after.

Case II.—Another victim came under my notice whose infatuating habit betrayed itself in sweaty, clammy hands, stinking feet, and mouth always full of saliva. I felt compelled to question her, for her own sake, and she confessed that as a child living in the quiet country, her chief delight was to go and sit up in trees for hours to gratify her sinful pleasure, under the pretence of cracking nuts. . . .

Only a few weeks ago, a married woman told me that she had carried on the practice for years, not knowing that the thing was sinful. She was then a confirmed sufferer from hysteria and hallucinations of the brain. Her husband told me that he feared from her strange actions at times that she was going out of her mind. I feel bound to say here and now, that there are many occult and seemingly unexplainable cases of mental and moral aberration, which are undoubtedly, attributable more or less to the baneful effects of the continuance of this secret habit, or excess of venery. . . .

—*Shun Bad Books and Bad Pictures.* . . . Never read a questionable poet; some of the cleverest poets have written things so vile that a devil might blush at them. Never read a questionable author of any kind, and especially eschew sensational novels which open the heart to licentiousness. Never look a second time at a picture or a statue which excites lustful feelings.

—*Shun all Questionable Places of Amusement, such as Theatres, Music Halls, &c.* They are dens of impurity behind the scenes, and the majority of plays tend, like sensational novels, to turn young minds in wrong directions. . . .

Priscilla Barker, *The Secret Book. . .for women and young girls*, 1888, pp. 7–9, 12–13, 26.

166. Vice, Insanity and Ovariotomy (1890)

[Discussions of the British Gynaecological Society, 8, 22 October 1890].

Referring to masturbation, he [Dr. Savage] raised the question as to whether this was a symptom or a cause of the disease [of insanity]. One met with young persons in whom masturbation developed on the establishment of menstruation as an untaught vice, and in a certain proportion of the cases insanity occurs through or with excessive masturbation. It was in this class of cases that the question arose as to whether it was justifiable to remove the ovaries. He suggested that the matter was one well worthy of consideration at the hands of the Society. So far as operative measures went, he said he had little personal experience. There certainly were cases in which the existence of insanity might possibly be referred to some disorder of the uterus or ovaries, and he insisted upon the diagnostic value of hallucinations of the sense of smell as an indication of the existence of troubles of the reproductive organs. He had remarked the liability to hallucinations of the smell in confirmed masturbators of both sexes. In one case at Bethlem Hospital in which there was ovarian disease this symptom was present to a marked degree. The ovaries were removed, but though the patient ceased to be subject to the hallucinations she remained insane....

He [Dr. Heywood Smith] was convinced that masturbation was far more common in females than was supposed, and with regard to ovariotomy—in spite of what had been said by a well-known ovariotomist at another Society—he had not found the removal of the ovaries to have any effect in lessening the sexual appetite. No operation had so marked a beneficial effect in these cases as clitoridectomy. When this operation failed it was probably because it had not been done as freely as had been recommended....

'Discussion on Sexual Function and Insanity', *The British Gynaecological Journal*, Vol. 6 (1890–1), pp. 407–8, 421.

167. The Grave Dangers of an Evil Habit (1902)

The dangerous habit of voluntarily produced excitement, to which alone the term 'masturbation' is due, may be formed by both the male and the female, and it is found even in the child as well as the adult.

In the child, however (it being immature in body), it is the dependencies of the brain, the nervous system, which come more exclusively into play in this evil habit. . . . This mental suggestion may be produced by the irritation of worms, by some local eruption, by the wickedness of the nurse, occasionally by malformation or unnatural development of the parts themselves. There is grave reason also for believing that transmitted tendency to sensuality may blight the innocent offspring. . . .

My attention was painfully drawn to the dangers of self-abuse more than forty years ago by an agonized letter received from an intelligent and pious lady, dying from the effects of this inveterate habit. She had been a teacher in a Sunday-school and the delight of a refined and intelligent circle of friends. But this habit, begun in childhood in ignorance of any moral or physical wrong which might result to her nature, had become so rooted that her brain was giving way under the effects of nervous derangement thus produced, whilst her will had lost the power of self-control.

It will thus be seen that there are two grave dangers attending the practice of masturbation. The first evil is the effect upon the mind through the brain and nervous system from evil communications or evil literature. The mind is thus prematurely awakened to take in and dwell upon a series of impressions which awaken precocious sexual instinct. This precocity gives an undue and even dominating power to this instinct over the other human faculties. . . .

The other grave danger incurred by the practice of masturbation is the risk of its becoming an overmastering habit, from the ease with which it can be indulged; also from the insidious and increasing power of the temptation when yielded to, and from its association with the times when the individual is alone, and particularly the quiet hours of the night.

In the adult who yields to solitary vice, Nature's marked distinction between the beneficent effect of spontaneous healthy relief and the injurious action of self-induced irritation is destroyed. Individual self-control, the highest distinctive mark of the human being, is abandoned. In this way the evil habit may become a real obsession, leading to destruction of mental and physical health, to insanity, or to suicide....

Elizabeth Blackwell, *Essays in Medical Sociology*, 1902, Vol. 1, pp. 36–7, 42–3.

168. Auto-erotism and its Danger Zones in Women (1909)

Great care must be taken not to direct the attention of the [adolescent] girl to her sexual organs, nor to sexual things. It is for this reason that an active life out of doors with many varied interests outside of herself should be encouraged. Her reading must be carefully guided. Introspective habits should be discouraged, and an objective life cultivated....

A strong instinct of repugnance impels us to gloss over this section [i.e. masturbation in women] of preventive gynecology, and to revolt when sacrilegious hands are laid on our ideal of purity. But the family practitioner is under obligation to see that the mother warns and watches her growing girl; he may no longer ignore the prevalence of the danger; he must recognize the marks of the yielding to this temptation in time to help; and he cannot avoid some study of auto-erotism in women if he would give effective counsel at critical periods....

... the secretiveness of the girl lessens the chances of detection or confession of a solitary indulgence that is self-taught. Among the crowded poor and the ignorant foreign population evil communications are facile. But in any individual, in adolescence, the soil is fertile, with its emotional and affectional fervors and introspective intensities.... Add to the monthly rush of blood to the genitals, the friction of the napkin, the suggestiveness of the hot-water bag, the lying awake in day dreams in bed the first day of the period, and we may well fear such arousing at some time during the seventy periodical opportunities between puberty and nubility.

The danger zones are these: Infancy; puberty and the years immediately following; school and factory life; engagement; marital maladjustment; widowhood; the pre-climacteric sexual activity; and any long period of nervous intensity or breakdown. Rare before puberty, the usual time of beginning is just afterward, and the average time of excess is within the next four years.

GENERAL CAUSES.—Parents who are intemperate, whether through weakness of will or excess of passion, transmit such tendencies. Among neurasthenics more than half have been masturbators at some time, and the most pronounced cases are very generally found among them. The two great main causes, however, are: defective education, and its result, defective self-control. Ignorance of the simplest sex knowledge, infirmity of body, absence of absorbing and healthful occupation, insufficient out-door exercise, lack of a constant stream of elevating influences and stimuli—all these favor the habit, particularly where, as in certain natures, there is capacity for an overplus of sexual passion. Among the most potent factors are undoubtedly these three: Emotional excesses, when feeling fails to be translated into action, whether it be roused to frequent intensity by novel, or theatre, or sermon; self-indulgences, such as late rising, and all idleness, sulky reticence, and hysterical outbreaks; and intimacies of the person, whether the liberties be with other girls, or with boys and men.

PREVALENCE.—We have no means of estimating the frequency either of minor degrees of self-abuse or its occurrence among healthy individuals. . . . For women of loose life and certain peasants there are figures showing a very frequent occurrence. Among women of a good class there are some indications that it is by no means uncommon, as for instance, where one thousand consecutive gynecological cases showed well-marked vulvar hypertrophies in over one-third. By one-third of this third, full admission was made, so that it is fair to attribute the findings in the remainder to the same cause, especially as categorical denial was forthcoming in only one in fifty. . . . Tell-tale hypertrophy of longitudinal folds and the frequent pigmentation often render the habit easy to recognize in an early stage.

After puberty the habit may be mental, vulvar, vaginal, urethral, mammary, or any combination of these. The fifth is presumably rare, but the occasional hypertrophies and pigmentations about the nipple point to breast congestion as a feature of some cases. The psychic form of solitary sexual indulgence is most difficult of all to study or describe, its shadings are so various, its ignorances of actuality so colossal. Vaginal masturbation is rare because of the fear of harming the hymen and thus destroying virginity...the extent of the need of watchfulness can never be grasped unless it is known that when self-abuse has reached its keenest pitch in certain individuals the effective pressures or frictions are so simple that a girl can reach the climax in bed with her mother without suspicion. A roll of bedclothes or nightdress held between the upper thighs, or, prone, beneath the vulva; the heel, brought up against the pudenda; vulvar contacts with the corner of a piece of furniture or the key in a drawer—any one of these may constitute an individual process. The vaginal douche tube and hot water excite very few women, and the bicycle saddle is to be exonerated; the sewing machine in large shops has, however, been accused of fostering the habit....

Contrary to the usual belief, the day is as much to be feared as the night...it must never be forgotten that women bear sexual excesses better than men—better, that is to say, physically; worse morally. With some the solitary orgasm is said to be no more fatiguing than the normal relation, with others it is infinitely more so....

EFFECTS.—The physical results of self-abuse, in all but the extreme cases, seem to be surprisingly small. Endometritis, vaginal catarrh, and trigonitis result from long indulgence. Neurasthenia is probably coincidence rather than consequence. Protracted masturbation, not associated with sexual images, tends to apathy or aversion toward the sex-act, but the contrary is true where there is longing for normal gratification. In the excessive forms of the vice, as with relaxed pelvic floors, the capacity for pleasure in coitus is lost. If the physical evils are not many, the moral penalties, on the contrary, are disproportionately great. The undermining of self-respect, the tortures and the shame react on the general health surely and frequently and deeply. But there is no diagnostic behavior or appearance...in general it can, in my view, be safely said that no well-marked area of corrugation about the female genitals is produced in any way but by pressures....

The physician is the moral sanitarium directly responsible [for preventive treatment]. It is for him to urge on the reserved woman what she will call the most difficult task of her life. Her telling is to be matter of fact, yet reverent; neither vague and sublimated, nor specific and suggestive; not too casual, yet not so freighted with import and interest as to arouse curiosity and invite experiment....

CURATIVE TREATMENT.—Confession, however fragmentary, is a long first step toward recovery. 'Remorse for sexual sin is still the religious teacher's great opportunity.' The doctor may 'show great things and difficult,' urge the immediate action that will break loose from the particular vicious association, start work to uplift others, and secure a promise to report. These, with strong mental suggestion of control, will go far.... Our motto should be, 'To replace is to conquer.' The taking up of an outdoor hobby, like a nature study, can bring about that muscular fatigue which is found to be the best single remedy for the male. Swimming, hydrotherapy, gymnastic games, skating, tennis, golf, wheeling and horseback—all are good, but hard to get in cities. Forced nutrition is usually needed, and a general upbuilding. Tea, coffee, and alcohol are cut off. A hard bed with minimum covering in a cool room; immediate evacuation of the bladder when first conscious, and prompt rising, followed by the cold spray or cold spinal douche, are desirable. Bromides help over crises, whatever the period of the month or the day temptation comes, and valerianates spread this quiescence further, where bromides would disturb.... In conclusion it may be said that whatever the divergence of opinion concerning danger or diagnosis, prevalence or effects, we can agree that there is on us the troublous duty of moral prophylaxis, the need of sane instruction of the teachers of children, formulation and comprehension of what the danger signals are, and the mastery of means that will strengthen the body and energize the will. Inasmuch as we do it not—

Dr Howard A. Kelly, *Medical Gynecology*, 1909, pp. 72, 291–8.

169. The Erotic Girl and Nervous Woman (1913)

Every nervous ill and weakness is accentuated by masturbation. The frequent and unnatural excitation of the sexual organs reacts on the sexual centre, and morbid imaginative impulses are excited with consequent fits of mental depression and sense of fatigue—and the erotic girl merges into neurasthenic womanhood. All such influences are accentuated previous to and at the time of the menstrual epoch, and are still more pronounced if there be dysmenorrhoea with ovarian crises of pain. On the one hand, there may be scanty flow; or menorrhagia and weakening loss on the other....

Dr H. MacNaughton-Jones, 'The Relation of Puberty and the Menopause to Neurasthenia', *The Lancet*, 29 March 1913, p. 880.

4.4 Clitoridectomy: The Baker Brown Controversy

170. Surgery and the Female Sex (1854)

There is no branch of surgery more open to improvement than that which relates to those accidents and diseases incident to the female sex, which admit of no relief except from the hand of the surgeon....

Isaac Baker Brown, *On Some Diseases admitting of Surgical Treatment*, 1854, Preface.

171. Baker Brown (1866)

The class of diseases on which I shall dwell are those depending on (or arising from) a loss of nerve tone, caused by continual abnormal irritation of a nerve centre....

Long and frequent observation convinced me that a large number of affections peculiar to females, depended on loss of nerve power, and that this was produced by peripheral irritation, arising originally in some branches of the pudic nerve, more particularly the incident nerve supplying the clitoris, and sometimes the small branches which supply the vagina, perinaeum, and anus....

... objections have been advanced against the morality of the operation [clitoridectomy], and I am here at a loss how to give an answer, for I can hardly conceive how such a question can be raised against a method of treatment which has for its object the cure of a disease, that is rapidly tending to lower the moral tone, and which treatment is dictated by the loftiest and most moral considerations. I may here observe, that before commencing treatment, I have always made a point of having my diagnosis confirmed by the patient or her friends ... I never operate or sanction operation on any patient under ten years of age, which is the earliest date of puberty....

The patient having been placed *completely* under the influence of chloroform, the clitoris is freely excised either by scissors or knife—I always prefer the scissors. The wound is then firmly plugged with graduated compresses of lint, and a pad, well secured by a T bandage.... A month is generally required for perfect healing of the wound, at the end of which time it is difficult for the uninformed, or non-medical, to discover any trace of an operation....

I. Baker Brown, *On the Curability of certain forms of Insanity, Epilepsy, Catalepsy, and Hysteria in Females*, 1866, pp. 3,7,12, 16–18.

172. Caustics or Clitoridectomy for Female 'Epilepsy'? (1866)

Dr. Bantock is pleased to ask my opinion relative to the differences between extirpation of the clitoris and the application of caustics [in the treatment of epilepsy].

In answer to that I would say that, setting aside my own impression that we have scarcely more right to remove a woman's clitoris than we have to deprive a man of his penis, and in spite of Dr. Bantock's superior judgement and great experience in these matters, it is my firm belief that the latter proceeding—viz., the application of caustics—is much more desirable, because the effect of the caustic can be kept up for as long a period as the medical attendant pleases, and may, if necessary, be re-applied; whereas, with regard to extirpation, directly the part is healed peripheral irritation may be had recourse to again over the remaining branches of the pudic nerve. And certainly those who resort to clitoridectomy are very much afraid of this, or why should they insist on long-continued watching after it? Then again, it must strike any one who gives the subject a moment's consideration that when it is necessary for the success of an operation that careful and unceasing observation of the patient should be kept up for six or even twelve months afterwards, it is very questionable whether the watching minus the operation would not succeed equally well.

There are few, if any, diseases to the cure of which a medical man has so much difficulty in certifying as epilepsy, as it is a well-known fact that any new treatment is generally followed by marked though temporary improvement; and therefore statistics are of very little use until a long period has passed after the apparent success. I am sorry that females have not as much knowledge of the clitoris as we have, for if that were the case I am sure there are very few who would consent to part with it, and when questioned about it afterwards say, 'Oh, I have only had a little knot removed.' Verily they know not the nature of that little 'knot'....

Harry Gage Moore, L.R.C.P., 'Clitoridectomy: To the Editor of THE LANCET.', *The Lancet*, 23 June 1866, p. 699.

173. Clitoridectomy as a Cure for Sterility? (1866)

SIR,—Mr. Gage Moore states it as his '*impression* that we have scarcely more right to remove a woman's clitoris than to deprive a man of his penis.' Is Mr. Moore really serious? If so, he has no hesitation in opposing his *impressions* to the facts which have already been recorded by Mr. Baker Brown in his recent work.... The justification of any operation is the result; and seeing that it has been indisputably proved that *sterility* has been cured by *this* operation, surely I need not argue the question of 'right'.

But I ask Mr. Moore whether he means to imply that the excision of the clitoris is equivalent to amputation of the penis? If he does I shall not argue against the physiological error implied in such supposed analogy, but beg to refer him to his text books.

Mr. Moore further states that it is his 'firm belief' that 'the application of caustics is much more desirable.' It is enough to say in reply that even extirpation is not sufficient in some cases; that in these caustics are as worthless as water; and that, however *firm*

Mr. Moore's *belief* may be, it cannot for a moment hold its ground against the *facts* which experience has brought forth.

So long as Mr. Moore will argue from *impressions* and *beliefs*, and will refuse to test the matter and distrust the good faith of other workers, so long may fruitless discussion be kept up....

Geo. Granville Bantock, 'Clitoridectomy. To the Editor of THE LANCET.', *The Lancet*, 14 July 1866, p. 51.

174. Tacit Approval for Mr. Baker Brown's Operations? (1866)

SIR,—During a short stay in London early in March last, I availed myself of the opportunity of being present at the [London] Surgical Home to witness some of the operations (for which that establishment has a reputation) performed by Mr. Baker Brown. Amongst others were one or two for the removal of the clitoris as a means of cure for certain kinds of epilepsy. Although very dexterously performed, I confess the operation appeared to me at the time something very unusual, inasmuch as there was no positive local disease, but a healthy organ made the subject of an unnatural use, and thereby, according to Mr. Brown's view, a cause of disordered nervous action. And this impression was not much affected by Mr. Brown's statement, 'that although the wound produced by the operation appeared large, yet its healing was so beautifully accomplished as almost to defy detection.' But when, in addition, he stated that he had the approval of Dr. Brown-Séquard and other eminent men for this mode of treating such epileptic attacks; and, further, that any or all of the gentlemen then assembled (numbering, I should say, forty or fifty middle-aged practitioners) were quite at liberty to watch his cases and inquire for themselves, I came to the conclusion that this operation must have some curative power. I particularly observed the fossa on the side of the perineum, which Mr. Brown describes as so characteristic of this kind of masturbation, and caused by the pressure of one of the fingers.

I do not take upon myself to say whether or not the operation is a justifiable one, but I am certain, from Mr. Brown's invitation to the medical men present to examine for themselves, and his own pursuit of the practice, that he has strong reasons for believing the operation to be satisfactory...I must confess surprise at the reticence of the London practitioners, if, after the invitations given to them by Mr. Brown to witness his operations and the results, they have done so, and not expressed their opinions, and more especially so if those opinions have been unfavourable to the operation. I, as a distant practitioner [from Blackpool], regard the absence of controversy on their part in our journals as a tacit approval of the operation. As a stranger to Mr. Baker Brown, I was very much pleased with his kindness and courtesy of manner, his frankness and candour in replying to any questions raised, and—last, though not least—with his coolness and dexterity as an operator. In conclusion, I take the liberty of stating, from personal experience, that Mr. Brown and the resident medical officer afford every facility to medical men for investigating these cases.

John Pickop, M.R.C.S.E., 'Clitoridectomy. To the Editor of THE LANCET', *The Lancet*, 14 July 1866, pp. 51–2.

175. 'This Very Questionable Operation' (1866)

SIR,—Whether excision of the clitoris is useful or admissible in the treatment of epilepsy, is a question of such vital importance to the female portion of our community that it is imperative on every member of the profession to come forward and give his experience and opinion on the subject without fear or partiality.

The causes of epilepsy are various: their name is legion. Masturbation may be one of these; but he who looks upon this vice as a leading cause takes, I think, a very contracted view of the subject. Masturbation is generally considered a prevalent vice amongst the young of both sexes; and the epileptic, often, perhaps generally, of weakened intellect, is more likely to be guilty of this and other excesses than the healthy. But who is to decide in what relation the disease and the vice stand to each other as cause and effect, supposing masturbation to have preceded the epilepsy? The thing is, I believe, impossible, and the *post hoc ergo propter hoc* argument is not sufficient when the existence of a clitoris is at stake. In confirmation of my view take the following case:—

A young lady, now aged sixteen, became afflicted with epilepsy at, I think, seven years of age. She was then placed under the care of one of our leading physicians, who advised that she should be watched, and it was found that even at that early age she was in the habit of practising masturbation. After years of suffering, time or treatment brought a respite. At fifteen, when she first menstruated, the fits returned, and a few months ago Mr. Baker Brown was consulted, and recommended an operation. This was deferred, and in the meantime my opinion was asked by a friend of the family. I advised that no operation should be permitted. The parents, however, wavering, as well they might, between two such opposite opinions, again consulted the family physician, and he proposed that the operation should be performed under his own supervision. This was done (not by Mr. Brown), and the fits became *for a few weeks less numerous*, as they will do under any new treatment. Previous to the operation they were ten per week. *Now they are the same.*

But in Mr. Moore's patient, Mr. Brown and Dr. Bantock assert that the disease was 'hysterical mania'. This fact, however, is clear: *whatever the disease, the operation was useless.*

But, Sir, I ask why have recourse to this very questionable operation whilst we possess a drug of such undoubted efficacy in epilepsy as the bromide of potassium? Given in doses of not less than ten grains, and continued for months or years after the fits have disappeared, having recourse to it again and again should threatening symptoms recur, the epileptic may cease to be an epileptic so far as the fits are concerned.

Dr R. S. Sisson, 'Clitoridectomy. To the Editor of THE LANCET.', *The Lancet*, 28 July 1866, p. 114.

176. Baker Brown Defends Clitoridectomy (1866)

SIR,—I trust I may now claim sufficient space in your columns to reply to the several objections which have been urged against excision of the clitoris, both in THE LANCET and elsewhere.

First of all, with a forgetfulness of physiology scarcely credible in these days, the opponents of the operation have declared that it 'unsexes a woman'. The objection is as old as the operation itself.... Putting aside all theory, the fact that several of my patients have become pregnant after the operation, is a complete reply to this objection.... In the face of the most indisputable evidence that the clitoris is *not* an *essential* part of the generative system, the expression 'mutilation of the person,' so freely employed, might be passed over as possessing no meaning other than that in which it would be applicable to numerous recognised surgical proceedings....

I am not ignorant of the value of rousing the patient to efforts of self-control [in cases of masturbation]. Indeed I have seen many recoveries by the patient's own firm will; but the cases in which moral effort suffices are not those in which I have recourse to the operation.

A still more visionary objection has been propounded in the theory that a recognition of the frequency of self-abuse might lead to the suggesting of it to the pure-minded. Such a notion would only be entertained by those who could applaud the idea of 'an experimental surgery which delights to *crawl* about the female pudendum' and by those who were determined to shirk the question as one for impartial and scientific investigation. These may fitly consort with the bigots who refuse the boon of chloroform in labour, on the ground that Providence intended women to bring forth in sorrow.... In that numerous class of cases comprised under the term hysteria and I may add, spinal irritation, the operation is almost invariably successful, while the bromide of potassium or ammonium seldom affords the slightest relief....

It has come to my knowledge that there are cases under the care of some of my most strenuous opponents in which masturbation is the cause of disease, rendering the patient bed-ridden and life a burden, without the slightest prospect of relief from the *skilful moral* treatment of those very practitioners; and, for my part, I fail to appreciate the refinement or sentimentalism which refuses to adopt a curative method because it shocks the delicate feelings of one who does not object to go on treating year after year, in its development, a disease he has no means of arresting. Is it not more honest to attempt a radical cure than to accept fees for an attendance confessedly useless?

The numerous facts I have collected at the London Surgical Home are, as they always have been, open to the strictest investigation, and I beg to state that I am willing to nominate, *jointly with* THE LANCET, a commission to report on the subject. Should such a commission report in favour of the operation, it would at once become recognised; while in case of an adverse verdict I would abandon the practice.

My confidence as to the result is mainly based on the facts which have been gathered at the Home, but is further strengthened by my experience in analogous instances; for whenever I have proposed any novel proceeding, it has at first been opposed, but afterwards generally adopted. Thus, when I became convinced that ovariotomy was justifiable, I was only allowed to perform it at my own hospital (St. Mary's) under protest of most of my colleagues. My treatment of ruptured perineum encountered the most determined opposition, headed by a physician distinguished for his opposition to everything new....

These and other instances, in which my ideas have at first been condemned, but afterwards accepted throughout the world, encourage me to think that in my last proposal, notwithstanding the opposition it has excited, a calm investigation of my facts will ultimately demonstrate its value. I therefore confidently await the judgment of the profession.

I. Baker Brown, 'Clitoridectomy. To the Editor of THE LANCET.', *The Lancet*, 3 November 1866, p. 495.

177. The Current of Opinion against Baker Brown's Operation (1866)

At the Obstetrical Society on Wednesday evening last [5 December] a more than usually lively discussion followed the reading of a paper by Dr. Tanner, 'On Excision of the Clitoris as a Cure for Hysteria.' It would be difficult indeed to give an idea of the remarkably bold manner in which a peculiarly delicate subject was handled, and the little that was left to the imagination of those who listened to the discussion. Even the winter of life failed for once to command the respect which is ordinarily considered its due, and the habits of sundry ladies more than seventy years old were expatiated upon in a way to prove that, although age may induce continence, it is not necessarily accompanied by chastity. The current of opinion certainly ran strongly against Mr. Baker Brown's operation. Member after member rose to record his experience of the utter failure of the proceeding in arresting, except whilst the wound was unhealed and the patient restrained, the vicious habit which led to its performance. A very few instances were noted in which improvement appeared to follow, but no satisfactory evidence was forthcoming that this was of a permanent character. On the whole the remarks were temperate and to the point, and there seemed generally a disposition to allow that Mr. Brown, whilst doubtless mistaken in his premises, was at least genuine in his opinion and open in his mode of proceeding. But there were not wanting those who protested with considerable indignation against a mutilation which it seemed had often been performed without the knowledge or consent of the patient or her friends; which, at least in one case (and this was allowed by Mr. Brown himself), had been inflicted upon a sufferer from spinal disease, since dead, under a mistake in diagnosis; and which confessedly required, in order to its success, such a system of moral and physical restraint as would seem to render any operation at the least unnecessary. Whilst we cannot but acknowledge that Mr. Brown defended himself with much spirit and no little skill in fence against the attacks which met him from every part of a crowded room, we are sure that, in a subject which excites such strong prejudice, something much more convincing than general assertions of success after indefinite intervals, or skilful appeals *ad justitiam*, will be required ere the profession will feel disposed to imitate a proceeding which if it be useless is a lamentable mistake, and if it be unnecessary is a cruel outrage.

[Anon.], 'Medical Annotations. Clitoridectomy.', *The Lancet*, 8 December 1866, p. 639.

178. Dirty Subjects and the History of Clitoridectomy (1866)

[Clitoridectomy: Leading Article]

Very little was urged on scientific grounds for or against the proposal of Mr. Baker Brown [concerning clitoridectomy, at the Obstetrical Society of London meeting of 5 December 1866] ... it is urged against Mr. Brown, that he is so possessed with the idea of the universality of the habit of self-abuse, and its power of producing innumerable evils, that he resorts to the operation with lamentable frequency.... Dr. West expresses, not one whit too strongly, the disgust which reasonable and thinking men must feel at the public discussion, before mixed audiences, of sexual abuses. It is a dirty subject, and one with which only a strong sense of duty can induce professional men to meddle; and then it needs to be handled with an absolute purity of speech, thought, and expression, and, as far as possible, in strictly technical language.

[Report of Obstetrical Society of London meeting of 5 December 1866]

... Dr. AVELING said that, as it was proper to commence every subject with its history, he would take the liberty of opening the discussion by expressing his surprise that the history of clitoridectomy had not been more fully gone into. It was not a new operation, and he could not help thinking a large amount of useful practical information might be gathered from the numerous authors who had written upon the subject. It was remarkable also, that no reference had been made to, and no explanation given of, the singular fact that, for eighteen hundred years, hysteria was treated by excitation of the clitoris. From the time of Galen up to the last century, this method of treatment was constantly recommended....

British Medical Journal, 15 December 1866, pp. 664–5, 674.

179. Doctors For and Against Clitoridectomy (1866)

[Obstetrical Society of London discussion]

Dr. Williams stated he did not believe that clitorotomy [sic] was a justifiable operation for the cure of hysteria, epilepsy, &c. It was true we were ordered, if a member offended us, to cut it off; and he thought that the clitoris was not the offending member, but the arms and hands; these, then, were the members that should be cut off. Of course he did not seriously recommend the amputation of the arms, but there can be no reason why they should not be put under restraint by being fastened behind the back. Indeed, it appeared that something of this kind was done after the excision of the clitoris....

[Dr. Routh] Want of success, particularly at the beginning of trials, was common both in medicine and surgery. Doubtless clitoridectomy was sometimes unsuccessful ... clitoridectomy should not be practised until all other means, prosecuted over a long period, had failed, and never except after consultation with a brother practitioner, wherever practicable. As offering a chance of recovery a patient should have the option to try it, all circumstances being freely explained to her....

[Dr. Tyler Smith] The fact was that the prepuce or foreskin [in the male] was a very unimportant structure as compared with the clitoris. As regards sensation, the clitoris was the analogue of the male penis, and was the organ of sexual sensibility in the female ... the removal of the clitoris in cases of hysteria and self-abuse could not be justified. We might as well think of removing the penis in cases of masturbation in the male.

Dr. GREENHALGH considered that the frequency and evil effects of self-abuse in the female had been greatly exaggerated. He did not believe that it led to idiocy and epilepsy as had been assumed; that girls suffering from these affections were occasionally addicted to such a habit he did not deny. He did not believe that the clitoris or nymphae had anything to do with the habit, but that it must be rather referred to a peculiar mental condition requiring moral control.... He consequently regarded clitoridectomy as a useless, pernicious, and most unjustifiable operation for the purposes for which it had been recommended to

Mr. Isaac B. Brown....

[Mr. Baker Brown] ... said that his operation did not alter sexual excitement on marriage, and that not only had many of his patients borne children after clitoridectomy, but he had now five cases in which, from previously having disliked marital intercourse and preferred self-abuse, the state of things had been entirely changed after his operation....

'Medical Societies. Obstetrical Society of London. Wednesday, Dec. 5th, 1866...', *The Lancet*, 15 December 1866, pp. 667–9.

180. The Expulsion of Mr. Baker Brown (1867)

OBSTETRICAL SOCIETY OF LONDON

A SPECIAL meeting of this Society was held on Wednesday evening last, at the rooms of the Medico-Chirurgical Society, for the purpose of considering and balloting upon the proposition brought forward by the Council at the previous meeting for the expulsion of Mr. Baker Brown. There was a very large attendance of Fellows, who began to assemble long before the commencement of the proceedings, and some difficulty was experienced in providing for their accommodation. The total number of Fellows attending in the course of the evening was 237, of whom, as will be seen from the declaration of the ballot, 232 voted and 5 abstained from voting. The chair was taken at eight o'clock, by the President, Dr. Hall Davis....

[Mr. Seymour Haden, proposing the resolution]...We have to remember, gentlemen, what we are as the Obstetrical Society of London. We have to remember that in choosing the particular branch of medicine which we follow, practising as we do among women particularly, nineteen-twentieths of us, we have constituted ourselves the true guardians of their interests, and in many cases in spite of ourselves we become the custodians of their honour. We are, in fact, the stronger, and they the weaker. They are obliged to believe all that we tell them, they are not in a position to dispute anything that we say to them. We, therefore, may be said to have them at our mercy. We have our patients, who are

women, we being men, at our mercy. I think, under these circumstances, that if we should depart from the strictest principles of
honour, if we should cheat and victimise them in any shape or
way, we should be unworthy of the profession of which we are
members (hear and applause), and certainly unworthy of being
members of this Society....

The motives which have induced me to bring it [the resolution]
forward may be included, perhaps, in what I should call the
growing insensibility on the part of the profession to the inroads
of quackery, and to the consequent decline of the profession in
public opinion...the quack of the present time has found out that
he can obtain and base his operations upon an actual professional,
legitimate footing...two forms of quackery which strongly affect
this Society...the diagnosis of disease which has no existence, in
the laying of women upon their backs for weeks and months
together, and in the daily ministration of cauterisations and
leechings of people who have literally nothing the matter with
them. (Hear.)...[second] the pretended cure of real disease by
means which have more or less a secret, unpublishable, compro-
mising character. I think that is a fair definition of the form of
quackery which we are called this evening to consider...an
operation which is in itself a mutilation....

[Dr. Barnes] ... Now, I ask Mr. Brown who is present—(there
he sits)—if he will deny that fact in this room, if he will say here
that he never operated upon a patient without the knowledge of
herself or of her friends or of her husband? [After a short pause
Dr. Barnes proceeded.] I think he dare not say it. There are
twenty men in this room who could confute him on the spot.
(Hear.) ... this form of clitoridectomy, this form of mutilation
without the knowledge and consent of the patient or her
husband, had become a matter of public scandal....

Mr. BAKER BROWN.—Mr. President and gentlemen, I am
glad that at last I have an opportunity of speaking, for I think you
will agree with me, and all those who have not made up their
minds before they have heard my reply, that never in the whole
history of medicine was such an unfair proceeding taken as has
been taken by the Council. (Hear.) I have been charged by them
with all sorts of offences. They have met in secret council again
and again. They have never intimated to me, in the slightest
degree, what their charges were: they have never called me before
them to ask what I have done, or what explanation I would give.

(Oh, oh!) I appeal to the sense of the meeting for common fairness; I have not had it from the Council: I appeal with confidence to the general meeting. I say that they have left out to-night one of their gravest charges: and why? Because my answer completely upsets their accusation against me—that of a want of truth. Instead of investigating the subject of clitoridectomy as scientific men, instead of examining the subject, which I have challenged them to do again and again, they have evaded the subject, and tried to get rid of it by expelling me ... I maintain, without any boasting whatever, that there is not a single man—not even Dr. Barnes himself—who has been so open in his practice as I have been ... I had a conviction that the operation of clitoridectomy was a justifiable operation.... Clitoridectomy is nothing more nor less than circumcision. ('oh, oh,' and hisses)....

THE PRESIDENT.—It is the manner in which the operation is performed, not the operation itself, which we have met to consider. It is the ethical question....

[Mr. Brown] I repeat, I have done this operation because I believe it to be a justifiable operation. I have done it to the best of my judgment in a way which I consider professional. I may err—we all may err—but if I have erred, call me before you, and show me where I have erred. You have not shown me yet....

[Dr. Tyler Smith] Now, I say that we, the Council, have not entered into the question of the operation of clitoridectomy in itself at all. We have avoided this matter. We have confined ourselves to the consideration of the question in ethics arising out of the modes in which it has been performed....

A few minutes before twelve the scrutineers handed the result of the ballot to the President, who announced that the numbers were as follows:—

For the removal of Mr. Brown ...	194 votes
Against his removal	38 votes
Non voters	5 votes

The scrutineers added, 'Thus it appears that the motion of the Council for the removal of Mr. Brown from the Obstetrical Society, is carried by 36 votes above the required majority of two-thirds'....

Obstetrical Society of London special meeting, 3 April 1867, reported in *The Lancet*, 6 April 1867, pp. 429–35, 439, 441.

181. The Ring Plan or Clitoridectomy Continued (1886)

[Dr Fenton Jones]
His practice had been to interfere only in cases [of masturbation] where free and full confession had been made; then to remove the nymphae completely where there was hypertrophy of one or both, leaving the clitoris intact. In cases of admitted masturbation and yet no enlargement of the lesser lips, he ran a thick silver wire under the clitoris and clamped it round into the form of a loose ring, which was left *in situ*. This, in his hands, had proved a most successful mode of treatment. It made a break in the habit; its presence as a foreign body interfering at first with any pleasurable sensations arising from the act of self-abuse, and for a long time it serves as a moral reminder to a patient anxious to abandon the practice. The ring can be removed without the slightest difficulty if marriage is about to take place, or if it is considered desirable to do so for any other reason.

He had seen the clitoris removed, but it was ineffectual without taking away the nymphae as well. He did not himself see any particular harm in this operation; but as sentimental objections had been raised in certain quarters, the procedure of ringing the clitoris was a ready way out of the difficulty. There was, at all events, no mutilation or removal of parts, and it was undoubtedly efficacious in a large number of cases....

[Dr Heywood Smith]
As to the question of clitoridectomy, and its comparative disuse since it had been said to have been abused, we ought to do the best for our patients irrespective of popular prejudice. Dr. Heywood Smith maintained that in proper cases clitoridectomy held out the best prospect of curing masturbation, and he boldly confessed that he had done the operation several times with the happiest results. He, however, acknowledged that in some cases of nymphomania it had failed. In one case sexual excitement became so intense at times that it rose to positive pain, and the patient had to get out of bed and writhe on the floor because of it. In this case clitoridectomy had relieved her for a time, but after some months the excitement and pain recurred, though not to so great an extent as before.

[Dr Bantock]

The question of treatment [of masturbation] was a very difficult one. It was not improbable that the removal of the clitoris—and the labia minora should be included—might be of essential benefit in the early stage, but later it was sure to fail. Then came the question of the removal of the appendages ... he feared that little could be hoped for from the mere removal of the appendages....

[Dr C.H.F. Routh]

As regarded clitoridectomy, he believed it was very efficacious in some cases, but useless in others. He had performed it only three times, one case being complicated with syphilis. In all a cure had followed, but he thought after the condemnation of Mr. Brown's operation, and its certain failure in many other cases, it was wiser never to undertake it except after full consultation with another practitioner.... He had not tried the ring plan [of Dr Fenton Jones: see above] in such cases, but he had cut down to the bone on each side of the clitoris through both crura, and so destroyed sensation in the clitoris. The branches of the pudic nerve were cut asunder, and did not reunite under nine months or thereabouts. By that time the habit might probably have been overcome ... he was sure clitoridectomy did not remove sexual sensations. Mr. Baker Brown had instanced cases where women who had never before experienced any pleasurable sensations before the operation, did so during the subsequent natural intercourse with their husbands, and it was a known fact that the Jewish Abyssinian women—in whom clitoridectomy was always performed as a religious rite—were acknowledged to be very sensitive in their sexual orgasm, so much so that some of the Abyssinian men became Jewish proselytes to marry these women....

'Discussion on Nymphomania', Meeting of the British Gynaecological Society, 8 December 1886, *The British Gynaecological Journal*, Vol. 2 (1886–7), pp. 504, 506–7, 509–11.

4.5 Birth Control

182. Classical Method

... wherefore, since if the parts be smooth conception is prevented, some anoint that part of the womb on which the seed falls with oil of cedar, or with ointment of lead or with frankincense, commingled with olive oil. If the seed remain within for seven days then it is certain that conception has taken place; for it is during that period that what is known as effluxion takes place....

What is called effluxion is a destruction of the embryo within the first week, while abortion occurs up to the fortieth day; and the greater number of embryos as perish do so within the space of these forty days....

Aristotle, *History of Animals*, 583a–583b, *The Works of Aristotle*, ed. J.A. Smith and W.D. Ross, Vol. 4, Book VII. 1, Oxford 1910.

183. The Female Remedy against Conception (1838)

The remedy, for preventing conception, shocks the mind of a woman, at the first thought; but prejudice soon flies. To weak and sickly females, to those to whom parturition is dangerous, and who never produce living or healthy children, it [birth control] is a real blessing, as it is in all cases, where children are not desired. It will become the very bulwark of love, the promoter of wisdom, of beauty, of health, and happiness. The remedy has long been known to a few in this country, and to the aristocracy in particular, who are always in search of benefits which they can peculiarly hold, and be distinct from the body of the labouring people. On the continent of Europe it has been long very generally practised....

Girls would not then [with birth control] be seduced as they are now. Those women who chose to have lovers would neither be degraded nor brutalised, nor made miserable in consequence thereof as they now are ... the great good which would result from physical preventives would be, that alliances would be more early formed, and would be lasting. Girls would not then surrender themselves to the caprice, the injustice of men, nor become victims to their cruelty, as they do now....

... before sexual intercourse, the female introduces into her vagina a piece of sponge as large as can be pleasantly introduced, having previously attached a bobbin or bit of narrow riband to withdraw it, it will be found a preventive to conception, while it neither lessens the pleasure of the female nor injures her health.... There is nothing unnatural in the circumstance, further than it is unnatural to use precautions against any other natural evil, such as a fever, a storm, or a beast of prey ... prevention is alike moral and legal, while destruction of the foetus is degrading, immoral and illegal....

Richard Carlile, *Every Woman's Book or What is Love?*, 1838, pp. 25–6, 31–2, 38, 42–3.

184. Conjugal Onanism in France and England (1879)

Our French medical contemporaries, who see so much more of this system [of conjugal onanism] than we do, are very condemnatory of this vile habit. Thus, Bourgeois, in his work on the Passions, says: 'Conjugal onanism is a real social pest. Every fraud is a choked germ rendered unproductive—an indirect infanticide!' Indeed, for the full development of this crime we must look mainly to France. Great and noble as that nation has been, and I know yet will be, it has tasted deeply of the pleasures of immorality. It can scarcely be otherwise when wholesale crime [i.e. prostitution] is licensed and encouraged by the State.

Onan was a criminal, and was sorely punished in consequence. [see Genesis 38. 8–10] But now-a-days science has devised other fraudulent aids. Nor will I dwell upon them; suffice it to say, that Onan's crime is imitated; coverings are used by males, plugs and injections by females, to complete their shame. It is almost defilement even thus cursorily to allude to these vile practices.

It has been reserved, however, for some of our own people to discover a fifth method. In a debate before the Medical Society of London last session on the use of intra-uterine stems, devised originally for uterine diseases, we were credibly informed that they were also used by some ladies of high position, and continually worn by them, with a view to *prevent* conception. Thus often it happens that malicious art perverts good intentions. . . .

First, let me state that I look upon conjugal onanism as a great moral crime. It is perverting a noble attribute to vicious propensities. It is feeding a lustful impulse, and in the most degrading manner lowering the status of a woman. It is even doing that which an animal actuated solely by instinct would never do. It is destroying in the beginning what, under God's blessing, might have matured into a living soul, and proved a blessing to humanity. Masturbation is mean and bad enough, and much to be reprehended, because it is fostered by a filthy spirit which can no longer control the sexual impulses. But here, at least, there is no partner in the sin, and no pure woman is degraded thereby. Conjugal onanism places both the man and the woman below the instincts of the brute creation.

But, secondly, like all crimes, it cannot be, and it is not, practised with impunity. The effect on the health of both men and women is very injurious . . . conjugal onanism is a frequent cause [for women] of chronic metritis . . . leucorrhoea . . . menorrhagia and haematocele . . . hysteralgia and hyperaesthesia of the generative organs . . . cancer in an aggravated form . . . ovarian dropsy and ovaritis . . . absolute sterility . . . mania, leading to suicide and the most repulsive nymphomania are induced thereby in many cases. . . . Among men, general nervous prostration, mental decay, loss of memory, intense cardiac palpitations, mania, conditions which also lead to suicide, are given [by Bergeret and other French authors] as the results of conjugal onanism . . . as conjugal onanism is at present practised very rarely, I believe, in this country [England], we are not, as professional men, open to receive the confessions of the unfortunate victimised women as the doctors are in France....

These habits [of conjugal onanism] are injurious in other ways. 1st. They lead to a diminution of population. 2nd. They produce a deterioration in the physical strength of a race, and they bring about great demoralisation.... Those who expend by excesses their virile power must engender a weakened offspring...the French armies conquered the world under the first Napoleon. The very Prussians were overcome. Under the third Napoleon how was the position changed! If the generals proved less competent, the men, accustomed to waste their strength in unholy debauches, were, like the luxurious nations of old, less able to cope with the sturdy sons of the North, and in their turn they were conquered: and the Commune proved that brutality had taken the place of courage, and Socialism of manliness....

Let the passions be kept down by athletics, hard mental work, and industrial occupations; and if we cannot afford to keep a wife, let us not seek to gratify sexual lust by unholy and debasing practices. Let us not lower the character of a woman by making her the lewd plaything for our vices. Let us remember she must hereafter bring up our children.... Let the mothers do their duty by their children, and suckle them as they are bound to do, and so they shall not procreate more frequently than is consistent with health. Ameliorate, improve, raise her moral position. Use her as a helpmate worthy of an honourable man, not as a vessel for unbridled lust....

C.H.F. Routh, *The Moral and Physical Evils likely to follow practices intended to act as Checks to Population*, 1879, pp. 9–17.

185. The Anti-social Note of 'Preventive Measures' (1899)

It is only fair to turn as well to reject another of the worst features of the Free Love school. 'Preventive measures' [i.e. birth control] constitute this, as means of deceit.

It has actually been sometimes argued that they in themselves are a sufficient shield and excuse for illicit sexual indulgence, because of the riddance from consequences they procure! 'Why assume responsibilities where none are entailed?' say these advocates. 'Why publish a most private and sacred matter which can only concern those who immediately engage in it?'

Now, it is because this latter statement is untrue; and because the emotions awakened by the consummation of sex-union—whether followed by or prevented from natural consequences—are so deep and far-reaching, and of such hygienic value, that no civilised state is justified in ignoring them in regard to the health of its component parts.

Therefore, whatever place may be ultimately assigned the Malthusian doctrine for hygienic reasons, in a progressive moral code it is perfectly clear that this false note—this anti-social note—from the would-be social deceivers will not be found there. As well cater for an empty world!

The natural and usual consequences of the union of man and woman is a child.

Evolution has unfailingly brought this by the hand before the eyes of the whole world by sex-relations.

Only, therefore, with her eyes upon a child, her heart open to its needs, can Progress hope successfully to provide for human needs, by perfecting sex-relations in a high moral code. . . .

Effie Johnson, 'Marriage or Free Love', *The Westminster Review*, Vol. 152, July 1899, p. 94.

186. A Revolt Against 'The Curse of Eve' (1907)

I can say from personal experience that a desire for limitation of family is at work through all classes of the English-speaking peoples, certainly among the more provident of all classes. It would indeed be surprising if the infallible guides along this new path were celibate or childless men like Father Bernard Vaughan, the Bishop of London, and Mr. Sidney Webb.

It may be true that if we examine carefully those 'superlative deceivers'—statistics, with reference to greater longevity we shall find that the real birth-rate has not declined at all, but that is not the real issue. Wanderings in Europe, the United States of America, and the British colonies have made it impossible for me to doubt that there is a real revolt amongst women against bearing as many children as their mothers and grandmothers bore ... in the confidence of speech between woman and woman one hears the same ideal expressed—the restriction of the number of children within a limit consistent with the health and vigour of the women who bear them, and with the means of giving each child the best possible start in life. ... It is the ideal of wifehood and motherhood that has changed. ...

With rational regulation of births the survival rate of infants is raised, and ultimately the marriage rate. ... What opportunity for wise upbringing had a woman I know, on whom fell the housework and a fair share of shop-work and stock-tending, and who for twenty years was either carrying or nursing a babe? 'Do you think,' she asked me one day, 'that if I had known how to prevent it I would have had fifteen children?'

'The curse of Eve' is a phrase that one hears drop glibly from the pulpit. Is it for men to press the curse on women so remorselessly as to give them no mitigation? Could any man do so who realised his debt to mother, sister, nurse?...It is practically certain that with a smaller number of births the proportion of deaths would be less. ... Nothing but the regulation of the number of children can make early marriage possible. ...

I need hardly say that I am fully aware that the withholding of recognition by the medical profession and society generally that the mother's claim [to restriction of family] is right within proper limits is producing great evils. If the doctor passes by on the other side, the quack is always at hand. Father Vaughan's hearer who 'refused to add greatly to his income by giving such advice' could have saved much suffering by a few minutes' conversation. The recent jeremiads will tend to prolong such evils, and on that ground call for protest.

It is quite unlikely that in this matter the conscience of the race will reject as evil means advisedly adopted to attain an aim which commends itself as good. A few years ago it was the use of anaesthetics at child-birth that was denounced as an avoidance of the curse of Eve. How hopelessly unchivalrous Adam has always been about that unrejected apple!... The untheological mind cannot reconcile itself to the theory that God sends the scourges while the Devil sends the antidotes and gives us the brains to discover and apply them.

Irene M. Ashby MacFadyen, 'The Birth-Rate and the Mother', *The Nineteenth Century*, March 1907, pp. 429–35.

187. Preventing Conception a Real Sin (1915)

Nothing should be done by either husband or wife to prevent conception. Not infrequently a young couple agree that they will postpone the commencement of a family until, in their opinion, their financial position or other circumstances make it convenient. Unfortunately, in many instances the postponed child never arrives. When, after some few years of marriage, the couple conclude that they are ready and willing to accept the offered blessing, they find to their disappointment and sorrow that the wife is no longer apt for conception. It is difficult to explain exactly why such disabilities should arise. It is quite possible that the preventive measures taken were such as did not appear to entail any injury to the wife; all the same, she may be found to be suffering from congestion of the internal generative organs, or, even without any evident disease or trouble, her health is less good than it should be, and in spite of an honest although belated effort to carry out the duties of the married state, no results follow. Probably there is some subtle nervous injury which cannot be seen by the doctor and is only vaguely felt by the patient, but the fact remains that in many instances the desire for children which arises some years after marriage is never gratified.

In the evidence offered to the Birth-rate Commission several specialists ... agreed that women who had few or no children were more liable to become nervous and invalidish. By no witness was any specific injury alleged; it appeared to them to be simply that, as is the case in other natural instincts, either the desire or the power to carry it into effect depends on its proper and timely gratification.... The witnesses were also careful to emphasise the fact that gratification of desire apart from marriage is only too likely to lead to the contraction of disease which has far-reaching and disastrous effects....

A young woman who cannot, or will not discharge these paramount duties [of wife and mother] is depriving her family and the nation, the present and the future generations, of the benefits which she, and she alone, can offer. It is therefore a real sin when a young married woman refuses to bear a family or neglects the nurture and the welfare of her children, in the pursuit of pleasure, or even in the performance of works which are indeed good, and which ought to be accomplished, but not by her....

Mary Scharlieb, *The Seven Ages of Woman*, 1915, pp. 73–5, 273.

188. The Census Report for 1911 (1918)

... It is perhaps only to be expected that the more conscientious, the more thrifty, and the more lovingly desirous to do the best for their children people are, the more do they restrict their families, in the interests both of the children they have and of the community which would otherwise be burdened by their offspring did they not themselves adequately provide for them. Those who are less conscientious, less full of forethought, and less able to provide for the children they bear, and more willing to accept public aid directly and indirectly, are more reckless in the production of large families. Of course there are many individual exceptions, but they do not affect the general tendency. These facts are most significantly borne out by the statistics of the birth-rates of different types of people. For instance, in the Census Report for 1911 (as published and analysed in 1912), we find that the total birth-rate per thousand married men under 55 years old is 162; but that the birth-rate for the upper and educated classes on this basis is only 119, while that of comparatively unskilled workmen is 213 and over. The detailed analysis of trades and occupations is most interesting, and should be read in conjunction with a memory of the wages and social environment of the various homes. Reckoning per thousand married men below 55 years old, the average number of children is as follows:

Anglican clergy ...	101	Policemen	153
Other ministers of religion	96	Postmen	159
		Carmen	207

Teachers, professors,		Dock labourers	... 231
etc.	95	Barmen	234
Doctors	103	Miners	258
Authors, editors,		'General labourers'	... 438
etc.	104		

The above figures apply only to children born of average married people; when the vicious and feeble-minded people reproduce, they do so more recklessly....

Dr Marie Stopes, *Wise Parenthood*, 1918 (11th edn., 1923), pp. 17–18.

189. The Fashion of Birth Control (1925)

If instead of birth control every one would preach drink control, you would have little poverty, less crime, and fewer illegitimate children... I speak feelingly; for as my brother Harold John Tennant and I were the last of twelve children, it is more than probable we should never have existed had the fashion of birth control been prevalent in the [eighteen] eighties.... It may be bad to have too many children, but it is worse to have too few....

Margot Asquith, *Places and Persons*, 1925, pp. 268–9.

190. Violent Proceedings, and a Bad Remedy (1847–9)

[Edward Stanley to his wife, Mrs. Henrietta Stanley, 9 November 1847]

MY DEAREST LOVE

This your last misfortune is indeed most grievous & puts all others in the shade. What can you have been doing to account for so juvenile a proceeding, it comes very opportunely to disturb all your family arrangements & revives the nursery & Williams in full vigour. I only hope it is not the beginning of another flock for what to do with them I am sure I know not. I am afraid however it is too late to mend & you must make the best of it tho' bad is best....

[Mrs. Stanley to her husband, Edward Stanley, 9 November 1847]

DEAREST LOVE

A hot bath, a tremendous walk & a great dose have succeeded but it is a warning....

[Edward Stanley to his wife, Mrs. Stanley, 10 November 1847]
I hope you are not going to do yourself any harm by your violent proceedings, for though it would be a great bore it is not worth while playing tricks to escape its consequences. If however you are none the worse the great result is all the better....

[Mrs. Stanley to her husband, Edward Stanley, 10 November 1847]

I was sure you would feel the same horror I did at an increase of family but I am reassured for the future by the efficacy of the means....

[Lady Eddisbury to Lord Eddisbury, 1 December 1848]

... I have felt very low for some time I much fear there is a very unpleasant cause for my malaise, & tho' I conclude it will come to an untimely end the remedy is a bad one.

[Lady Eddisbury to Lord Eddisbury, 30 November 1849]
... As to my prospects, I feel well, not at all sick. Williams says she is sure I am not with child & that all will come right. I really would not swear either way.

[Lady Eddisbury to Lord Eddisbury, 5 December 1849]
I have to give you the most pleasing intelligence, that my apprehensions are dispersed. It is a most singular circumstance, I have done nothing one way or another. I certainly do wish some time or other to have another baby but not next June as I would rather see after the girls....

Nancy Mitford (ed.), *The Ladies of Alderley*, 1938, pp. 142–4, 185, 218–9.

191. Ethics and 'The American Sin' (1886)

[27 October 1886]
Private
Dearest Father,
I saw that a book called 'Ethics of Marriage' was sent to you, & I am writing this to ask you to lend it me. You may think it an unfitting book to lend, but perhaps you do not know of the great battle we of this generation have to fight, on behalf of morality in marriage ... I think it sad & useless for any one to know of these horrors unless they are obliged to try & counteract them—for when one once knows of an evil in our midst, one is partly responsible for it. I do not wish to speak to Mama about it, because when I did, she in her innocence, thought that by ignoring it, the evil would cease to exist.

What is called 'the American sin' is now almost universally practised in the upper classes; one sign of it easily seen is the Peerage, where you will see that among those married in the last 15 years, the children of the large majority are under 5 in number, and it is spreading even among the clergy, & from them to the poorer classes. The Church of England Purity Society has been driven to take up the question.... As a clergyman's wife, I have been a good deal consulted, & have found myself almost alone amongst my friends & contemporaries in the line I have taken. ...

It is almost impossible to make people see it is a sin against nature as well as against God. But it is possible to impress them on the physical side—Dr Mathews Duncan, Sir Andrew Clark & Sir James Paget utterly condemn the practice, & declare the physical consequences to be extremely bad. But they have little influence. If you quote them, the answer always is 'They belong to the past generation—they cannot judge of the difficulties of this one'... you cannot help becoming aware of the present sad state of things. It is what frightens me about England's future. It was a sign of decay in the Roman & Greek Empires.

Mary [Gladstone] Drew to William Gladstone, 27 October 1886, Glynne-Gladstone MSS. [St. Deiniol's Library, Hawarden].

192. Moral Differences between Contraceptive Methods (1906)

... I did not enough dissent when you said you thought *all* checks [i.e. contraceptives]... stood morally on the same level ... those checks which involve self control, i.e. the time checks [i.e. intercourse during the 'safe' period?] differ in kind ... also differ in kind from the wholesale prevention of procreation [i.e. via the sheath?] hand in hand with unlimited license... I agree with you that the sins of the flesh if actually weighed in the balance with the sins of the spirit, would be not nearly so blame worthy in themselves....

Mary [Gladstone] Drew to Edith Lyttelton, September 1906, Chandos Papers, II, 3/28 [Churchill College, Cambridge].

193. Birth Control in the Aristocracy since 1875 (1911)

... really it is a tremendous and awe inspiring fact that since 1875, the educated and aristocratic classes have more than halved their families, so that the fittest are rapidly decreasing while the less fit, the diseased, the feeble minded, the unhealthy alone increase (except in the case of Jews, R.C.'s and the clergy, blessings be on them)—I have been steeped in Eugenic literature ever since that visit to Eton last year in Lent when Edward inoculated me, and here [in Cape Town, South Africa] there are one or two enthusiasts who fear the Mother Country is rapidly demoralising, because like Rome, Greece & Spain, the best among them are forcibly limiting or refusing parenthood....

Mary [Gladstone] Drew to her sister, Agnes Wickham, 13 April 1911, Mary [Gladstone] Drew Papers, BL Add. MS. 46230, f. 166.

194. French Letters and Healthy Married Life (1901)

[8 September 1901: an upper-class lady to her fiancé]
...Georgie has asked her masseuse about those F.L. [French letters, contraceptive sheaths]...I told you about 6 dozen!! ought to be enough even for us I think. We need to have several other things as well all of which is a bother but I suppose it's as well to be on the right side as regards certainty. I hope you won't leave those letters around—they may surprise people not a little. I long to be held tight in your arms....

[9 September 1901]
...Please Darling the masseuse who is to buy those things wants to know your size!!...

[10 September 1901]
...You mustn't misunderstand me here. You know I love babies but I do so want to enjoy my married life when everything will be so perfect without being ill or miserable. I should adore to have a child who could call you father but we can afford to wait being both young—don't you think. Don't get worried at what I am going to use—they are absolutely safe....

[19 September 1901]
...Have just received a parcel from Paris and opened it having taken one out for you to look at, have wrapped the rest up and given to Clara for safe keeping.... How do you think they will work?? Georgie says you can get them right up and certainly nothing could ever get passed—I shouldn't think—how about fit—are they too big? I can't help laughing at my sending you this—Please don't open the enclosed in [the] Mess....

An upper-class lady to her fiancé, 8–10, 19 September 1901.

PART 5

From Menopause to Death

Introduction

Victorian and Edwardian models of the fate of women who survived the perils of childbirth, and lived to their forties or older, were deeply contradictory. If the primary meaning of female life was achieved through maternity, then the woman's world after reproduction was necessarily characterised by the loss of meaning. The social expression of this reductionist biological viewpoint was that 'all women over fifty should be shot' (Cicely Hamilton, 1912 [205]). Women who could no longer bear children were reduced to the performance of secondary social roles such as household management, and even these duties were conceived as progressively impaired by the physical degeneration associated with the menopause and ageing. Conversely, the medical stereotypes of these last stages of the female life cycle also recognised that women lived longer than men, and generally survived in better health than elderly men.

The menopause was seen as the great climacteric of the woman's life cycle, the critical period of the end of menstruation. Physical decline, disorder and diminished functions were emphasised as the general characteristics of the onset of the menopause (e.g. Laycock, 1840 [195]; Barnes, 1873 [199], etc.). Dr Ryan (1841) [196] painted the most grotesque picture of the change of life, when 'All the characters of puberty and the peculiarities of women cease'. The change was represented as the de-feminisation of woman: 'the breasts collapse in most cases, the fullness of habit disappears, the skin shrivels...and the women become corpulent, and lose the mild peculiarities of their sex'. There were long lists of the extensive symptoms of 'the change of life', such as Tilt's one hundred and twenty infirmities, sub-divided into 'seven distinct modes of suffering'. Tilt (1857) [198] pioneered the medical recognition of the menopausal syndrome, and criticised earlier medical books in which 'the critical time and its infirmities are generally dismissed with half a page.' Tilt aimed to establish a scientific, quantitative base for the treatment of the illnesses of middle-aged women, and his analysis was markedly more sophisticated than the caricatures of the 1840s. But Tilt's basic assumption remained that the menopause was the cause, and the one hundred and twenty symptoms were the inevitable result.

However, a modern scientist has concluded that: 'Excluding hot flushes, no evidence of a menopausal syndrome was found' (Carl Wood, 1979, p. 497: see bibliography). That is, the menopausal syndrome, with its extensive lists of symptoms, was a medical invention to explain a great variety of different conditions. Culture rather than biology was the decisive influence for the special Victorian view of the menopause, and for the ways in which women adjusted to the change of life. For some writers today, the end of the fertile period is not necessarily a 'change of life' at all—it depends to a large extent on the variety of approved social roles for women (van Keep, Greenblatt and Albeaux –Fernet, 1977, pp. 6–7: see bibliography).

A number of medical and popular authors contributed to the 'menopausal myth' after Tilt's pioneering work. Dr Barnes (1873) [199] outdid Tilt in emphasising the significance of the change of life: 'The climacteric perturbation is often even more severe and more marked than what is observed at any previous period of life.' Dr Barnes was especially interested in 'nervous aberrations' and so tended to focus on the 'irregular determinations of blood to the head' and associated nervous conditions which he saw as consequences of the menopause. J. C. Webster (1892) [203] accepted the idea of the menopausal syndrome and elaborated the psychological and physical symptoms and their 'varying combinations'. Dr Galabin (1893) [204] also characterised the menopause in terms of 'climacteric disturbances', especially those 'nervous disturbances' which manifested themselves as irritability, depression or insanity. Lionel Weatherly (1882) [202], in contrast, thought that doctors over-emphasised the inevitability of ill health during the menopause, and he stressed the value of observing the 'law of hygiene' and seeking early treatment.

Women's experiences of menopause were another secret,

private world, rarely recorded. The euphemism ('change of life'), the foreign phrase (*'temps de la vie'*), or silence, were characteristic responses, exemplified in Mary Haldane's (1880) and Louisa Antrim's (1908) letters [201]. The social convention was to reserve this subject for specialist medical texts and journals, or the more scientific advice books for women. Cicely Hamilton (1912) [205] was unusual in drawing attention to the social implications of the menopausal myth, particularly because she confronted her contemporaries with the delicate subject of sexual desire in women over fifty. Dr Braxton Hicks (1877) [200] had simply assumed that 'woman passes on to old age better than man, because free from sexual activity and its many demands on the powers of the system at this later period of life'. Presumably the older men then either turned to pre-menopausal women, or exhausted themselves and died from this terminal necessity.

There was an extraordinary paradox in the male accounts of the menopause and the subsequent ageing process in women. At the same time as the menopause was represented as a climactic epoch of reproductive decay, it was also the transitional stage to improved health for women, when they reverted to 'the neutral man-woman state' (Braxton Hicks, 1877 [200]), or when, 'like the body, their mental faculties assume a masculine character' (Tilt, 1857 [206]). The end of menstruation was also perceived as the source of better and healthier lives: 'There is less of passion, less disappointment, less mortified vanity, and fewer causes for indulgence in evil tempers and foolish caprices; while those mental ills which unavoidably happen are soothed by more or less of religious feeling' (Laycock, 1840 [195]). Dr Ryan (1841) [196] also noted that after the change of life 'women often enjoy better prospects of health and of long life' than men, though the price was that they 'become remarkably corpulent'.

Since menstruation was seen as a major cause of ill-health, the menopause allowed good health to be re-established. Menstruation was the defining feature of female physiology, so its absence allowed women to become 'neutral' or to assume the 'masculine character'. However, Dr Braxton Hicks (1877) [200] rejected Tilt's view of the de-feminisation of the woman's consciousness after menopause, 'because there remains impressed upon the mind, memory, and nervous system the reflection of the woman'. He believed that the middle-aged and elderly woman remained under the subjection of her gender and its biology to the end. Indeed, 'losing sexuality and its various impulses, she becomes more capable of rendering herself useful' in society at large.

The point of transition to old age was not clearly fixed in the minds of Victorians and Edwardians, though the menopause was seen as the final stage before death. Relative old age began about forty-five rather than sixty-five in nineteenth-century Britain (see F. B. Smith, *The People's Health 1830–1910*, p. 316), though 'the richer classes' had higher life expectancies than the majority of the population. Doctors were rarely interested in the medical problems associated with ageing, though the elderly were a significant source of medical income. Geriatrics, the science dealing with the health and welfare of old people, was not developed until the twentieth century. Old age was not a condition which could be treated with success, since the patient always died. But Victorian doctors did not expect cures for many diseases, and were accustomed to providing comfort where they could not cure.

The history of Victorian and Edwardian experiences of ageing can never be fully written, because ageing was largely a private experience. The history of private prayer would have to feature prominently, as part of the ritual of Christian preparation for death. Agnes King's (1911) [209] prayers illustrate the personal anxieties, family concerns, and religious preoccupations which must have dominated the later years of many women, for whom 'every day it is harder'. Women complained to each other about the physical problems of ageing, such as rheumatism (Ann Clive, 1899, 1903 [207]), but there was no way to restore lost elasticity. The elderly were especially vulnerable to viral infections such as influenza, which achieved epidemic status seven times in nineteenth-century Britain. But doctors could do no more to cure influenza than heart disease, and the burdens of old age were shared between the elderly and their families, or 'covered by the earth'.

Death was a dominant and common experience for Victorian and Edwardian men, women and children. Death was not monopolised by the elderly, nor was it hidden away in hospitals. Childbirth and childhood were frequently associated with illness, death and mourning (Conquest, 1848 [210]; see also Part 3). The

Victorian and Edwardian ways of death were very distinctive, as individuals and families struggled to come to terms with the prospective and actual loss of loved ones. Anxiety before death was all the more marked because doctors were often uncertain or ignorant about the nature of the illness and its prognosis. William Gladstone's private record of the sufferings and death of his beloved daughter Jessy in 1850 [212] provides an exceptionally revealing insight into the Victorian family. Gladstone's religious beliefs established the mental framework for his experience of death in the family: 'O how much better will she be cared for than in this sad and evil world. His will be done.' Gladstone took the small coffin with him by train for the family burial service, making 'three changes of carriage' on the long journey from Chester to Scotland with the dead child. Even with his intense religious convictions, the death of Jessy provoked a deep personal crisis for Gladstone as he endeavoured to accept God's will.

Although death was a more frequent experience for Victorian and Edwardian families than today, its emotional impact was not diminished. Religious faith was the essential support which gave positive meaning to many family deaths (e.g. Acland, 1851 [213]; Brontë, 1848 [216]; Curzon, 1904 [217]; Lyttelton, 1857 [219], etc.). But by 1851 half the population of England and Wales no longer attended Church services, as urbanisation and industrialisation gradually undermined the habit of religion for the masses. From the 1860s Charles Darwin's writings helped to raise doubts about religion among the educated classes, some of whom turned instead to spiritualism to try to establish contact with the 'continuous life' of the departed (e.g. Lyttelton, 1902–36 [214]). There was a special pain with the death of a young child (e.g. Mitford, 1938 [211]). As Lady Selborne (1914) [215] wrote, 'I never think the doctrine of immortality of the soul is the same comfort with regard to a baby that it is with regard to older people'. The process of grieving often began during the final illness and continued after the funeral service. Many families encouraged talking about their dead—sharing the emotional effect of their loss (e.g. Ridding, 1914 [215]). Letters were exchanged with lengthy recollections of the lives of departed relatives, and detailed memoranda sometimes lovingly composed on all the events leading up to the death (e.g. Gladstone, 1850 [212]; Curzon, 1904 [217]; King, 1870 [218]).

If possible the family assembled at the deathbed and experienced the process of dying with their relatives, sometimes over a period of days or even weeks. Death was usually a domestic experience because few people chose to die in hospitals, which had reputations as places of accelerated mortality. Doctors did visit some of the dying at home, but as outsiders who left the family on the centre stage. The deathbed scene could be an intensely meaningful and emotional rite which helped the dying as well as the family left behind (e.g. King, 1870 [218]). The common social experience of the death could be communicated in conversation or correspondence with relatives and friends. The sight of the dead person was an important part of the acceptance of death for the family (e.g. Curzon, 1875 [220]). Even suicide could be integrated within the Victorian and Edwardian conventions of death, though with difficulty (e.g. Courtney, 1905 [221]). The record of the details of this 'family event', and the virtues and 'flaws' of character which resulted in the 'Temporary Insanity', were part of a social process of mourning in which everyone had a place and an importance after death, however that death had occurred. The dead lived on in the memories of their families, refreshed by a re-reading of the diaries, memoranda and letters in which those deaths had been recorded, or revived by looking at a photograph or sketch from their past.

5.1 Menopause

195. The Morbid Phenomena of Menopause (1840)

The vigour of the reproductive system begins to decline about the age of forty or forty-two; and from this period to the age of forty-nine, there is a state of system exceedingly analogous to that of the period during which it was first developed. The morbid phenomena are, however, favourably modified by circumstances. Age has blunted the sensibilities in some degree. There is less of passion, less disappointment, less mortified vanity, and fewer causes for indulgence in evil tempers and foolish caprices; while those mental ills which unavoidably happen are soothed by more or less of religious feeling. The hysteria is of the sthenic or cachectic type; the uterus and mammae, or, if the patient have not had children, the thoracic viscera are principally affected; asthma, angina pectoris, menorrhagia, neuralgia of the mammae, and their concomitants, are observed; and when the catamenia cease, if the health be not re-established, gout, hypochondriasis, or general cachexy, supervenes, and cancer attacks the reproductive organs or their glandular appendages....

Thomas Laycock, *A Treatise on the Nervous Diseases of Women*, 1840, p. 143.

196. The Climacteric Period (1841)

CESSATION OF MENSTRUATION.—SENILE STERILITY.—The menstrual secretion ceases, in temperate countries, about the forty-fifth or fiftieth year, sometimes so early as the twenty-fifth (Haller, Dewees, Velpeau); and again, not until the fifty-fifth, sixtieth, sixty-fifth. . . .

When menstruation is about to cease, the period is called critical, 'the change, or turn of life, the climacteric period;' and many important changes take place in the constitution at this epoch. All the characters of puberty and the peculiarities of women cease, the breasts collapse in most cases, the fullness of habit disappears, the skin shrivels, and appears too large, and loses its colour and softness, and many diseases develop, occasionally and rarely, in the womb, ovaries, and breasts, which had lain dormant for years. The cheeks and neck wither, the eyes recede in their sockets, and the countenance often becomes yellow, leaden-coloured, or florid, and the women become corpulent, and lose the mild peculiarities of their sex. When this period has, however, passed, women often enjoy better prospects of health and of long life than the other sex, and become remarkably corpulent. This period is also designated 'the climacteric, the critical time, the critical age;' and often before its arrival the menstruation is irregular, may be absent for weeks or months, the abdomen becomes tumid, there is loss of appetite in the morning; and the woman considers herself pregnant, which is scarcely ever the case. . . .

The cessation of menstruation, however, is often preceded by gradual derangement of health; there is nervousness, with all its Protean symptoms, or more serious diseases appear; so that moderate purgation is often of the greatest advantage.

The disorders most common at this period are hypo-chondriasis, nervous irritability, indigestion, derangement of the digestive organs, costiveness, diarrhoea, intestinal and other haemorrhages, spasms in different parts of the body, giddiness, apoplexy, and severe or transient pains in the back, loins, inferior extremities, and different parts of the body. Chronic complaints are often aggravated, and organs predisposed to disease very often suffer. Disorganizations of the uterus, ovaries, mammae, rectum, and bladder are very frequently developed. Daily observation in hospital, dispensary, and private practice, confirms the correctness of this statement. The more general opinion, however, is, that most women are generally exempt from such diseases.

The menstrual function rarely ceases without more or less disorder. In some cases the cessation is preceded by a gradual diminution, or an increase of quantity of the menstrual secretion, amounting to haemorrhage. The evacuation may recur every three or six weeks, and there is often severe mucous leucorrhoea. In many women it ceases without any inconvenience whatever, and better health may be enjoyed than at any former period of womanhood. In others, especially those who lead a luxurious life, the 'critical age' is, rarely, an epoch of licentiousness. Pregnancy is often suspected by such persons, but it rarely exists. . . .

It is very manifest from the preceding account of this function, that every process of female economy to the climacteric age, is affected by the periodical secretion; and women very properly ascribe most of their diseases to the derangement of this important function. . . .

TREATMENT.—The chief indications of treatment are to employ general or local bleeding, purgation, low diet, &c. in persons of full habit. When the women are delicate, nervous, or hysterical, anodynes, anti-spasmodics, tonics, &c. will be required. . . .

Dr Michael Ryan, *A Manual of Midwifery*, 4th. edn., 1841, pp. 71–3, 75, 347.

197. 'The Turn of Life' (1845)

But although the tendency to mental disorder prevails to the greatest extent during the period of menstruation,—that is, from the age of fifteen to forty-five,—yet it must be acknowledged that the natural cessation of this function is with women a most critical period; and indeed the woman herself is not wholly insensible to the important revolution which menstruation produces in the female economy: hence the emphatical expression, 'the turn of life'. Women dread this period, because hitherto occult or latent diseases now manifest themselves; hence tumours and cancer of the breast, various distressing affections, even cancer of the womb itself, pulmonary diseases, indigestion, dropsy, etc., form but a small proportion of the formidable category of ills to which women become liable, and from which they often suffer at this period. . . .

Samuel Mason, *The Philosophy of Female Health*, 1845, p. 3.

198. The History, Infirmities and Treatment of the Change of Life (1857)

The few works written on the subject of this inquiry [the change of life] led me to believe that they would not afford me much assistance. In treatises on diseases of women, I have found very little to help me, because the critical time and its infirmities are generally dismissed with half a page. In none of our classical works have I found diseases of the c.[hange] of life brought within the range of the laws of general pathology, and no general principles of treatment are laid down for the guidance of others. Perhaps the deficiencies of medical literature are corrected in the daily routine of practice, though some eminent practitioners are of a different opinion. They do not pretend that nothing is done to relieve the sufferings of women, but not enough, that a placebo is given where systematic treatment is required. Thus, Sir C. M. Clarke, commenting on the diseases of this epoch, states that 'It is not unusual with women to refer all their extraordinary sensations to 'the c. of life,' and to consider that, when they have thus accounted for their diseases, they have at the same time cured them; and in this, most medical men, judging at least from their practice, seem to be of the same opinion'....

The c.[hange] of life not only determines some diseases for the first time, but finding also the germs of others, such as gout, cancer, &c., it gives them an additional impulse so as to renew health, or curtail life. Previous authors affording little information, I have endeavoured to obtain a correct bead-roll of the infirmities entailed by the c. of life, and have set down very minutely whatever could be detected morbid in 500 women....

TABLE XIX
... [plus 108 other infirmities]

Nervous irritability	459	[91.8%]
Flushes	287	[57.4%]
Pseudo-narcotism	277	[55.4%]
Dorsal pain	226	[45.2%]
Epigastric faintness	220	[44%]
Headache	208	[41.6%]
Abdominal pain	205	[41%]

Perspirations	...	...	...	...	...	...	...	201	[40.2%]
Leucorrhoea	...	...	...	...	...	...	...	146	[29.2%]
Hysterical state		...	...	...	...	...	...	146	[29.2%]
Flooding	...	...	...	...	...	...	...	138	[27.6%]
Sick headache	...	...	...	...	...	...	...	92	[18.4%]

This would give to each of the 500 women 7 distinct modes of suffering, the prognosis of which, with the exception of cancer, organic diseases, and the worst forms of mental suffering, is not serious; but they are often tedious, ever-recurring, and destructive of peace and happiness. . . .

SEDATIVES.—. . .The utility to be derived from sedatives has been so admirably pointed out by. . . Sir H. Holland. . . 'Here opium is the most certain and powerful of the aids we possess; and its use is not to be measured timidly by tables of doses, but by fulfilment of the purpose for which it is given'. . . . These remarks are in every way applicable to diseases of the c. of life . . . in many cases, the systematic use of camphor, lupulin, hyoscyamus, and opium are required. . . .

E. J. Tilt, *The Change of Life in Health and Disease*, 2nd edn., 1857, pp. 7, 70–1, 82, 97–9.

199. The Climacteric Perturbation (1873)

CLIMACTERIC CONVULSIVE DISEASES.—At the 'turn of life,' when the ovario-uterine functions are ceasing, the nervous system, it is well known, exhibits frequent and various perturbations. Thus we find giddiness, vertigo, actual syncope, a pseudo-paralysis marked by numbness and comparative loss of power of one side, impairment of memory, mental irritability, restlessness, culminating in some cases, especially where the nervous diathesis exists, in epilepsy, and even in insanity. Probably few women pass through this epoch without some nervous perturbation. It is a stage of transition and of trial for all. Vertigo, some degree of loss of memory, some disposition to utter *mal-a-propos*, to use the wrong syllable or word, some sense of distrust in the power of self-control, are extremely common.

These perturbations may persist for months, even for years, before the balance is restored. During a great part at least of this transition period the ovarian influence may be traced. There is more or less periodicity in the nervous disorder; and when the uterus and ovaries have undergone complete senile involution or atrophy, when all menstrual discharges have ceased, these disorders commonly subside or change their character.

The climacteric perturbation is often even more severe and more marked than what is observed at any previous period of life. Thus many women may have passed through the trials of puberty and of child-bearing without serious nervous disorder, and will break down at the menopause. Often, no doubt, this is the climax, the last ounce of a long-troubled sexual life. Exhausting labours, consequent uterine disease, the cares incident to the rearing of a family, tell at last, so that when the irregular and futile efforts which mark the close of sexual life are made, the nerve-force, missing its proper destination, breaks out in various aberrations. These nervous aberrations commonly entail irregular deviations from the proper order of the blood-distribution, as well as alterations in the quality of the blood. That menstruation exerts a depurating action on the blood is an old idea. I believe it is a correct one. At any rate, when there is no longer a normal attraction or afflux of blood to the pelvic organs, the subject becomes liable to irregular determinations of blood to the head. . . .

Dr Robert Barnes, 'Lumleian Lectures on the Convulsive Diseases of Women', *The Lancet*, 26 April 1873, pp. 586–7.

200. The Menopause and the Neutral Man-Woman State (1877)

. . . there is one other subject which must not be omitted. I mean the period called 'change of life', the 'climacteric', 'cessation of menses', 'turn of life', or, by the French, the 'ménopause'. These terms are applied to women; but the term 'climacteric', 'turn of life', is also applied to man. In him the change is more gradual, as puberty is . . . the menopause in women . . . is definitely attended by the involution of the ovary; the cessation of its activity ... and almost invariably the power of conception is lost....

But it is quite certain that all the tendency to various troubles, to which I have partly alluded as belonging to females, principally after puberty, now cease, or at least do so after a time. All the local uterine irritations, engorgements, and fluxes; all the reflex symptoms, neuroses, vomiting, neuralgias, headaches, pass gradually off; and then, when the change is complete, the woman passes much into the state of one who has had her ovaries removed, having a tendency to revert to the neutral man-woman state; yet not entirely so, because there remains impressed upon the mind, memory, and nervous system the reflection of the woman; in manifold ways recalling to her actions and movements that manner and style she had in earlier life.

But, after the change has been completed, we generally find her system improved; not disturbed by the periods, nor pregnancy, nor by the multitudinous reflex symptoms which distracted her attention; losing sexuality and its various impulses, she becomes more capable of rendering herself useful. She is less of the woman she was than a man is a man at the same time of life. The study of the subsidence of menstruation tells us the same physiological facts as those which accompanied its origin; and further, they point out the essence of those complaints which, troubling the woman so long, subside at this epoch.... Thus, suffering all their menstrual life, women now generally become comfortable, stout instead of emaciated, composed instead of hysterical ... woman passes on to old age better than man, because free from sexual activity and its many demands on the powers of the system at this later period of life....

Dr J. Braxton Hicks, 'The Croonian Lectures on the Difference between the Sexes in regard to the Aspect and Treatment of Disease', *The British Medical Journal*, 21 April 1877, pp. 475–6.

201. Experiences of Menopause (1880, 1908)

I have just been administering a little eau de vie to Eliza [Sanderson]. She has continual diarrhea [sic], and I cannot think that it can be from other reasons than as an outcome of her illness, and really a safety valve. It is evident to me that it is the change of life but I never say so. She does not like it, and please don't hint of it to her, or to the world in general. This only between you and me this little observation.

Mary Haldane to her sister, Jane Sanderson, n.d. [1880], Haldane MSS, Acc. 5782, Box 1 [National Library of Scotland].

I have followed the advice (from the book which Jeanne found so helpful) for temps de la vie [i.e. time of life] and have no flushes now—I had one bout of relations [i.e. a period] a fortnight ago after 4 months absence but no more heats thank goodness. I am growing fat however much to my regret—all my clothes are tight. I feel India is my only chance of getting thinner....

Louisa Antrim to her sister, Mary, Lady Minto, 2 October 1908, Minto MS. 12439, f. 188 [National Library of Scotland].

202. Suffering and the Change of Life (1882)

MANAGEMENT OF HEALTH DURING THE CHANGE OF LIFE

This period is one that to the majority of women is fraught with a considerable amount of discomfort, if not actual ill-health; and I am convinced that sufficient attention is not paid to the curability of many of the complaints at this time, simply because it is falsely imagined that they are bound to occur and to continue till the period of the change of life has been passed.

Medical men, I am afraid, err too much and too often in the same way; and what is more common than to hear a doctor tell his patients, 'That she must expect to suffer in this way or that during this period'?

As at puberty, when the menstrual flow is first making its appearance, so now is the female subject to many conditions at variance with perfect health; and doubly important it is for her to follow out in their strictest sense all the ordinary laws of hygiene, as well as to seek advice from her medical man, should she find herself to be a sufferer from what she may wrongly suppose is an unpreventable outcome of the change of life....

As during the period of its first appearance, so of its last, the spirits become more or less depressed, headaches, etc. are complained of, and a general irritability of temper is noticed; all these symptoms after a time, however, are often followed by a fresh renewal of good health and strength.

This state of things may exist; but how often is it far different from this! How often is it that this period, as also the period of puberty, leaves the female broken in health, feeble, sickly, and unable to bear the brunts of life, with its trials and difficulties!...

Lionel A. Weatherly, *The Young Wife's Own Book*, 1882, pp. 90–1.

203. Character and Disposition at 'The Change' (1892)

Among the most striking phenomena [of the change of life] are those relating to the character and disposition. There is a depression of vital energy, the woman losing her former spring and vigour. She takes less interest in her work, becoming often indifferent to pleasures or duties, which once greatly interested her. If previously of a vivacious or impulsive nature, she may become calm and restrained. Some become dejected and downcast, fearing the onset of trouble or illness. Others become irritable, peevish, and restless, losing the power of concentrating their attention steadily for any length of time upon any subject. In some cases, women get an idea into their heads that something is wrong with them: they may consider themselves as suffering from a tumour, from heart or lung disease, or some other trouble.

In some cases women may become liable to outbursts of

temper more or less violent, so that they may become a great annoyance to their friends. . . .

Some women complain of a heaviness in the head; they feel stupid and dull, and inclined to sleep. In pronounced cases there may be developed a state of stupor or sleep which may last for hours. Other women become very forgetful even of their own or their children's names. In some cases there may be complete loss of self-control, or great fear that it may be lost; the woman may lose all interest in those she loves best, and she may even have an inclination to injure them, or she may think they wish to harm her. Sometimes there may be a slight suicidal tendency.

Sometimes there may be developed an intense desire to drink strong liquors, even in those who have never previously been accustomed to take alcoholic drinks.

Disturbances of stomach and bowels are very common. If a woman has suffered previously from indigestion, her troubles usually get worse at the change. A few cases, however, improve or get quite well. The causes of these disturbances are varied. No doubt, altered nervous stability is an important one. Anaemia, also, accounts for a considerable number of cases. There may be bad heartburn, nausea, a feeling of heaviness in the pit of the stomach, pain behind the breast-bone, or between the shoulders, disordered appetite, and constipation. It is rare to find a person with all these symptoms; they occur in varying combinations. In other cases there may be a great deal of trouble from wind in the stomach. Vomiting often occurs; it may be in connection with food, or between meals. . . .

Regarding the sexual appetite, many variations are found. In many women it disappears more or less completely; in some it remains unaltered, while in others it may increase in intensity. There can be little doubt that the first of these variations is to be considered as the most common. Cases in which there is a marked increase are generally due to some abnormal state, such as a tumour in connection with the internal genitals. . . .

Flushings and sweatings are very common occurrences at the change. The feelings of heat may be felt in several parts of the body, very often in the head. They are increased by nervous shock, emotion, excessive warmth, etc. In bad cases women may feel very weak or faint during an attack. Flushings may alternate with chills. The perspiration may take place over the whole body, or only in special parts such as the breast, neck, forehead, scalp, etc. ...

J. C. Webster, *Puberty and the Change of Life. A Book for Women*, 1892, pp. 40–3, 45–8.

204. Disturbances at the Menopause (1893)

CLIMACTERIC DISTURBANCES.—The cessation of menstruation at the menopause is frequently accompanied by constitutional disturbances of a well-known character, which often last over a period of several years. These are to be attributed, not only to the cessation of the periodical active hyperaemia and discharge of blood to which the system has been accustomed for some thirty-five years, but to that of the expenditure of nervous energy in a particular direction. The chief phenomena, therefore, are signs of plethora, with transient vascular disturbances, inducing flushings of the face, or feelings of heat, chilliness, or sinking in the epigastric region and other parts. Vicarious haemorrhages from the nose and rectum are frequent; the liability to cerebral haemorrhage is also increased. Any previously existing congestion or inflammation of pelvic organs is liable to undergo a temporary aggravation, after which, as a rule, it tends to subside. In many cases, especially when any previous uterine disturbance has existed, the diminution of menstruation is not gradual and progressive, but long periods of amenorrhoea are interrupted by profuse and often prolonged haemorrhage, which may arouse a suspicion of the existence of cancer.

Irregular discharges of nervous energy are usual, and may take the form of headaches, of epileptiform or apoplectiform attacks, or of hysterical manifestations, in those predisposed to that disorder. In other cases the nervous disturbance takes the shape of irritability or depression, which, when there is a constitutional proclivity, sometimes develops into insanity. Sometimes, again, women seek refuge in alcohol from low spirits, or from the pain produced by pelvic disorders or by indigestion, and the foundation of intemperance is not infrequently laid about this time of life. With the diminution of sexual activity is associated a tendency to corpulence and to deposit of fat about internal organs, which is apt to lead to neglect of outdoor exercise. To this cause are partly to be ascribed the digestive disturbances which often form the most prominent feature of the general condition. They consist mainly of constipation, inactivity of liver, and distension of the abdomen by flatus, with frequent spasmodic and painful contractions of the intestines.

TREATMENT.—No emmenagogue treatment should be adopted, unless the menopause appear to be coming on at a period very long anterior to the normal age; nor, on the other hand, should the intercurrent haemorrhages, which often afford a natural relief, be checked too suddenly, unless signs of anaemia appear. . . .

Dr A. L. Galabin, *Diseases of Women*, 5th edn., 1893, pp. 489–91.

205. 'Women Over 50 Should Be Shot' (1912)

Sex is only one of the ingredients of the natural woman—an ingredient which has assumed undue and exaggerated proportions in her life owing to the fact that it has for many generations furnished her with the means of livelihood. . . .

A friend of my own (who will forgive me for repeating her confidence) told me the other day of a happening in her life that, to my mind, exactly illustrates the awakening of class-consciousness amongst women. It was the careless speech of a man, addressed to her while she was still a very young girl, to the effect that all women over fifty should be shot. The words were lightly spoken, of course, and were probably intended half as a compliment to her manifest youth; certainly they were not intended as an insult. But their effect was to rouse in her a sense of insult and something akin to a passion of resentment that she and her like should only be supposed to exist so long as they were pleasing, only so long as they possessed the power of awakening sexual desire. She took them as an insult to herself because they were an insult to women in general; and, lightly spoken as they were, they made upon her an impression which helped to mould her life.

I give my friend's experience because it seems to me to be typical; because amongst women of my own class I know others who have felt the same rush of anger at the revelation of a similar attitude towards the sex they belong to; who have raged inwardly as they recognized that character, worth, intellect were held valueless in woman, that nothing counted in her but the one capacity—the power of awaking desire. That is an attitude which we who have become conscious of our class resent with all our souls; since we realize that to that attitude on the part of man, to compliance with it on the part of woman, we owe the degradation of our class. . . .

Cicely Hamilton, *Marriage as a Trade*, 1912, pp. 27, 182–3.

5.2 Experiences of Ageing

206. The Masculine Character of Women after Menopause (1857)

When the change [of life] is past, the mind emerges from the dark clouds in which it has seemed lost. Thankful that they have escaped from real sufferings, women cease to torture themselves with imaginary woes. They feel the ground grow steadier underfoot, they are less dependent on others,—for, like the body, their mental faculties assume a masculine character. The c. of life does not give talents, but it imparts a firmness of purpose to bring out effectively those that are possessed, whether it be to govern a household, to preside in a drawing-room, or to thread and unravel political entanglements. When women are no longer hampered by a bodily infirmity periodically returning, they have more time at their disposal, they are less subject to be led astray by a too ardent imagination, or by wild flights of passion, and the faculties of the mind may become endowed with new vigour....

When safely anchored in this sure haven, a woman looks back on the time when her health was disturbed by ever-recurring infirmities, by pregnancy with its eccentricities, by the perils of child-birth, and the annoyances of nursing. From the tranquillity she has attained, she may well revert to the long years when love, jealousy, and their attendant emotions often harrowed up her soul, presenting to the mind everything through the delusive prisms of passion. She will find how much her existence is changed from what it was, and will understand the saying of Madame de Deffand—'*Autrefois quand j'étais femme.*'...

E. J. Tilt, *The Change of Life in Health and Disease*, 2nd. edn., 1857, pp. 67–8.

207. An Experience of Old Age (1899, 1903)

[15 May 1899: aged 84]

... Now that I am by way of being 'as before' in mind, body and health, I do *not* find the recovery so perfect—very stiff joints in my knees so that I can no longer pick up a pin or stoop down for a fallen flower. But more than all, the noise of various voices more or *less* well modulated tries my nerves and I like my own company much better than I used to....

[20 March 1903: aged 87]

... This is a sad letter—I am so crippled with Rheumatism from the constant damp that I can hardly walk upright now. I know not if fine weather and Spring days will give me back my elasticity. I shall be 88 this year and I think a pair of crutches is more likely to be my portion....

Ann Clive to Mary, Lady Minto, Minto MS. 12423, fos. 118, 189 [National Library of Scotland].

208. Patients, Doctors and Death (1911)

... Please tell me something more explicit about Cousin Emily [Miss Emily Murray Macgregor]—now that you will have seen her—her doctor will probably know more about her than she will herself as they normally have a way of fibbing to their patients. Poor Cousin Emily—it would be better for her that she should go altogether than that she should remain almost helpless and her life would be worth nothing. When a person is very ill it is quite impossible for him to eat things—a doctor can't do it himself when he is ill—doctors spend their lives preaching what they don't practise. It is only a way of 'paving' the way when people die that they can say that they wouldn't have died if they had done what they told them. When people die after an operation—have you never noticed that according to the doctors the operation has always succeeded marvellously, and that they always die of something else. Doctors only think of their pockets. There is a proverb in some language that 'doctors' mistakes are covered by the earth'.

Lady Evelyn Murray to her brother, Marquis of Tullibardine, 12 April 1911, Athol MSS, 82/83/1 [Blair Castle, Scotland].

209. An Agony Worse Than Death (1911)

Oh God I know my mind is going. I cannot stem the tide of sleeplessness and sorrow. Keep me safe keep me safe. I beseech thee that I may not live long to be a burden to those I love so dearly. I have tried to see my way but I have failed all round. I know nothing I understand nothing. I only know that I want to do right, and some time to meet the dear ones again whom I have loved so much. This is an agony far far worse than death yet I know I must cling to life however useless and broken it is. Thou hast made my mind as well as my body take care of it I beseech thee. I am holding on with all my might but every day it is harder and some time I am sure I shall be able to hold on no longer. Oh God what then! be near to save me.... If I am to remain here on earth stricken show me how to be least trouble to my brother and all those whom I love, and in Thine own good time take me to heaven and let me meet those whom I have loved so dearly here.... Give me strength Oh God to go on and where I fail forgive me.

Show me how I can bear Elizabeth's [her sister] great suffering and teach me to say 'Thy will be done'. I cannot say it yet.

Agnes King, 'Prayers during the long struggle', 9 September, 30 November 1911, MacDonald Papers, P.R.O. 30/69/970.

5.3 Death in the Family

210. Mortality among Children (1848)

If it be a fact established on the most unquestionable evidence, namely, on the returns to the registrar-general of the mortality in England and Wales, that of the children born in LARGE cities nearly *a third* die before they attain the age of one year; and that the mortality in the early and most engaging periods of human existence is so great, that not less than one *half* die under *five* years of age, in the unhealthy districts of some large manufacturing towns; and that one *fourth* of all those born in England perish under the same age, surely it is of the highest importance that some efforts should be made to arrest the progress of such mournful and affecting ravages. ...

Until of late, in no country has the attention of medical men been so little directed to the state of infancy, as in this; and much of the mortality among children must be accredited to those whose duty it is to disseminate instruction on this subject in a popular and intelligible manner ... the remedial treatment of the diseases of infancy is frequently left to nurses, thoroughly imbued with the most dangerous prejudices ... it may, with justice, be affirmed that medical men have most criminally neglected the preventive treatment of disease, and to overcome and correct those prejudices and errors of mothers and nurses—the results of which, too long contemplated with indifference, they might prevent by their influence and their teachings.

Although this opinion may be considered by many as too strongly put forth, nevertheless, few will hesitate to acknowledge that a lamentable amount of ignorance prevails amongst the community as to the proper treatment of infants, with a view to the preservation of their health and the averting of disease; and if this be acknowledged, it cannot be denied that, had the means which are known to the medical profession, to accomplish these most desirable ends, been properly and prominently inculcated in their writings and teachings, less would now remain to be done. The opinions of nurses, and the practices which they follow, are too often, in truth, the cast-off doctrines of professional men of a former age. The profession, therefore, lies under the double duty not only of disseminating knowledge, but of repudiating the errors of their predecessors. . . .

Dr John T. Conquest, *Letters to a Mother*, 1848, pp. 111, 116–8.

211. Death of a Daughter: Mary (1849)

[Lady Eddisbury to Lord Eddisbury, Sunday night, August 1849]
MY DEAREST LOVE,
I am so fretted about dear baby I must write to you. Yesterday afternoon the little thing was uncomfortable & when the nurse came she could not suck from wind. She has continued poorly all night & today I was quite shocked when I came upstairs at the change which had taken place in the baby, so thin & its little hands cold & shrivelled. Dr. Locock ordered her castor oil & sal volatile which Williams had given. I had a very bad night, never closed my eyes, first from pain & then from the laudanum.
11 o'clock. I have just sent for Dr. Locock I am so uneasy about dear Baby.
7 o'clock Monday morg. Baby no better, pinched & blue Locock ordered brandy in her milk it is the nurses milk put down her throat in spoonfuls
6 o'clock. I think Baby is better, I have more hope.
12 o'clock. I am more & more anxious. Poor dear little lamb it looks so worn & piteous. When Locock comes again he is to decide about her being baptized. I shall be so wretched to lose her she is such a darling & I feel it quite a punishment for having said I did not wish for a child. I did not know how fast love grows for babies but as I sit by its cradle & hear its faint moans it goes thro' my heart. I feel very poorly quite knocked up. I am sure you will feel for the little soft thing you have watched the last fortnight as well as for me. She sleeps continuously & when she is roused to

take food her eyes look quite dead.

2 o'clock. It has been a cholera attack without pain, & now she is exhausted. She has no disease. I cannot now say what day I can go I feel I shall not have my little darling to bring.

[Lady Eddisbury to Lord Eddisbury, Monday night, August 1849]

MY DEAREST LOVE,

I closed my letter before with a gleam of hope, Dr. Locock came just as I had sealed it he said Baby was less *prostrate* than in the morning but he would not say she was at all out of danger—she was not safe. Within half an hour of his going the blue look came on again. I then decided upon having her baptized at once & a curate came & the dear little lamb was baptized Mary Ethelflida, I did not care what name for I fear she will not bear it long here, but you had said you liked that & I thought it would be best....

[Lady Eddisbury to Lord Eddisbury, 25 August 1849]

My dear little one would have been a month old today—you can have no idea how present she is to my mind, I am surprised at it myself, still I do feel most thankful that up to this time we have been spared other losses by this dreadful disease [cholera]....

[Lady Eddisbury to Lord Eddisbury, 15 November 1849]

I am just returned from Church—I at first felt very sorrowful, for the memory of that wee thing is still very present to my heart, but I can feel truly thankful that all the other dear ones have been spared & you my chiefest & greatest blessing. The churches were very well attended & the day observed everywhere. I believe this is the only country in which there has been a national acknowledgement of God's directing Providence in the cholera, & I believe it is not a mere outward form but that more & more are becoming every day religious. At such a time one's heart is very full & many thoughts crowd that cannot be expressed. I hope I may show the fruits of religion more than hitherto....

Nancy Mitford (ed.), *The Ladies of Alderley*, 1938, pp. 205–6, 208, 216.

212. Death of a Daughter: Little Jessy (1850)

[29 March 1850]
... Dear little Jessy's illness which has long been tedious, looked serious today: there was a total loss of appetite now for the 3d day, & of energy, and apparently some unconquerable obstruction in the bowels.

[2 April 1850]
... It was a day of much anxiety & pain. Last night the brain was in a fearful state of irritation & dear little Jessy spent it tossing, moaning, & screaming, chiefly in C.s arms, the rest in mine. With day came some diminution of the excitement: & Locock in the morning still held it most probable that the stomach was the cause. But at night he declared the head symptoms unequivocal. The moaning was much less but the head moved very constantly from side to side. The pulse was low, which he much disliked. The eyes very heavy. He says it is tubercular inflammation of the membranes of the brain, a most insidious form of disease: the danger imminent but the case 'far from hopeless': 48 hours he thinks will bring it to a point so as to make the issue clear. And now O Father can we readily yield her up to Thee? O how much better will she be cared for than in this sad & evil world. His will be done. My Catherine bears up wonderfully.

[8 April 1850]
... While they were here Locock came: and found Jessy in a state almost hopeless. We were deluded yesterday as to convulsions: for I now find Mrs Baker observed some. But without knowing this Catherine perceived through a mother's divining instinct that her darling had begun to give way in the deadly struggle. In the afternoon I prepared some little things by anticipation.

As the evening drew on all the signs grew worse, and our hearts again very sick yet I trust neither of us are so blindly selfish as to murmur at the Lord's being about to raise one of our children to Himself. Dr Locock's last visit left us no hope. C. and I with Mrs Baker sat in the room of death and watched the beloved child in her death battle, powerless to aid her. In the intervals of the thickening convulsions I read Mr Munro's excellent Letter, & wrote the necessary letters for the morning: until latterly when there was scarcely any spaces of repose between the tearings and tossings of the conflict.

[9 April 1850]

It is all over, and all well. The blessed child was released at two o'clock in the morning compassionately taken by her Saviour into the fold of His peace. I dwell on it no longer in this place: I must try to put together a few recollections of her little life. C. & I got to rest between 3 & 4. I was wakened in the morning by her weeping. The day was occupied with the communications & arrangements necessarily following the Death.

[10 April 1850]

... Today we had Jessy in the Boudoir. Flowers came from Scotland: and C. put them about her.

I wrote today this little inscription perhaps for the stone floor of the Chapel over her.

Underneath
Sleep the mortal remains of
Catherine Jessy Gladstone
Born July 27. 1845
Died April 9. 1850
'And in their mouth was
found no guile: for they
are without fault before
the throne of God.'
Rev. XIV. 5.

Catherine showed nervous weakness a little: but was much comforted by having Jessy near: I mean her body near: for of her spirit we know not: but that may be also near.

[11 April 1850]

... In the evening came the closing of the coffin & the last kiss upon the cold features of our Jessy. It was a pang for me; a deep one for a mother—who is going too to part from her sooner.

[12 April 1850]

Left C.G. at 5 3/4 AM: & went from Euston Square in a Coupee with the dear remains. Took Willy as far as Blisworth & there *consigned* him for Geddington. Closed my blind to have no other company than the thought of her who seems incessantly to beckon me & say 'Come Pappy Come': & of the land whither she is gone.... Notwithstanding precautions and assurances I had to pay in five parts and to make three changes of carriage.

[13 April 1850]
Reached Fasque between 8 & 9 A.M. Welcomed by Helen with deep emotion: & by all: particularly Hayman. At Eleven we had morning prayers, the funeral office, & Holy Communion: after which I saw the coffin set right under the spot where she used to kneel in infant prayer....

My Father did not converse much on business: & having slept ill went to rest after dinner.—I conversed with Aunt J. & again with Helen about our darling's life and illness....

I kept the key of the vault and was able to visit my Jessy there.

[15 April 1850]
... I could only pay one last visit [to the vault] being with my Father so much. Oh that I may carry away with me the seal of that Chamber.

W. Gladstone, *The Gladstone Diaries*, Vol. 4: 1848–1854 (ed. M.R.D. Foot & H.C.G. Matthew), Oxford 1974, pp. 196–8, 200–2.

[12 April 1850: rail journey with coffin]
She and I were alone all the way. It was a great privilege. In the interval we had so deeply enjoyed the presence of her lifeless frame, with the now gentle traces of suffering, and the surpassing peace and purity, and even majesty that invested her countenance.

W. Gladstone's memorandum on the death of Jessy Gladstone, Mary Gladstone Papers, BL Add. MS. 46269.

213. Death of a Daughter: Little Emma (1851)

You will be grieved to hear that a slight ailment of our dear little Emma Cecily proved to be scarlet fever or some form of it, and convulsions coming her little life soon ebbed out—God be praised for All his Mercies which are great indeed—I feel this to be a serious call to us and beg your prayers that it may be blessed to us. Dear Mary is well, and able to do all that is required of her. I suppose the little one's remains will be laid by her sister's. . . .

Thomas to Lydia Acland, n. d. [1851], Devon Record Office, Acland MSS (1148 M/16/2).

214. Death of a Son: Antony (1902)

Alas, Alas, I can gather him [her son, Antony] no longer, though my arms weary for him, though my heart aches for him . . . he was tired—too tired—and his heart slowly stopped—no pain, no sign,—only a flickering and flickering, which went out a little before ten . . . I kept away from the sight of him all through one day, till at last the day before he was buried . . . the agony of our loss had grown and grown, until it seemed that such a thing could not be borne . . . when I looked upon his face, the child in it was gone . . . all at once, swiftly, softly and silently, like falling snow, a wonderful peace and hope descended upon me. My tears were dried, my heart was healed. I felt him,—oh and I felt others too, very near to me. I could almost at the moment have cried for joy. It was Antony's last smile for me. . . .

[17 December 1936]
Some day far hence the messages which have come through about Antony from another life will be known and will bring proof to many that his life is only a stage in a greater journey. . . . This is no credulous dream of a fond mother: I have been allowed to see the evidence which exists of Antony's continuous life as well as that of others. . . .

Edith Lyttelton, memorandum on the death of Antony, 1902, 1936, Chandos Papers, II, 3/21 [Churchill College, Cambridge].

215. Death of a Grand-child: Johnny (1914)

I think Top has written to tell you of the death of dear little
Johnny. It was most sad for us all....
    I never think the doctrine of the immortality of the soul is the
same comfort with regard to a baby that it is with regard to older
people—at least from a mother's standpoint—because it is the
body that she loves at that age—the affection is the instinctive
animal affection, she wants to have it in her arms, to feel the little
fingers clasping hers. She does not know what the soul is like yet,
so she can only love that vaguely—but the other instinct is so
strong that she suffers cruelly if she loses her baby....

Maud, Lady Selborne to her son, Bobby Palmer, 18 November
[1914], Selborne Papers, MS Eng. lett. C. 454, f.173 [Bodleian
Library].

After the Service Top and Grace [Palmer] stole round to the tiny
grave with its pathetic little holly twigs and white flowers, side by
side with Father [Lord Selborne]—little Johnny's Great-
grandfather. Poor Grace! Her plain black clothes, her sad eyes, all
so touching. On Wednesday she talked to me about the sad little
death quite freely and very intensely. She had to stop speaking
sometimes....

Laura E. Ridding [née Palmer], 25 December 1914, 'Christmas at
Blackmoor', Selborne Papers, MS Eng. hist. c. 1018, fos. 60-1
[Bodleian Library].

216. Death of Emily Brontë: Pulmonary Tuberculosis, 1848

[29 October 1848]
... I feel much more uneasy about my sister than myself just now.

Emily's cold and cough are very obstinate. I fear she has pain in her chest, and I sometimes catch a shortness in her breathing, when she has moved at all quickly. She looks very thin and pale. Her reserved nature occasions me great uneasiness of mind. It is useless to question her; you get no answers. It is still more useless to recommend remedies; they are never adopted....

[23 November 1848]
I told you Emily was ill, in my last letter. She has not rallied yet. She is *very* ill. I believe, if you were to see her, your impression would be that there is no hope. A more hollow, wasted, pallid aspect, I have not beheld. The deep tight cough continues; the breathing after the least exertion is a rapid pant; and these symptoms are accompanied by pains in the chest and side. Her pulse, the only time she allowed it to be felt, was found to beat 115 per minute. In this state she resolutely refuses to see a doctor; she will give no explanation of her feelings, she will scarcely allow her feelings to be alluded to. Our position is, and has been for some weeks, exquisitely painful. God only knows how all this is to terminate. More than once, I have been forced boldly to regard the terrible event of her loss as possible, and even probable. But nature shrinks from such thoughts. I think Emily seems the nearest thing to my heart in the world.

[10 December 1848]
... Hope and fear fluctuate daily. The pain in her side and chest is better; the cough, the shortness of breath, the extreme emaciation continue. I have endured, however, such tortures of uncertainty on this subject, that, at length, I could endure it no longer; and as her repugnance to seeing a medical man continues immutable,—as she declares 'no poisoning doctor' shall come near her,—I have written, unknown to her, to an eminent physician in London, giving as minute a statement of her case and symptoms as I could draw up, and requesting an opinion. I expect an answer in a day or two....

[Tuesday, December 1848]
I should have written to you before, if I had had one word of hope to say; but I have not. She grows daily weaker. The physician's opinion was expressed too obscurely to be of use. He sent some

medicine, which she would not take. Moments so dark as these I have never known. I pray for God's support to us all. Hitherto He has granted it.

[21 December 1848]
Emily suffers no more from pain or weakness now. She never will suffer more in this world. She is gone, after a hard, short conflict. She died on *Tuesday*, the very day I wrote to you. I thought it very possible she might be with us still for weeks; and a few hours afterwards, she was in eternity. Yes; there is no Emily in time or on earth now. Yesterday we put her poor, wasted, mortal frame quietly under the Church pavement. We are very calm at present. Why should we be otherwise? The anguish of seeing her suffer is over; the spectacle of the pains of death is gone by; the funeral day is past. We feel she is at peace. No need now to tremble for the hard frost and the keen wind. Emily does not feel them. She died in a time of promise. We saw her taken from life in its prime. But it is God's will and the place where she is gone is better than that she has left. . . .

Charlotte Brontë, letters quoted by E. C. Gaskell, *The Life of Charlotte Brontë*, New York, 1857, Vol. 2, pp. 63, 65–8.

217. Anticipating Death after Miscarriage, 1904: Lord Curzon's notes on his wife's experience

3.40 am.   Thursday Sep. 22 [1904] Great pain into the night. Eyes.
8.15 am.   I'll do my best.
  (1)   Pain gone to the other side.
         Pulse better. Only 110, it was 130.
         Cable to my people; they ought to know. I have peritonitis.
         How are the little children?
  (2)   All right. Would you like to see them? No.
         My tongue is quite dreadful. It is cracked right across.

(3) Asked about Champneys and Barlow [doctors].
knew going to be operated on
said she knew it would kill her
said I must not say anything to make her cry
2.20 pm. Try and keep up. Make a good struggle. Keep your
strength.
I haven't got any
My darling, my beau. Dont make me cry.
3-8. From 3.30 to 5.30 things were at their worst. During this
time she was thrice nearly gone. Her hands and arms and
extremities become cold. I rubbed her arm and hand with brandy
and hot water bottles were put under feet and legs, even up to her
thighs.

She was most reluctant to believe that she was going and said
that she did not want to see the children till the end.

At intervals she gave me instructions about everything.
Dont let the children remain here. It is too cold for them. . . .
Dont take them to India. Ask Mama as my last wish to come
and take them to some warm place and look after them.

I asked her if she died whether she would wish to be buried at
Kedleston.

Yes I should love it.

Here she said, Dont put me in the ground. I have a horror of
being put in the ground (and at another time: I have a horror of
being buried alive.) Put me in the vault.

At one time when she thought she was going she asked me to
read through our favourite psalm, 'Lord who shall dwell in thy
holy tabernacle or who shall rest upon the holy hill' and I read it
through in floods of tears. She repeated the first two sentences
after me.

Then she asked me to read Tennyson's Crossing the Bar, and I
repeated the first verse. She said, 'But you must not mourn for
me'. At one moment when she was nearly going she said, Repeat
the Lord's Prayer, and I repeated it and she after me. . . .

I asked her whether in another world, if there was one, she
would wait for me till I could come. Yes, she said. I will wait.
When I said that we had loved each other long and been all in all
to each other, she asked that that might be inscribed on her tomb.
She asked that we might be buried side by side with a marble

effigy of each of us looking towards each other, so that we might one day be reunited.

Lord Curzon, '... notes made by me at Walmer Castle in September 1904 when my darling lay dying ...', quoted by Nigel Nicolson, *Mary Curzon*, 1977, pp. 176–80.

218. Death of Margaret Gladstone: Puerperal Fever, 1870

The sickness is so dreadful and nothing nothing does her [Margaret Gladstone] any good. All you can do is to pray for us ... we can hardly pray for ourselves. The abcess is disappearing without breaking, and the doctors now think there is some disease of the kidneys....

Elizabeth King to Margaret Henderson, 15 August 1870, MacDonald Papers, P.R.O. 30/69/852.

... After breakfast John [Dr Gladstone, Margaret's husband] said to her 'I think my love God is going to take you to Himself'. She said 'Do you' and after a moment added 'When?' He replied 'I think today'. After lying still a little, she said 'Bring baby Mamma'. When I came back with the little thing she looked to her husband and said 'John you dedicate our baby to God—be short—bring in the children—all'....
  ... The four little girls stood at the bedside. She took the hand of each and kissed each and said 'Goodbye'—I do not remember more words to them—John said will you shake hands with the servants. She assented with a slight nod but said she could not speak to them. They were all brought in with the children.... There was a great company in the room. John said 'will you shake hands with them.' She said 'Yes' and named Byhoe—so he came first then she said 'Cook' and Cook came. The wetnurse caught

her attention by sobbing, and never having seen her or heard of her, she [Margaret] looked inquiringly at John; he said this is baby's nurse. When she heard this, she tried to raise herself a little and said with deep earnestness in broken accents 'Do the best you can for baby—in God's name'. Then she shook hands with all the servants and said as loudly as she could 'Do the best you can for baby—in God's name—all of you'. They said 'we will' and left the room.... Once she said 'There is nothing in [the] world that John would not get for me and there is nothing I want but a cup of pure cold water'.... This was a very short time before her breath ceased ... John stood at her pillow and I was beside her on the bed till almost at the end. She motioned me off and crossed her hands on her breast and so passed very gently away.

Elizabeth King's journal of her daughter's, Margaret Gladstone's, death, 1870, MacDonald Papers, P.R.O. 30/69/852.

219. Death of Mary Lyttelton after 12th Labour, 1857

All her strength was given to her 12 children. I remember saying that the 12th baby was as the last gallant effort of the high-mettled racer. It was thus that 17 years of married life, and the birth of 11 children, were gone through by her with hardly a passing cloud....

On the 15th [August 1857] I slept not a wink.... At 3, she sent for me.... She asked if she was dying—I had just been to [Dr] Giles, and asked him if there was any hope. He said it was a state of the greatest possible danger; but there was still a faint hope. I therefore replied to her to that effect, softening it however a little. She then said the thought of her children was almost too much for her; spoke of them with some strong words of affection and said: They do so bring me back to life....

I urged her to take comfort in the thought, that if taken from us (as we word it) she might still believe that she would watch over and take interest in, possibly, even influence us, while unseen. And next, I told her to be assured as of the pure truth, that though no one ought to be told at such a time that they had nothing to repent of, yet in her behaviour to me and to the children, as far as man can speak, she had ever been as an Angel without spot.

... I found she was thinking of being helped through the prayers of those around her, to pass safely through Death.

Account by George W. Lyttelton, 4th Baron Lyttelton, of the death of his first wife, Mary, on 17 August 1857, Mary Gladstone Papers, BL Add. MS.46269, fos. 68, 81–2, 97.

220. Death of Blanche Scarsdale, Mother of 11 Children, 1875 (aged 37)

It is a very hard trial for us all and especially for poor Papa but we must try to bear it and comfort him—I have just written to Denman's and ordered black trousers for each of us ... I slept at 1 Grosvenor Crescent last night but was awoke this morning at twenty minutes to four and we drove here in a cab as fast as possible but we were too late—for dear Mama [Blanche, Lady Scarsdale] died at half past three quite peaceably, with no pain. We went in and saw her today, her face was like it used to be, with a happy smile on, but of course very grey and calm, like marble. Aunt Mary put white flowers all over the bed. We shall not see the dear face again.

George to Alfred Curzon, 4 April 1875, quoted by Kenneth Rose, *Superior Person: A Portrait of Curzon and his Circle in late Victorian England,* 1969, p. 37.

221. Death of Blanche Cripps: Suicide, 1905

... I must now record a family event ... but a very tragic one. Our Sister Blanche Cripps died by her own act in the early morning of the first day of June. [1905]—Maggie Hobhouse [her sister] brought us the news....

Before going to bed she kissed her Husband several times and told him how good he had always been to her—Later at 2 o'cl[ock] she went up to Stan and Harry [her young sons] and woke them to kiss them and tell them always to be good and loyal to their father and then I suppose she went and did it....

Her Husband having occasion to go into the Bathroom found her and he and the two poor youngest children spent the early hours of the morning in the vain attempt to bring back life. Except when those fits of temporary depression came on she was very happy, fond of her Husband and devoted to her children and I never saw young men more affectionate or nicer to their Mother—And she was a noble woman in many ways—generous—affectionate and with a good deal of talent and even force of character—but with some flaw in the brain which destroyed the sequence of her ideas—her memory for events and arrangements and her intellectual sympathy....

She had also I understand left directions with Fanny about her funeral and that she was to be buried with her head on a Bible and her feet on a Shakespeare.

... And so passes another of my eight Sisters—curiously like Theresa the wife of one of the Cripps brothers and the two middle Sisters of the family.

Kate Courtney [neé Potter], Diary, 4, 5 June 1905, Courtney Collection; Vol. 32, fos. 47–51 [L.S.E.].

Death Certificate entry for Blanche Cripps
Registration District: St Marylebone
1905 DEATH in the Sub-district of The Rectory in the County of London.
No.: 110
1.   When and where died: First June 1905 2 Stratford Place...
4.   Age: 52 years
5.   Occupation: Wife of William Harrison Cripps a surgeon (F.R.C.S.) England
6.   Cause of death: Suffocation/Strangulation by hanging When suspended with bandage placed round neck Suicide Temporary Insanity following fits...

222. Death of 'Lallie' Holt, 1906

... That Sister of mine [Lallie Holt] always knew what she liked
& though she often saw with blinkers on she saw far & absolutely
straight & clear....

   Betty & Molly were with her through the last days nursing her
devotedly. She knew she was going, spoke of everything being
nicely straightened out & gave Miss Parsons full directions about
the service the hymns & all the arrangements saying when this
was done 'now put that paper in your pocket & don't think about
it till the time comes: it is as good an hour's work as I have done &
I feel much better already'—She directed that her body should be
cremated & the ashes scattered. Dear old Lallie she was a bit of a
Martha about arrangements—& got very impatient with people
who left them to chance, her housekeeping was only too good...
Sister Holt as we sometimes called her was my eldest & nearest
Sister my constant companion for 20 years....

Kate Courtney [née Potter], Diary, 4 June 1906, Courtney
Collection, Vol. 32, fos. 126–30 [L.S.E.].

223. Death of Lady Cranbrook in Old Age, 1897

November 13 [1897]—'A quiet night but very tired' is this
morning's report. That troubles us, for the dear one, though
sleeping fairly and taking nourishment, runs down. We cannot
forget her age, which is against a rapid rally, but we hope. I saw
that Emy and Katie when they came to prayers looked very sad,
and no wonder, for the dear mother felt so weak that it struck
herself as sinking. We have telegraphed for Alfred, Gathorne, and
Evelyn. God help us all, and her! ... At a quarter to one o'clock
she slept into eternal rest, just passed tranquilly away without a
pang; a ray of sunlight came through the blinds on to the dear
face, and her last sigh was given while Mr Daubeny read the
commendatory prayer. What a fund of love has she taken from
the world, and what a blessed memory of unselfishness does she
leave! I can hardly realize that the companion of sixty years has

left me, but there was no response to my last kisses. She is with 'the loved and lost awhile' and her end was as she desired.

Diary of Gathorne Hardy, first Earl of Cranbrook, quoted in *Gathorne Hardy. First Earl of Cranbrook. A Memoir* (ed. The Hon. Alfred E. Gathorne-Hardy), 1910, Vol. 2, pp. 360–1.

Select Bibliography

This section provides an introductory list of bibliographies, documentary collections, and secondary books and articles relevant to the subjects and contexts raised in this volume. The place of publication is London unless otherwise stated.

Details of the primary sources used for documentary extracts are supplied after each document in the text. These authors are included in the Index, as well as the authors of secondary books and articles referred to in our introductions to the major sections.

Bibliographies

Kanner, S. Barbara, 'The women of England in a century of social change, 1815-1914: a select bibliography Part 1', pp. 173-206, in Vicinus, Martha (ed.), *Suffer and Be Still. Women in the Victorian Age*, Bloomington, Indiana, 1972.

————, 'The women of England in a century of social change, 1815-1914: a select bibliography, part 2', pp. 199-270, in Vicinus, Martha (ed.), *A Widening Sphere. Changing Roles of Victorian Women*, Bloomington, Indiana, 1977.

———— (ed.), *The Women of England from Anglo-Saxon Times to the Present*, 1980.

Stineman, Esther, *Women's Studies. A Recommended Core Bibliography*, Littleton, Colorado, 1979.

Documentary Collections

Bauer, Carol and Ritt, Lawrence (eds.), *Free and Ennobled: Source Readings in the Development of Victorian Feminism*, Oxford, 1979.

Bell, Susan Groag, and Offen, Karen M. (eds.), *Women, the Family, and Freedom. The Debate in Documents. Vol. 1, 1750–1880; Vol. 2, 1880–1950,* Stanford, California, 1983.

Davies, Margaret Llewelyn (ed.), *Life as we have known it by cooperative working women,* 1977.

——, *Maternity: Letters from Working Women,* 1978.

Hellerstein, E. O., Hume, L. P., and Offen, K. M. (eds.), *Victorian Women. A Documentary Account of Women's Lives in Nineteenth-Century England, France, and the United States,* Brighton, Sussex, 1981.

Hollis, Patricia [ed.], *Women in Public 1850–1900. Documents of the Victorian Women's Movement,* 1979.

Murray, Janet Horowitz [ed.], *Strong-Minded Women and Other Lost Voices from Nineteenth-Century England,* New York, 1982.

Riemer, Eleanor S., & Fout, John C. (eds.), *European Women. A Documentary History, 1789–1945,* Brighton, Sussex, 1983.

Secondary Books and Articles

Alaya, Flavia, 'Victorian science and the "genius" of woman', *Journal of the History of Ideas,* 38, 2 (April–June 1977), pp. 261–80.

Anderson, Michael, *Approaches to the History of the Western Family 1500–1914,* 1980.

Banks, J.A., *Prosperity and Parenthood. A Study of Family Planning among the Victorian Middle Classes,* 1954.

——, and Olive, *Feminism and Family Planning in Victorian England,* Liverpool, 1964.

——, *Victorian Values. Secularism and the size of families,* 1981.

Banks, Olive, *Faces of Feminism. A Study of Feminism as a Social Movement,* Oxford, 1981.

Beales, H.L., & Glover, Edward, 'Victorian Ideas of Sex', in Annan, Noel, *et al., Ideas and Beliefs of the Victorians. An Historic Revaluation of the Victorian Age,* New York, 1966.

Bell, E. Moberly, *Storming the Citadel. The Rise of the Woman Doctor,* 1953.

Bloch, Ivan, *A History of English Sexual Morals,* 1936.

Branca, Patricia, *Silent Sisterhood. Middle Class Women in the Victorian Home,* Pittsburgh, 1975.

——, *Women in Europe since 1750,* 1978.

Bullough, Vern and Voght, Martha, 'Women, menstruation and 19th century medicine', *Bulletin of the History of Medicine,* vol. 47, no. 1 (1973), pp. 66–82.

Burstyn, Joan N., 'Education and sex: the medical case against higher education for women in England, 1870–1900', *Proceedings of the American Philosophical Society*, vol. 117, no.2 (April 1973), pp. 79–89.

———, *Victorian Education and the Ideal of Womanhood*, 1980.

Cartwright, F.F., *A Social History of Medicine*, 1977.

Davies, Mel, 'Corsets and conception: fashion and demographic trends in the nineteenth century', *Comparative Studies in Society and History*, 24, 4 (October 1982), pp. 611–41.

Degler, Carl N., 'What ought to be and what was: women's sexuality in the nineteenth century', *American Historical Review*, vol. 79, no. 5 (December 1974), pp. 1467–90.

———, *At Odds. Women and the Family in America from the Revolution to the Present*, New York, 1980.

Delamont, Sara & Duffin, Lorna (eds.), *The Nineteenth-Century Woman. Her Cultural and Physical World*, 1978.

Donnison, Jean, *Midwives and Medical Men: A History of Inter-Professional Rivalries and Women's Rights*, New York, 1977.

Duffy, John, 'Masturbation and clitoridectomy: a nineteenth century view', *Journal of the American Medical Association*, vol. 186, no. 3 (19 October 1963), pp. 246–8.

Dyhouse, Carol, *Girls Growing Up in Late Victorian and Edwardian England*, 1981.

———, 'Working class mothers and infant mortality in England, 1895–1914', in Webster, Charles (ed.), *Biology, Medicine and Society, 1840–1940*, Cambridge, 1981.

Ehrenreich, Barbara and English, Deidre, *Complaints and Disorders. The Sexual Politics of Sickness*, 1973.

———, *For Her Own Good: 150 Years of the Experts' Advice to Women*, New York, 1978.

Figlio, Karl, 'Chlorosis and chronic disease in nineteenth-century Britain: the social constitution of somatic illness in a capitalist society', *Social History*, 3 (May 1978), pp. 167–97.

Fleming, J.B., 'Puerperal fever: the historical development of its treatment', *Proceedings of the Royal Society of Medicine*, 59 (April 1966), pp. 341–5.

Forbes, Thomas R., 'The regulation of English midwives in the eighteenth and nineteenth centuries', *Medical History*, vol. 15, no. 4 (October 1971), pp. 352–62.

Foucault, Michel, *The History of Sexuality. Volume 1: An Introduction*, New York, 1978.

———, 'What is an author?', pp. 113–38, in Bouchard, Donald F. (ed.), *Michel Foucault: Language, Counter-Memory, Practice. Selected Essays and Interviews*, Ithaca, New York, 1980.

Fryer, Peter, *The Birth Controllers*, New York, 1966.

Gay, Peter, *The Bourgeois Experience, Victoria to Freud. Vol. 1: Education of the Senses*, New York, 1984.

Gorham, Deborah, *The Victorian Girl and the Feminine Ideal*, 1982.

Graham, Harvey, *Eternal Eve: The History of Gynaecology and Obstetrics*, New York, 1951.

Harrison, Brian, 'Women's health and the women's movement in Britain: 1840-1940', pp. 15-71, in Webster, Charles (ed.), *Biology, Medicine and Society 1840-1940*, Cambridge, 1981.

Harrison, Fraser, *The Dark Angel. Aspects of Victorian Sexuality*, 1977.

Hartman, Mary and Banner, Lois W. (eds.), *Clio's Consciousness Raised. New Perspectives on the History of Women*, New York, 1974.

Himes, Norman Edwin, *Medical History of Contraception*, New York, 1970.

Hudson, Robert P., 'The biography of disease: lessons from chlorosis', *Bulletin of the History of Medicine*, vol. 51, no. 3 (Fall 1977), pp. 448-63.

Klein, Viola, *The Feminine Character: History of an Ideology*, New York, 1949.

Knight, Patricia, 'Women and abortion in Victorian and Edwardian England', *History Workshop*, 4 (Autumn 1977), pp. 57-69.

Lewis, Jane, *Women in England 1870-1950: Sexual Divisions and Social Change*, Brighton, Sussex, 1984.

McLaren, Angus, 'Women's work and regulation of family size: the question of abortion in the nineteenth century', *History Workshop*, 4 (Autumn 1977), pp. 70-81.

———, *Birth Control in Nineteenth-Century England*, 1978.

———, *Reproductive Rituals. Perceptions of fertility in Britain from the sixteenth century to the nineteenth century*, 1984.

Manton, Jo, *Elizabeth Garrett Anderson*, 1965.

Maudsley, Henry, 'Sex in mind and in education', *Fortnightly Review*, n.s. 15 (1874), pp. 466-83.

Mechling, Jay, 'Advice to historians on advice to mothers', *Journal of Social History*, 9, 1 (Fall 1975), pp. 44-63.

Mitchell, J. and Oakley, A. (eds.), *The Rights and Wrongs of Women*, Harmondsworth, Middlesex, 1976.

Mosedale, Susan Sleeth, 'Science corrupted: Victorian biologists consider "The woman question"', *Journal of the History of Biology*, 11, 1 (Spring 1978), pp. 1-55.

Munro Kerr, J.M., Johnstone, R.W., and Phillips, Miles H. (eds.), *Historical Review of British Obstetrics and Gynaecology 1800-1950*, 1954.

Parry, Noel and Jose, *The Rise of the Medical Profession. A Study of Collective Social Mobility*, 1976.

Parsons, Gail Pat, 'The British medical profession and contagion theory: puerperal fever as a case study, 1830–60', *Medical History*, vol. 22, no. 2 (April 1978), pp. 138–50.

Peterson, M. Jeanne, *The Medical Profession in Mid-Victorian London*, Berkeley, 1978.

Pollock, Linda A., *Forgotten children. Parent-child relations from 1500 to 1900*, Cambridge, 1983.

Poynter, F.N.L. (ed.), *The Evolution of Medical Practice in Britain*, 1961.

———, *The Evolution of Hospitals in Britain*, 1964.

———, *Medicine and Science in the 1860s*, 1968.

Rendall, Jane, *The Origins of Modern Feminism: Women in Britain, France and the United States, 1780–1860*, 1985.

Ricci, James Vincent, *One Hundred Years of Gynaecology, 1800–1900*, Philadelphia, 1945.

Robertson, Priscilla, *An Experience of Women. Pattern and Change in Nineteenth-Century Europe*, Philadelphia, 1982.

Roebuck, Janet and Slaughter, Jane, 'Ladies and pensioners: stereotypes and public policy affecting old women in England 1880–1940', *Journal of Social History*, vol. 13, no. 1 (Fall 1979), pp. 105–14.

Rowbotham, Sheila, *Hidden from History. 300 Years of Women's Oppression and the Fight Against It*, Ringwood, Victoria, 1975.

Shorter, Edward, *A History of Women's Bodies*, 1983.

Sicherman, Barbara, 'The uses of a diagnosis: doctors, patients and neurasthenia', *Journal of the History of Medicine and Allied Sciences*, vol. 32, no. 1 (1977), pp. 33–54.

Siddall, A. Clair, 'Chlorosis—etiology reconsidered', *Bulletin of the History of Medicine*, vol. 56, no. 2 (Summer 1982), pp. 254–260.

Smith, F.B., *The People's Health 1830–1910*, Canberra, 1979.

Smith-Rosenberg, Carroll, 'The hysterical woman: sex roles and role conflict in nineteenth-century America', *Social Research*, 39 (1972), pp. 652–78.

Suitor, J. Jill, 'Husbands' participation in childbirth: a nineteenth century phenomenon', *Journal of Family History*, vol. 6, no.3 (Fall 1981), pp. 278–93.

Van Keep, P.A., Greenblatt, R.B. and Albeaux-Fernet, M. (eds.), *Consensus on Menopause Research. A Summary of International Opinion*, Baltimore, 1977.

Veith, Ilza, *Hysteria: the history of a disease*, 1965.

Vicinus, Martha (ed.), *Suffer and Be Still. Women in the Victorian Age*, Bloomington, Indiana, 1972.

———, *A Widening Sphere. Changing Roles of Victorian Women*, Bloomington, Indiana, 1977.

Weeks, Jeffrey, *Sex, Politics and Society. The regulation of sexuality since 1800*, 1981.

Wohl, Anthony S. (ed.), *The Victorian Family. Structure and Stresses,* 1978.

Wood, Carl, 'Menopausal myths', *The Medical Journal of Australia,* 1 (2 June 1979), pp. 496–9.

Wood, Clive and Suitters, Beryl, *The Fight for Acceptance. A History of Contraception,* Lancaster, 1970.

Woodward, John, *To Do The Sick No Harm: A study of the British voluntary hospital system to 1875,* 1974.

Woodward, John, and Richards, David (eds.), *Health Care and Popular Medicine in Nineteenth-Century England. Essays in the Social History of Medicine,* 1977.

Youngson, A.J., *The Scientific Revolution in Victorian Medicine,* Canberra, 1979.

Acknowledgements

Copyright permission for manuscripts has been kindly granted by Sir Richard and Lady Acland (Acland MSS), The Duke of Atholl (Atholl MSS), The British Library (Campbell-Bannerman Papers), Lord Chandos and the Master, Fellows and Scholars of Churchill College in the University of Cambridge (Chandos Papers), The British Library of Political and Economic Science (Courtney Collection), Sir William Gladstone Bt. (Gladstone Papers), The National Library of Scotland (Haldane and Minto Papers), Mr Richard Hobbs (Hobbs-Derby/Gathorne-Hardy Papers), the Public Record Office on behalf of Mrs Sheila Lochhead (MacDonald Papers), and Lord Selborne (Selborne Papers).

The following publishers have kindly granted copyright permission for extracts from printed sources: The Bodley Head (Naomi Mitchison, *All Change Here*, 1975), Oxford University Press (*The Gladstone Diaries*, vol. 4: 1848–54, ed. M.R.D. Foot and H.C.G. Matthew, 1974), A.D. Peters and Co. Ltd. (Nancy Mitford, *The Ladies of Alderley*, Chapman and Hall, 1938), Weidenfeld and Nicolson Ltd. (Nigel Nicolson, *Mary Curzon*, 1977).

Index